100+ PAGES OF BUGS & INSECTS TO COLOR

AN ADULT CHILL PILL COLORING BOOK

COPYRIGHT © 2021 • ALL RIGHTS RESERVED
DANO JANOWSKI • ISBN: 9798593337788

Let your imagination take you away with wings to a place where life is beautiful all of the time and you don't have to worry or stress about a time limit for coloring these 100+ pages FULL of beautiful Bugs & Insects To Color. This is your ticket to ride.

Did you know... Coloring books are not just for children anymore. Researchers from around the globe have found that coloring has therapeutic mental health benefits, including a reduction from symptoms of depression and anxiety. Coloring allows your mind to take a much needed breather after a long busy day at work. Rediscover the art of slowing down in a fast paced world and get an Adult Chill Pill Coloring Book. Pick up some colored pencils, markers, crayons, or paint brushes, and color your way to a more relaxed person!

A relaxed attitude lengthens a person's life ~ Proverbs
In this fast paced world, it's important to slow down sometimes ~ Biker George

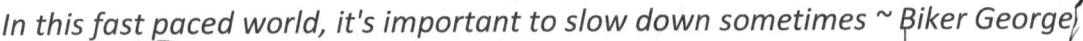

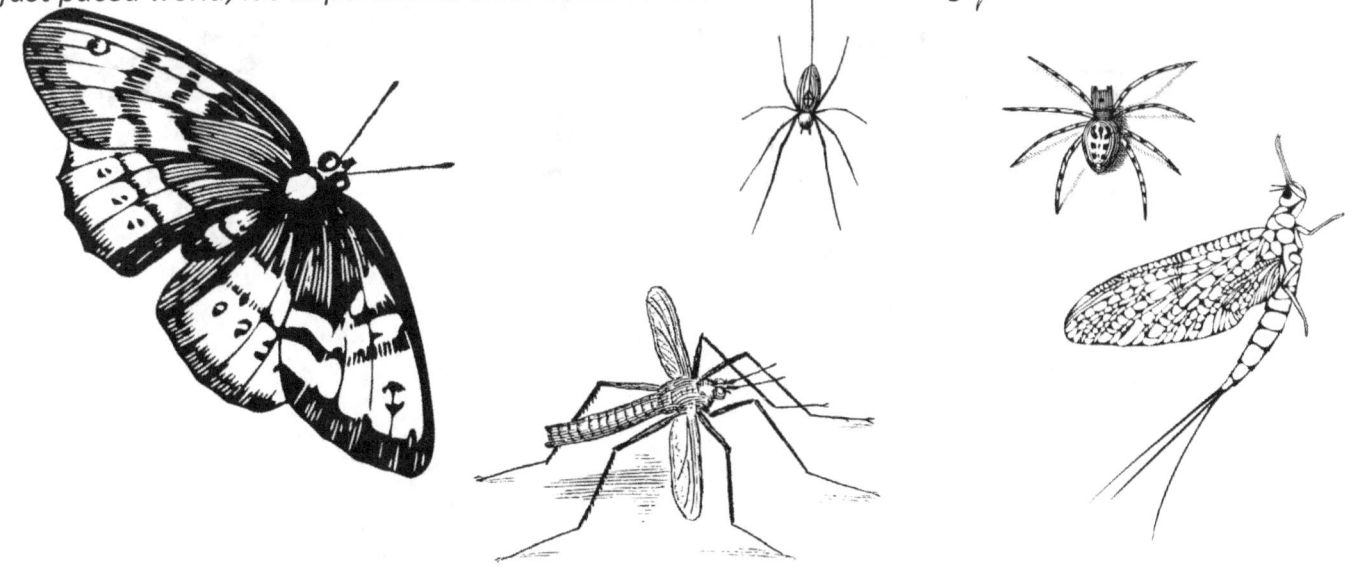

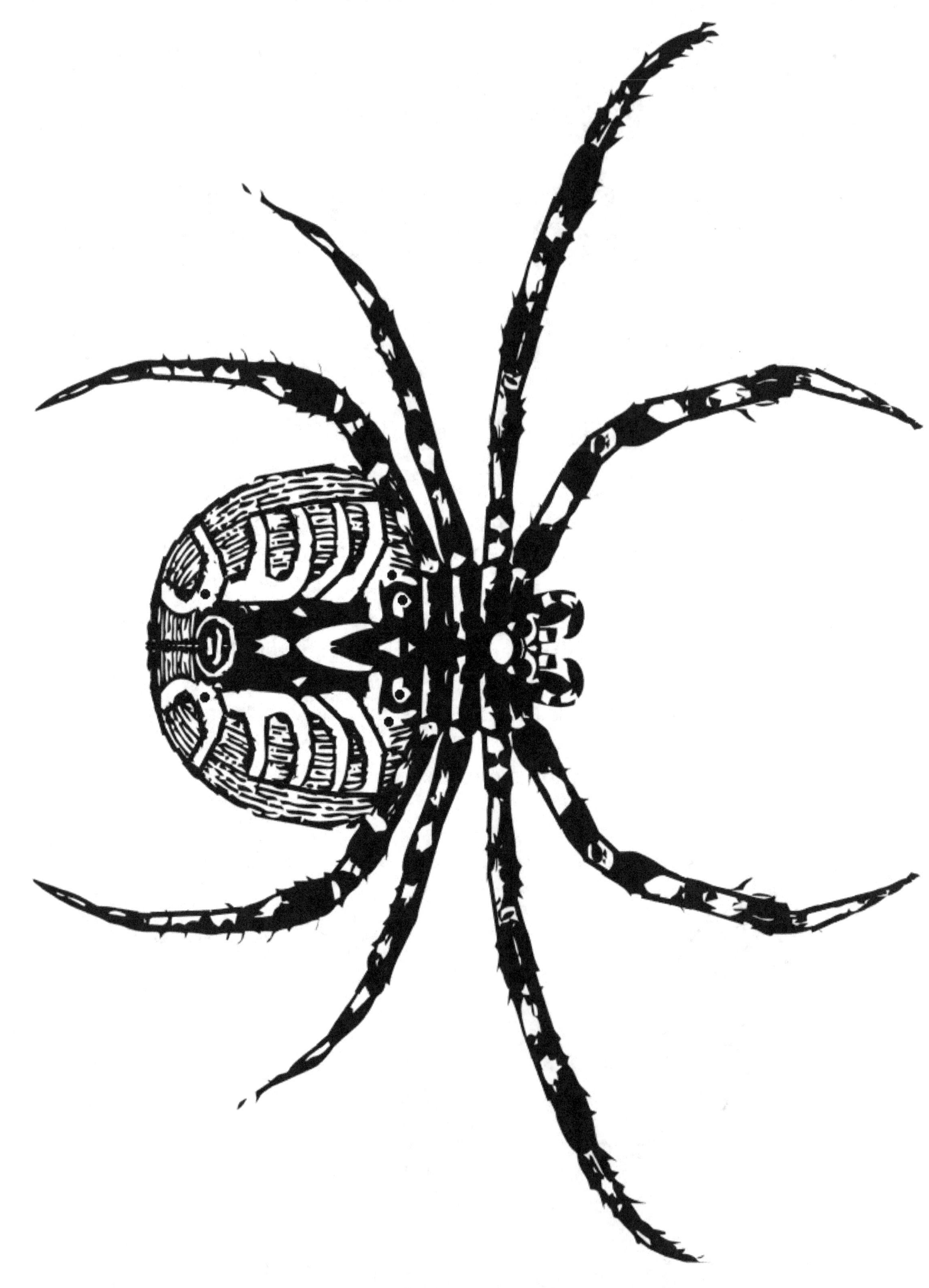

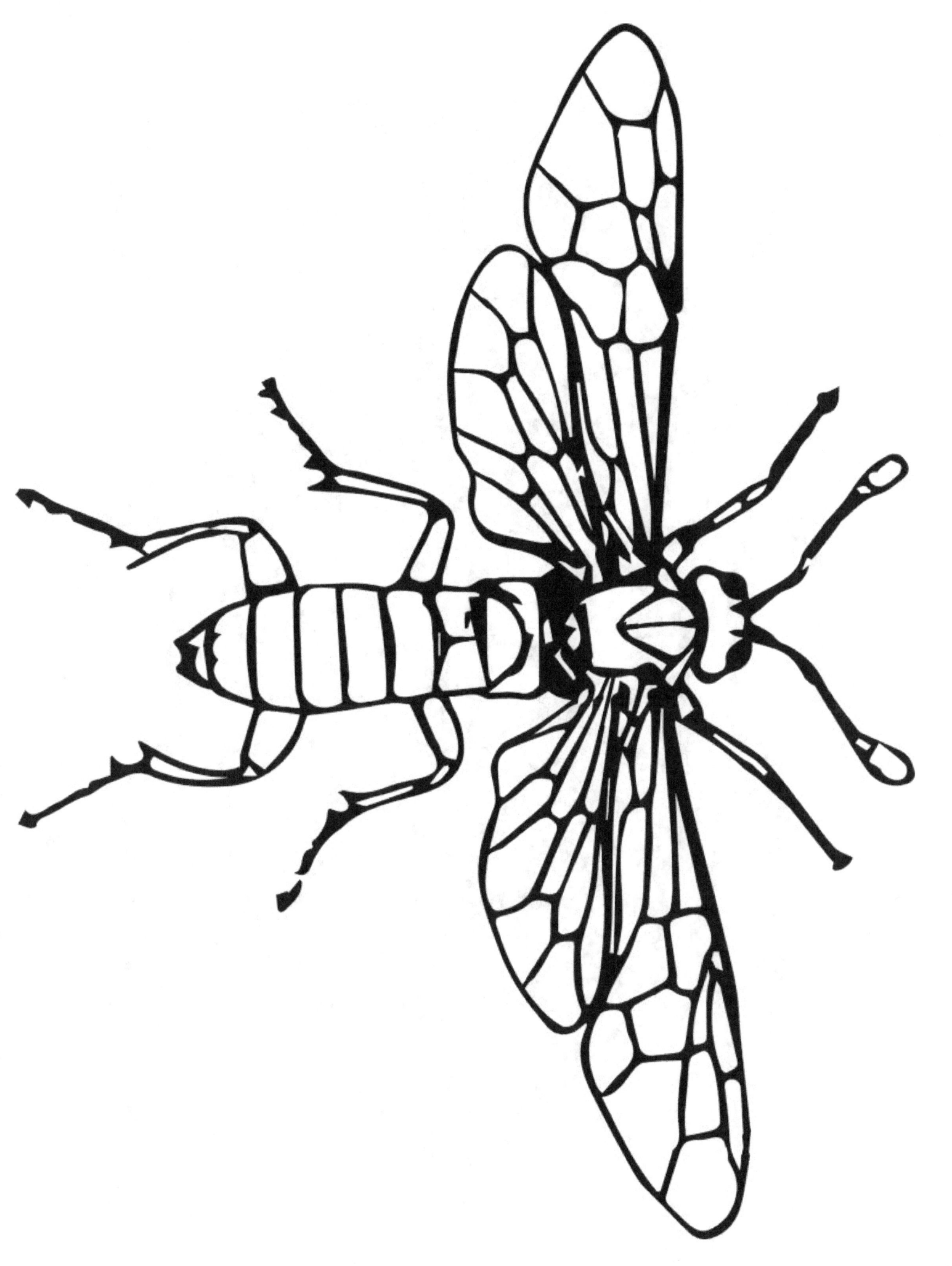

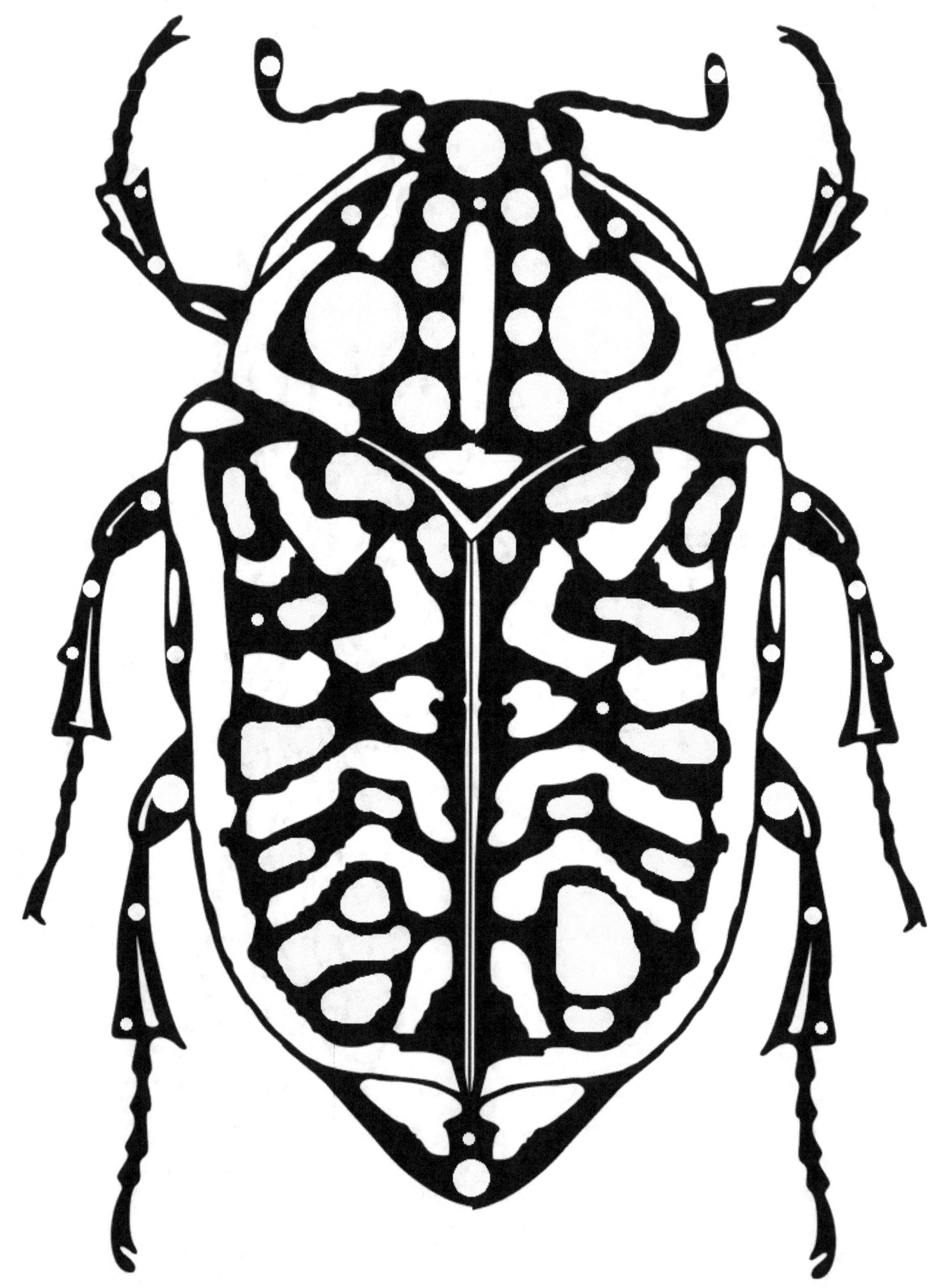

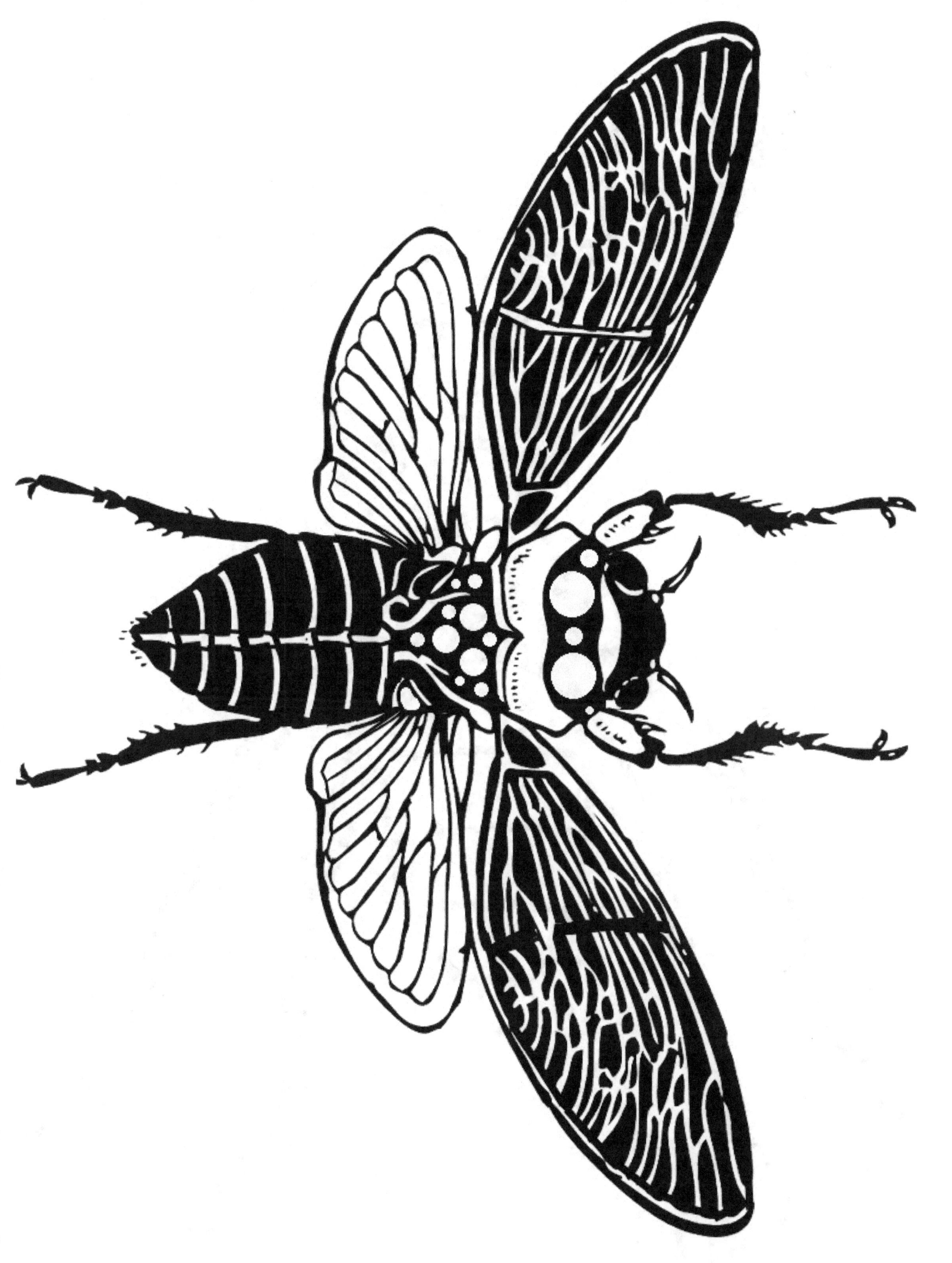

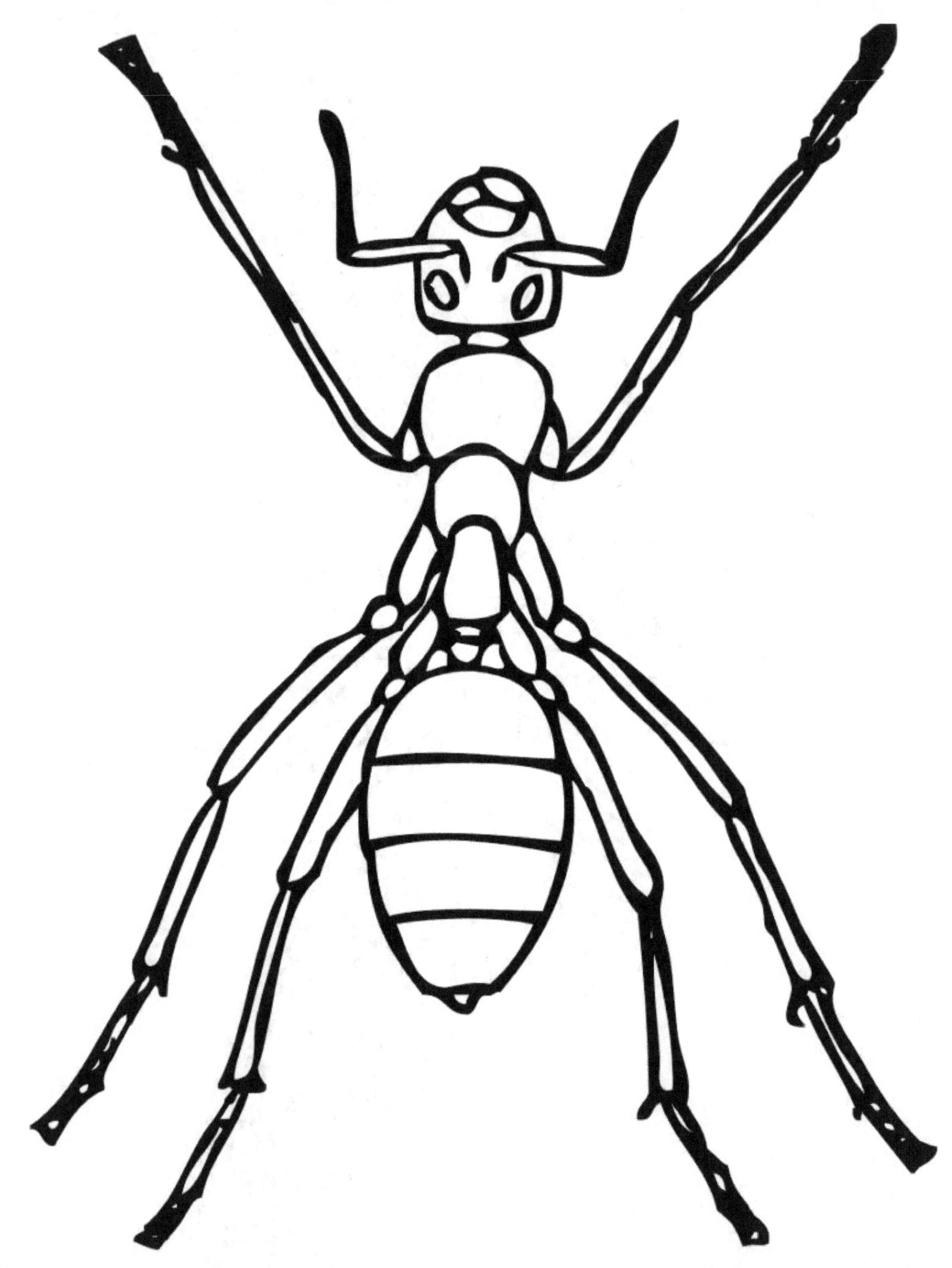

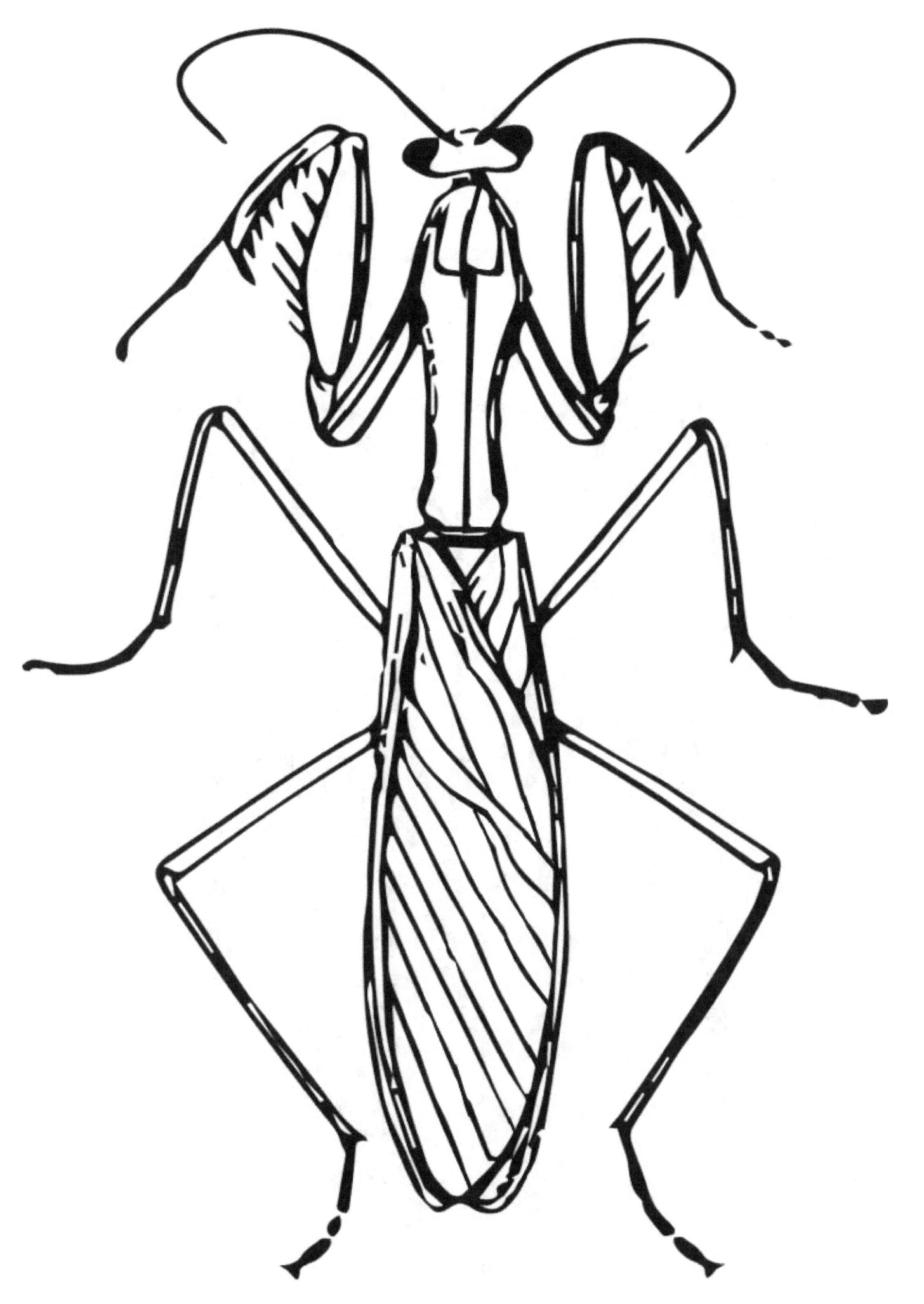

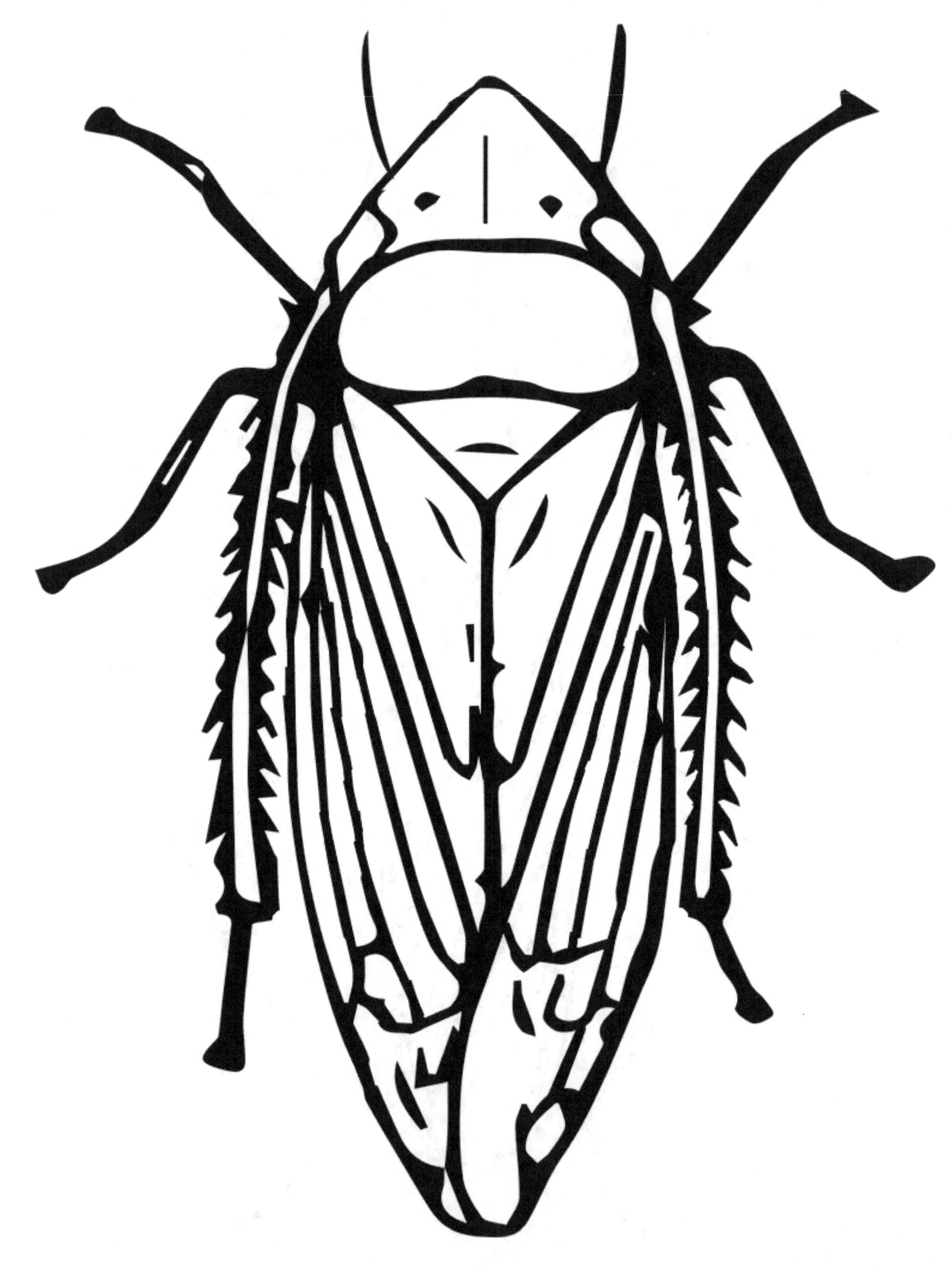

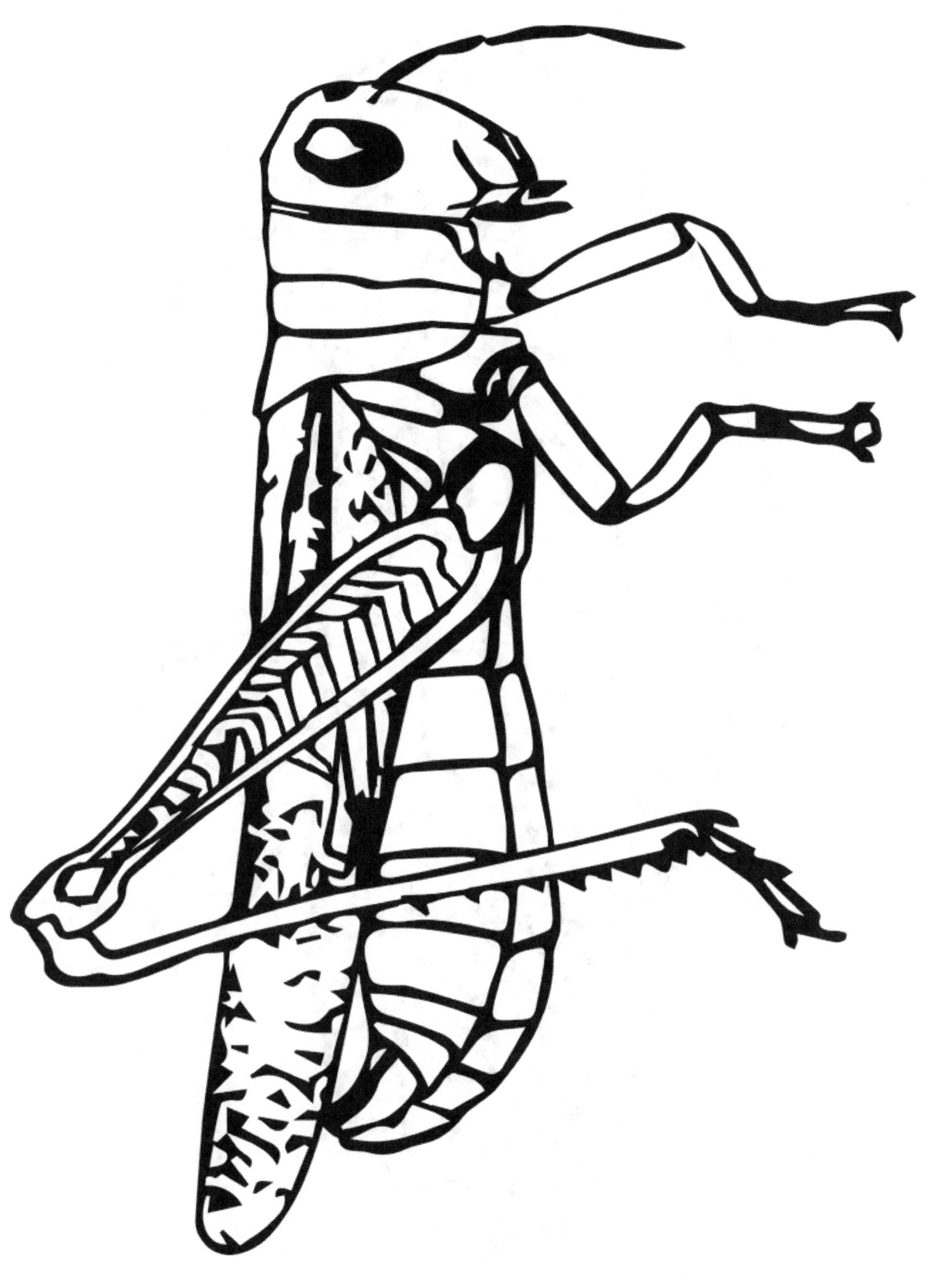

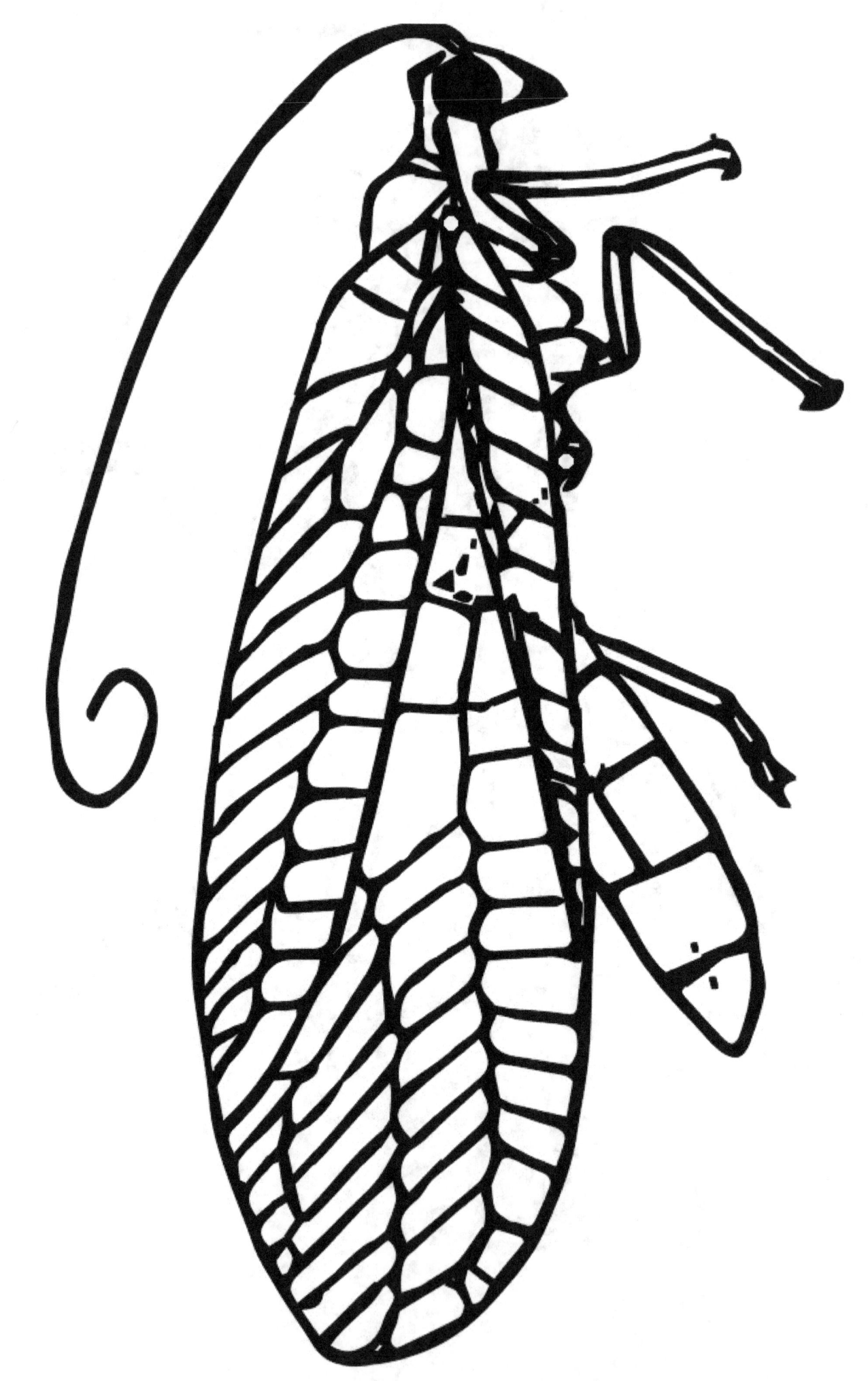

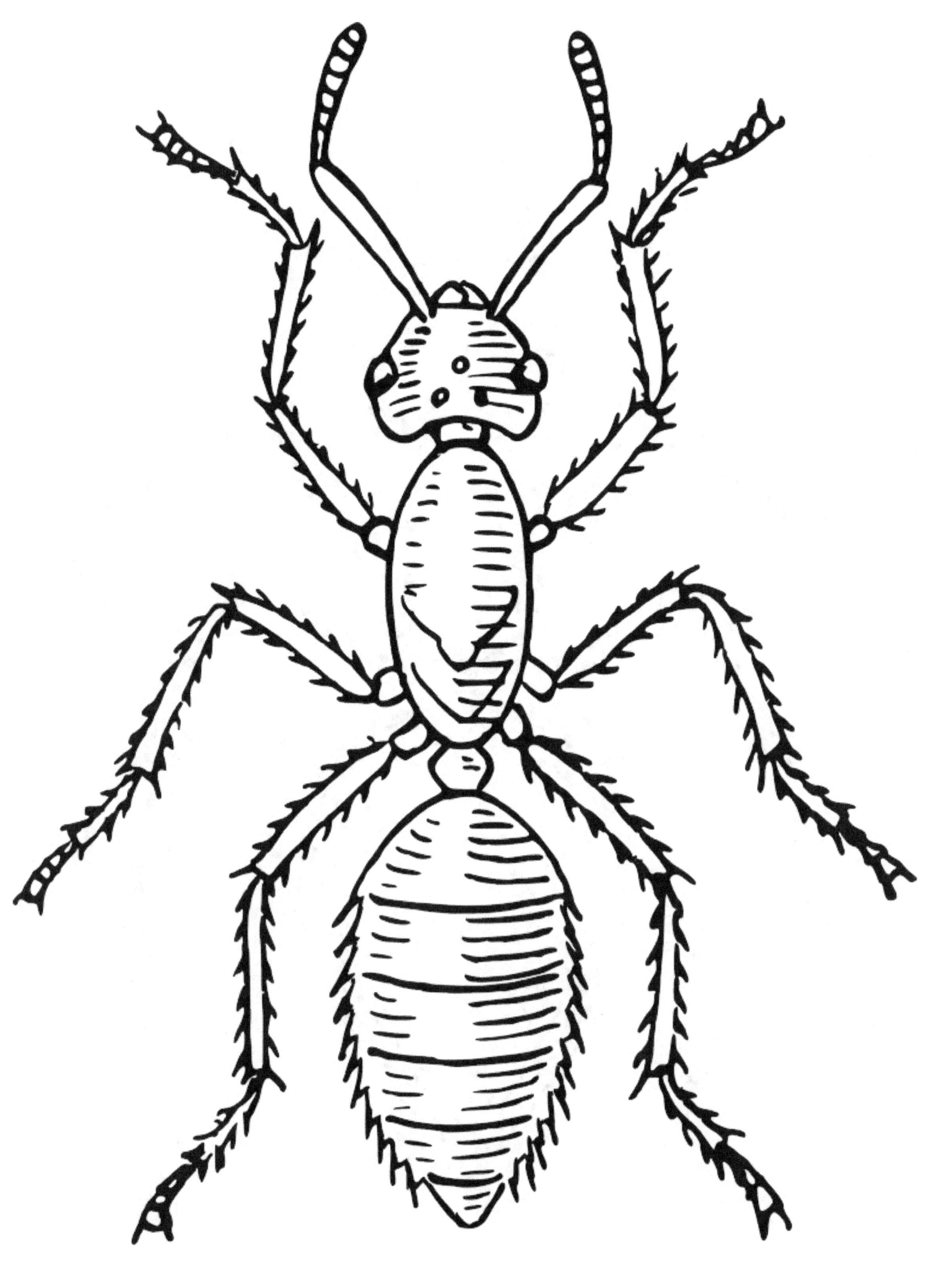

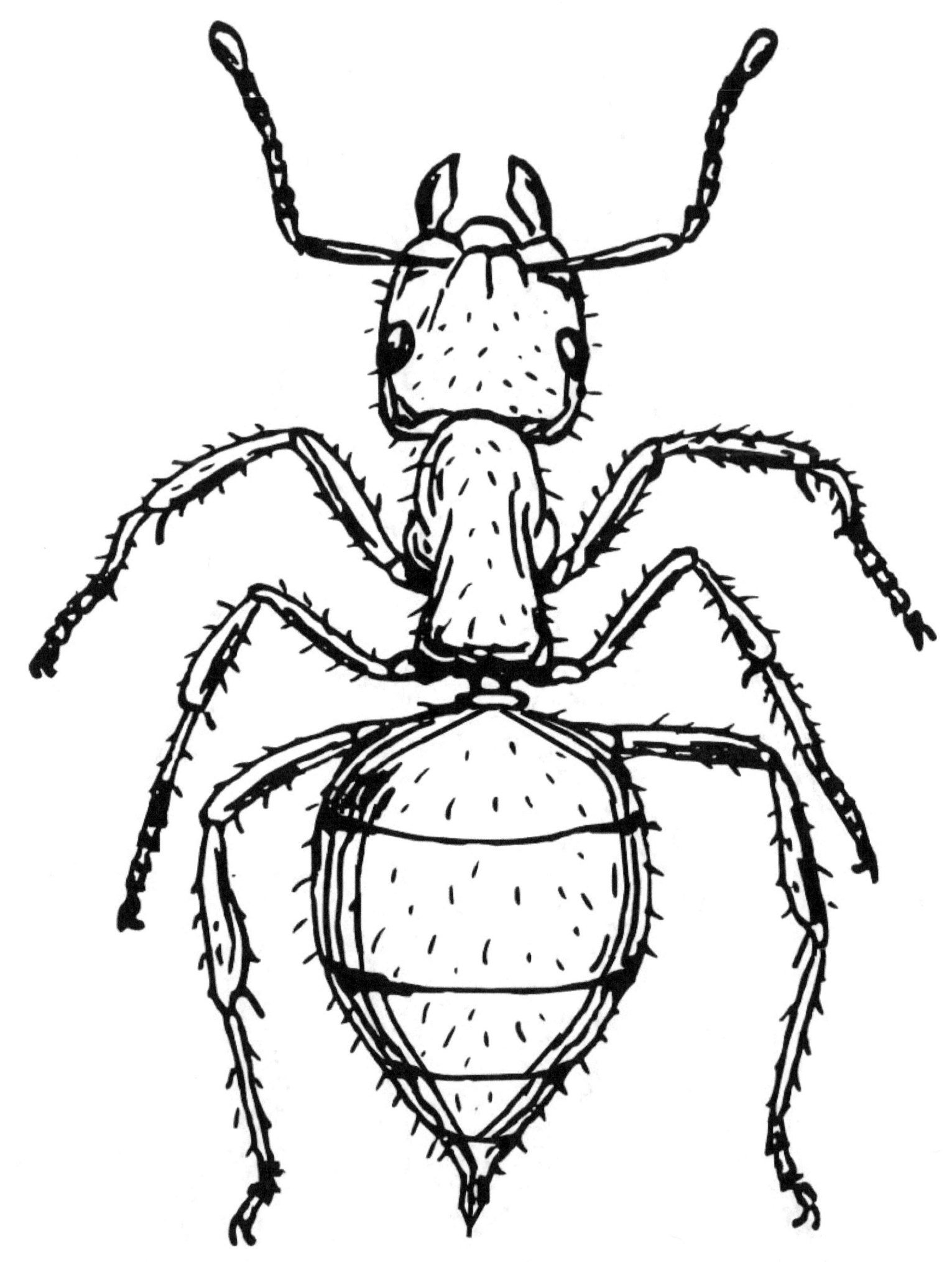

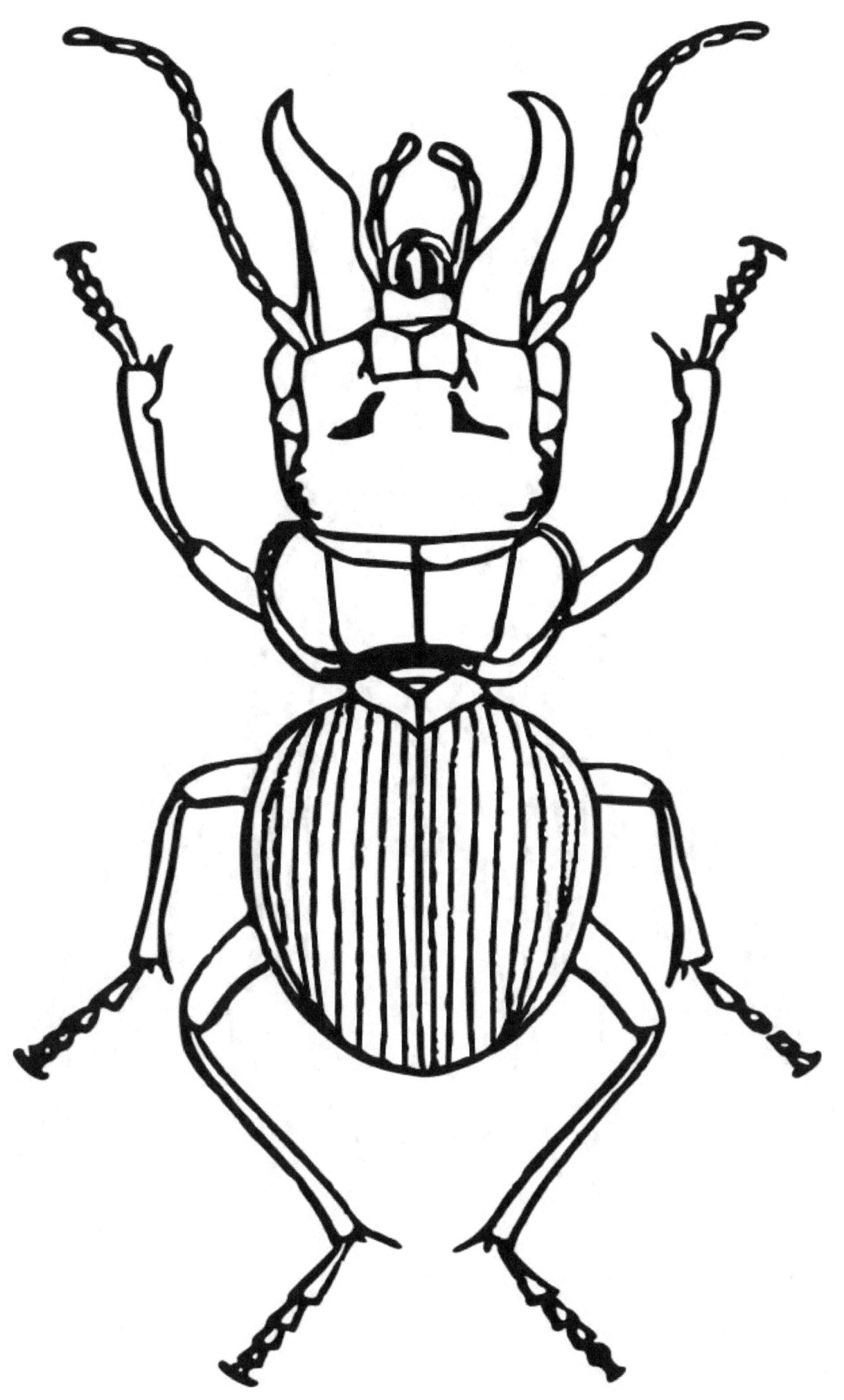

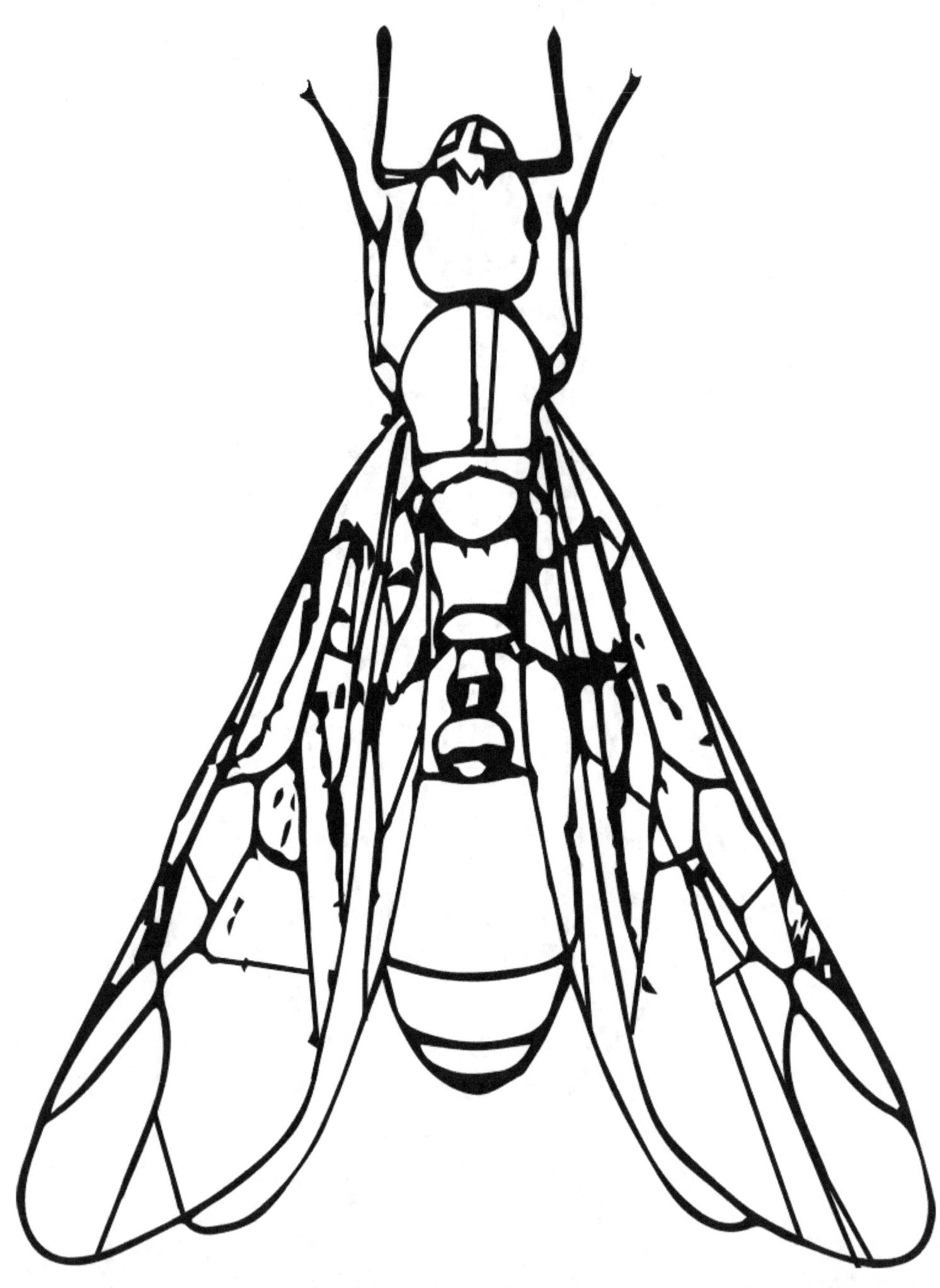

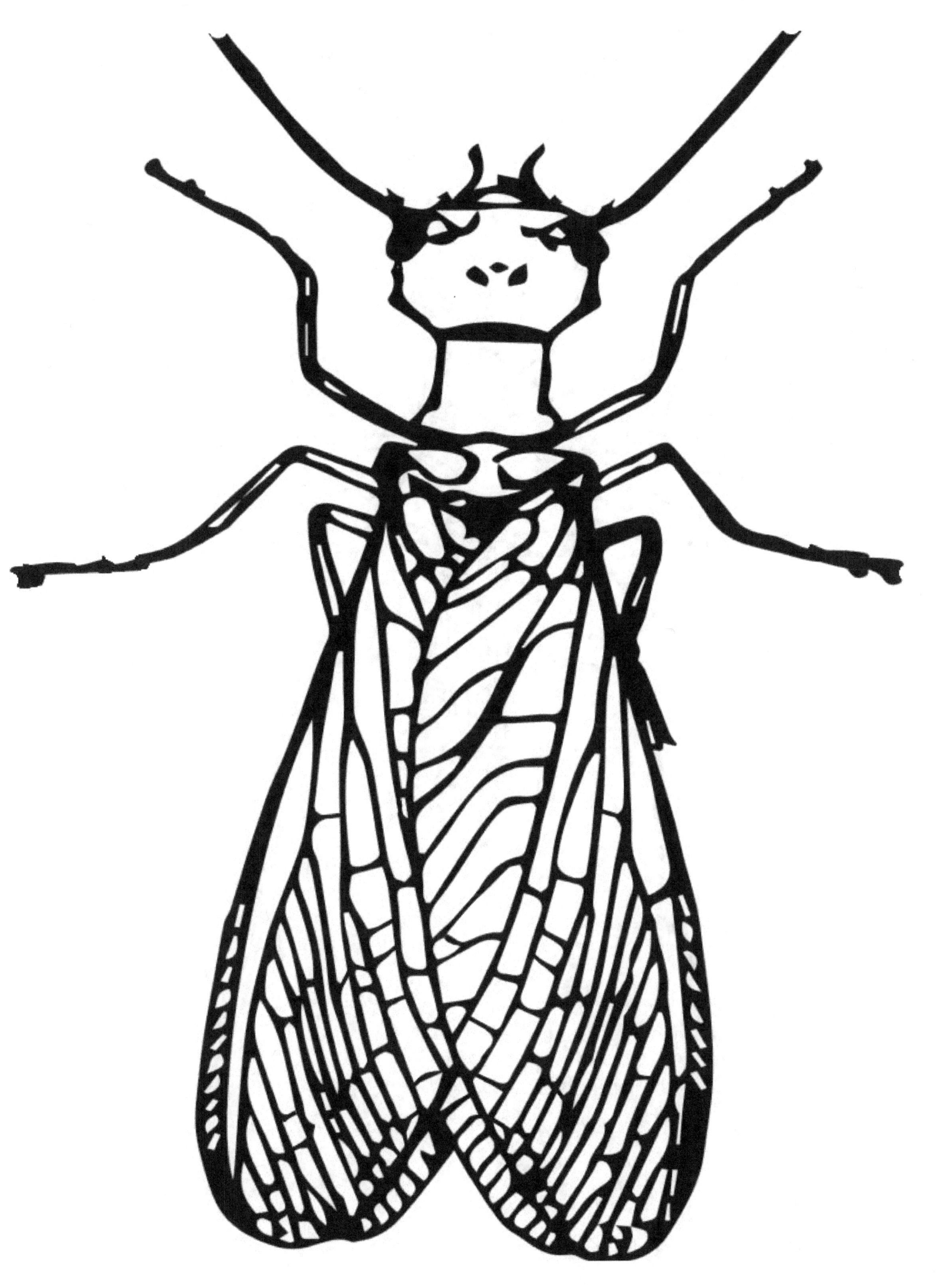

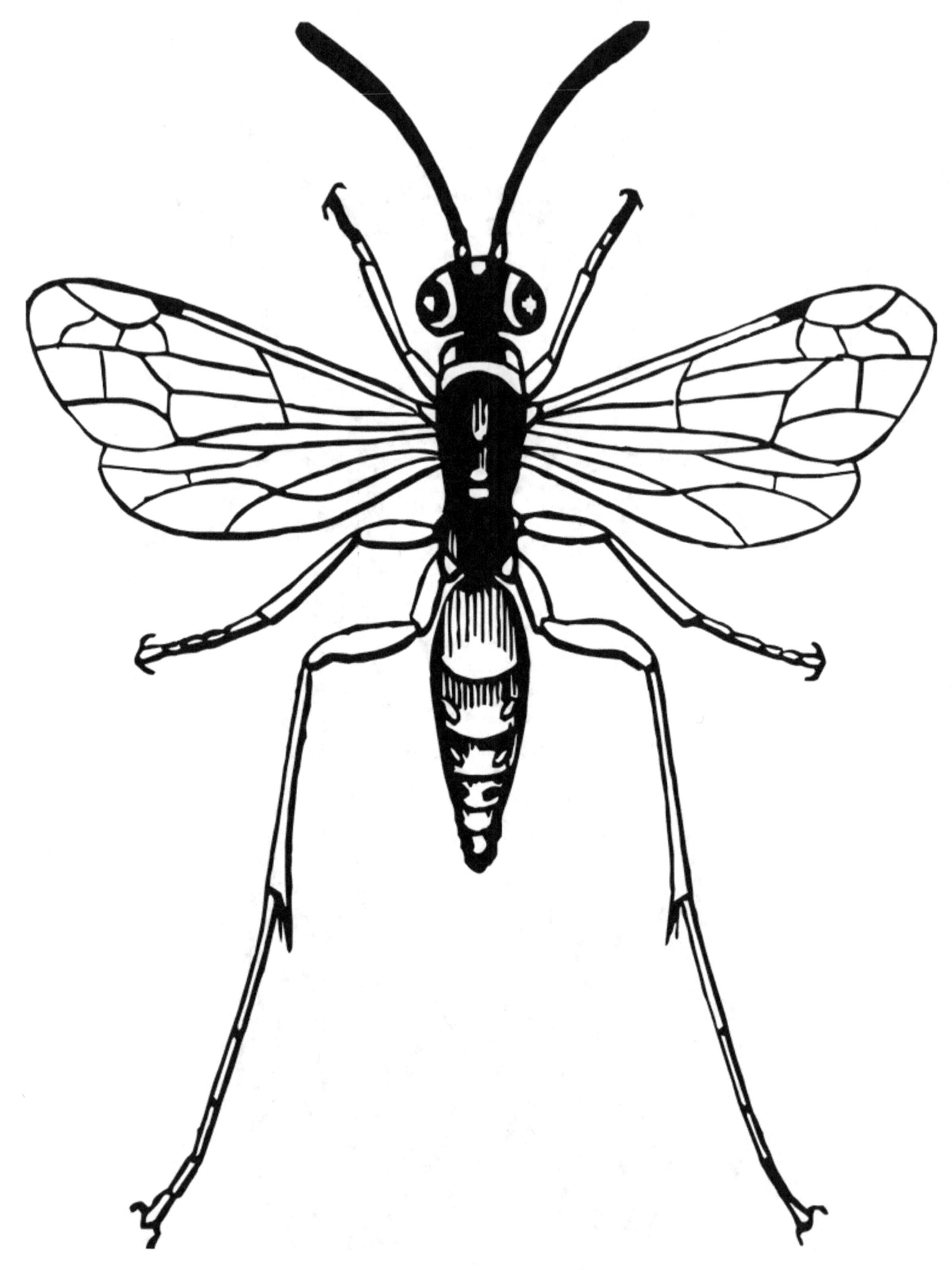

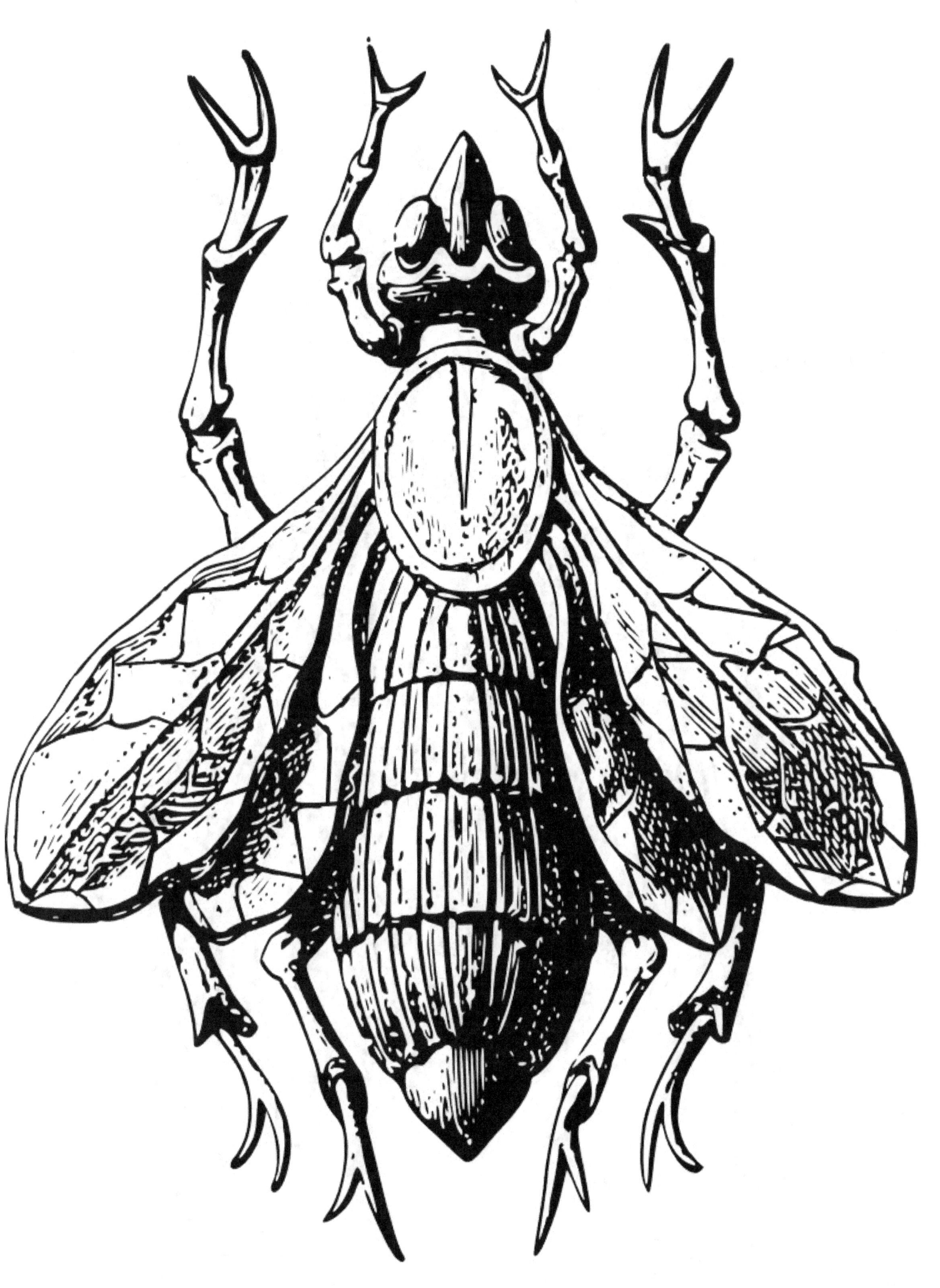

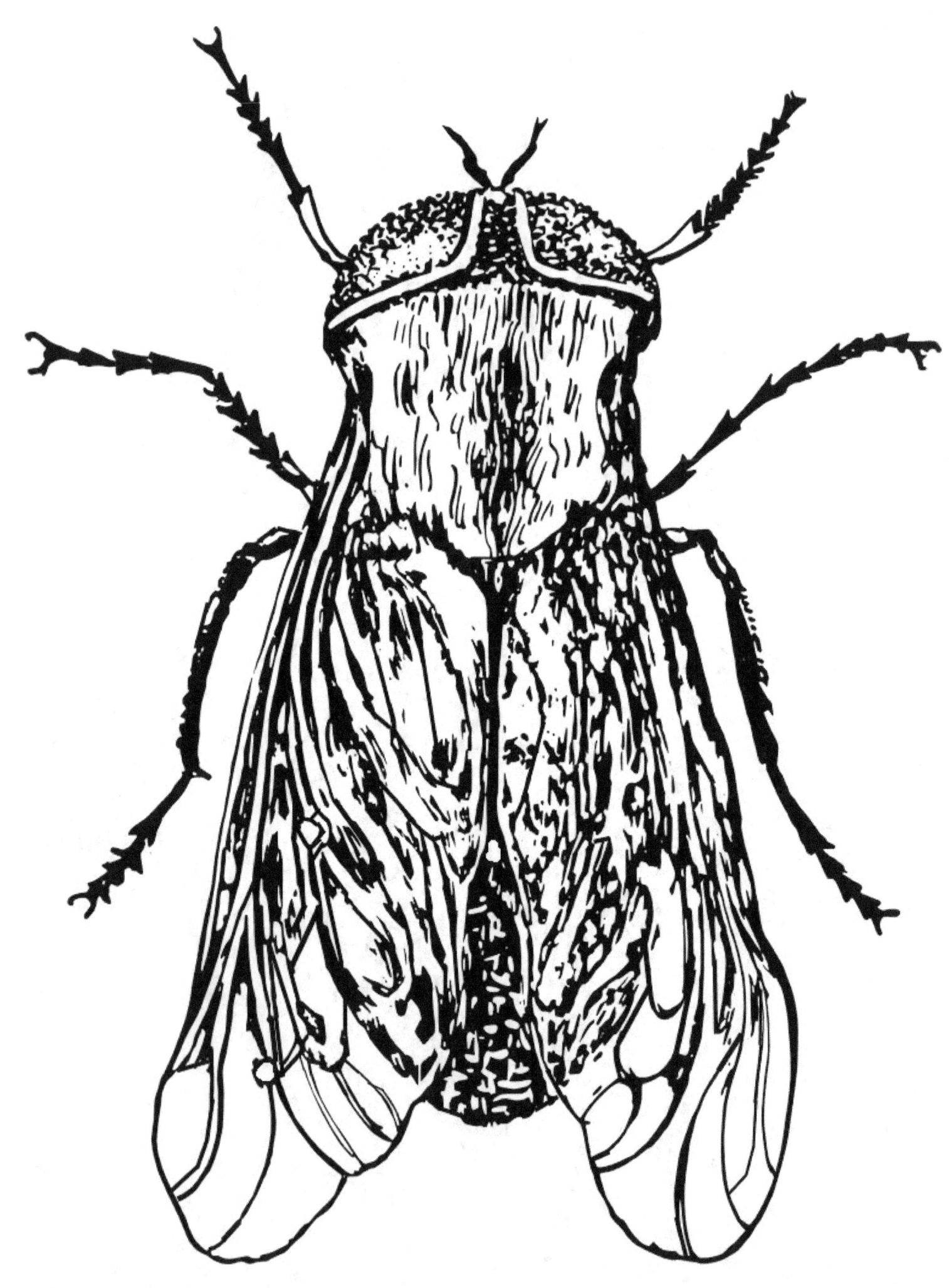

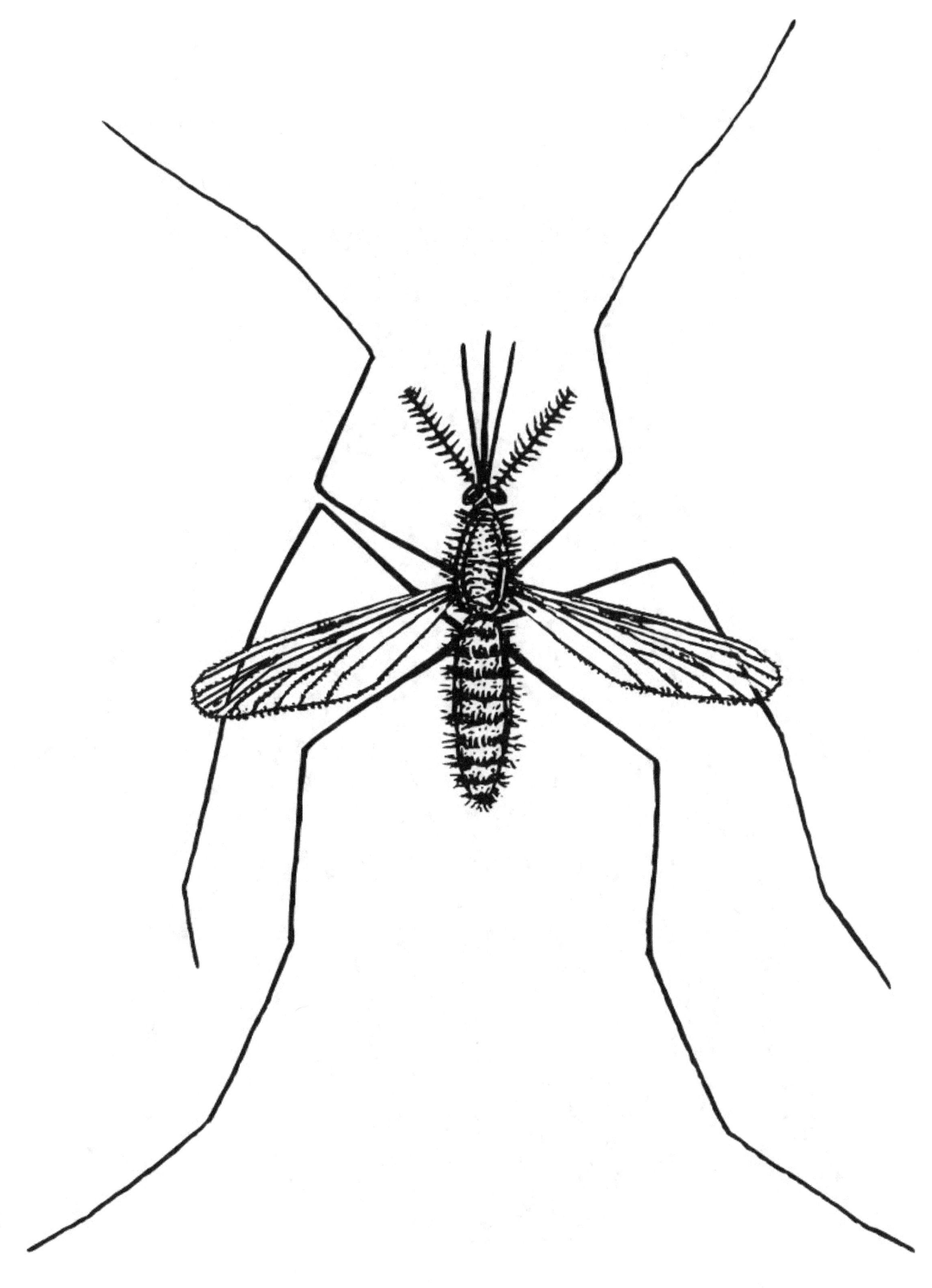

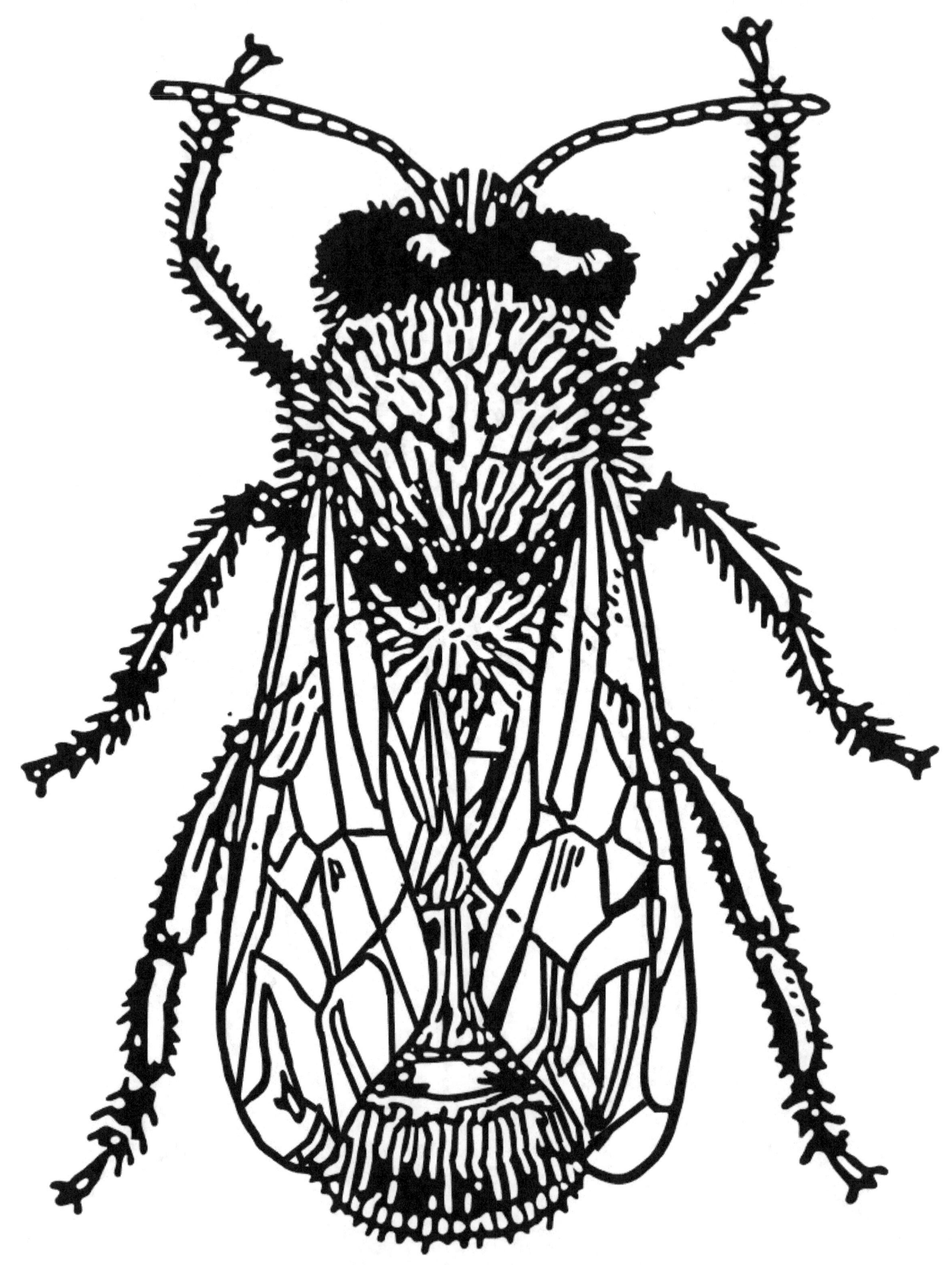

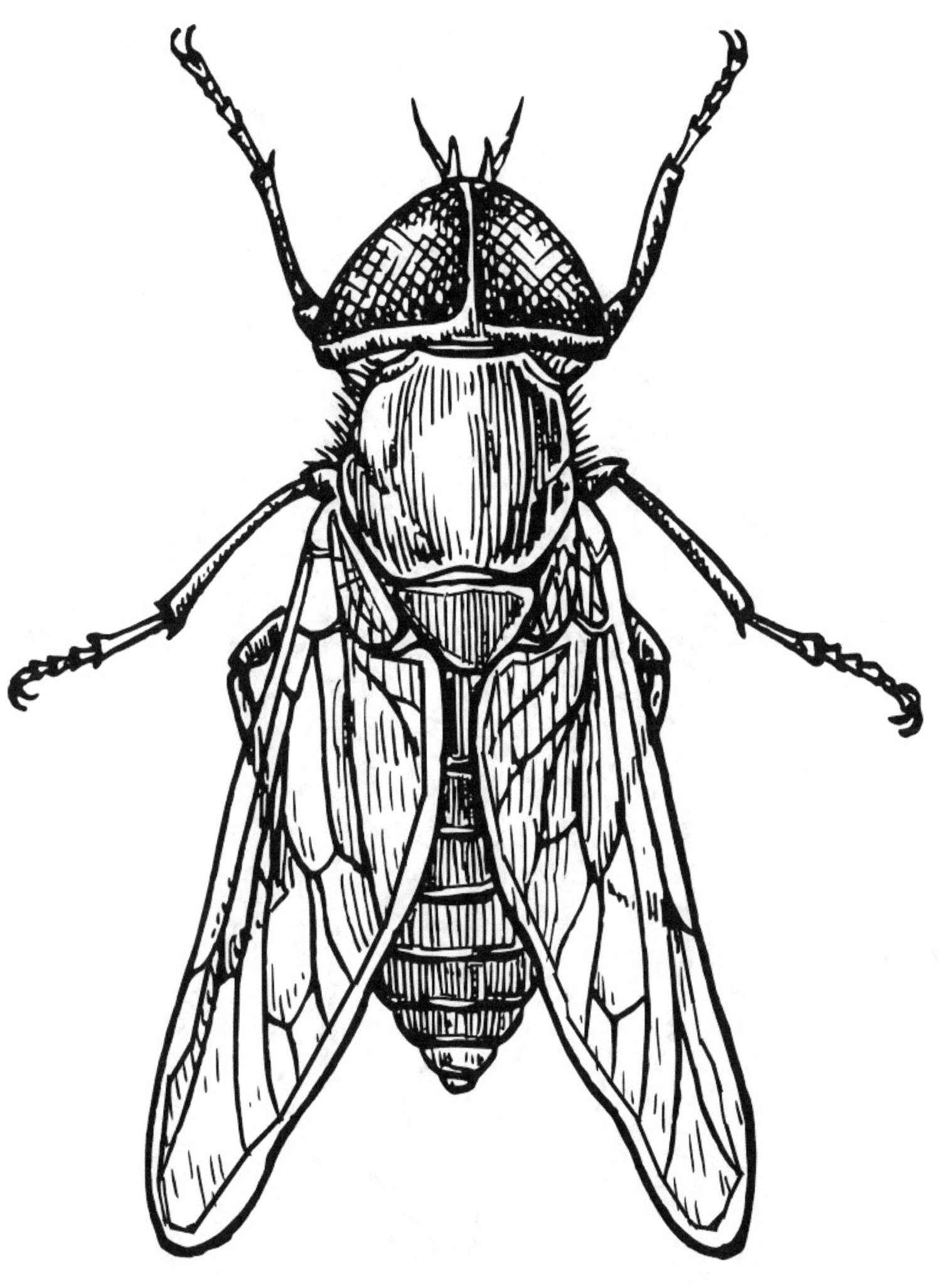

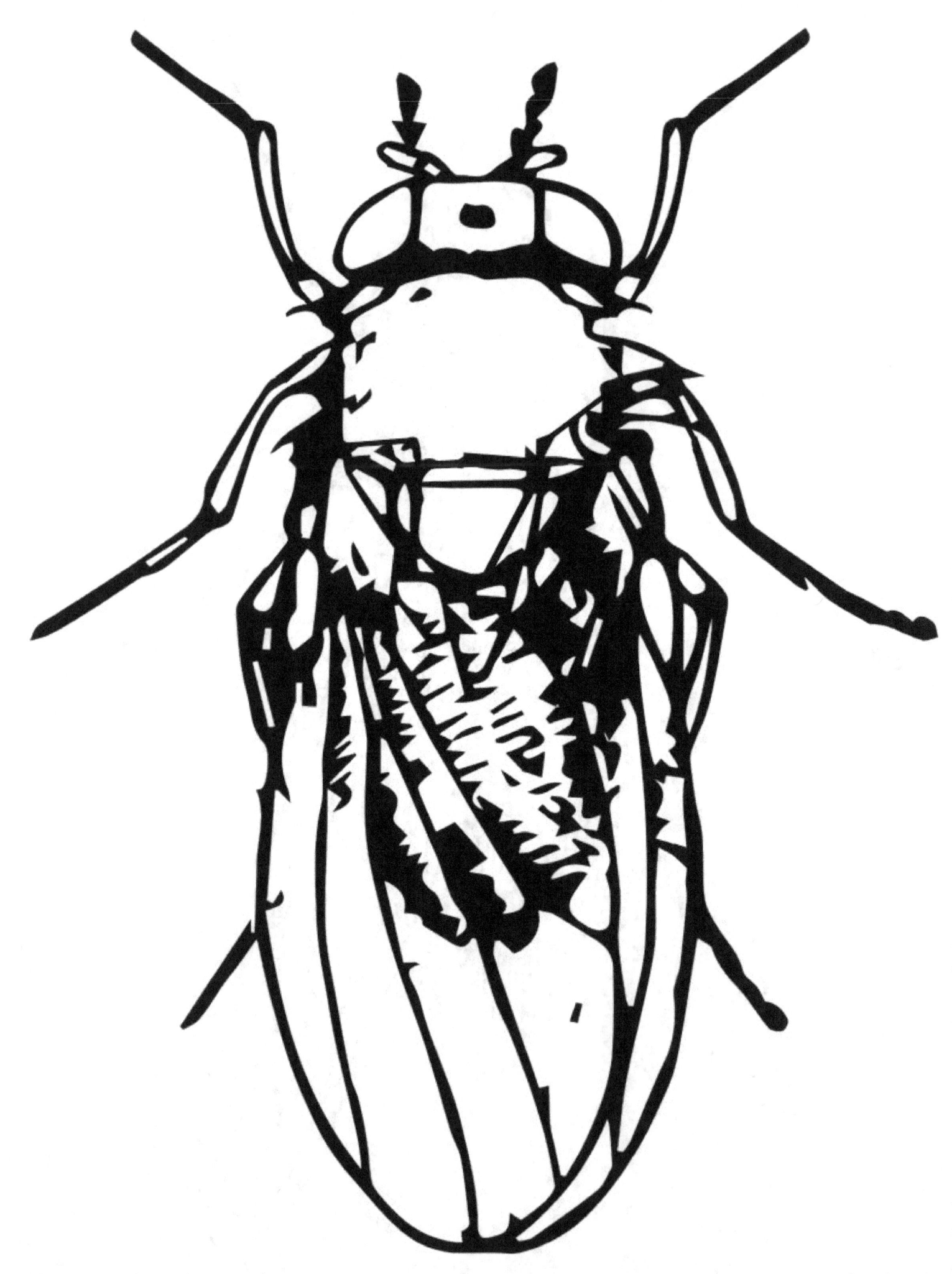

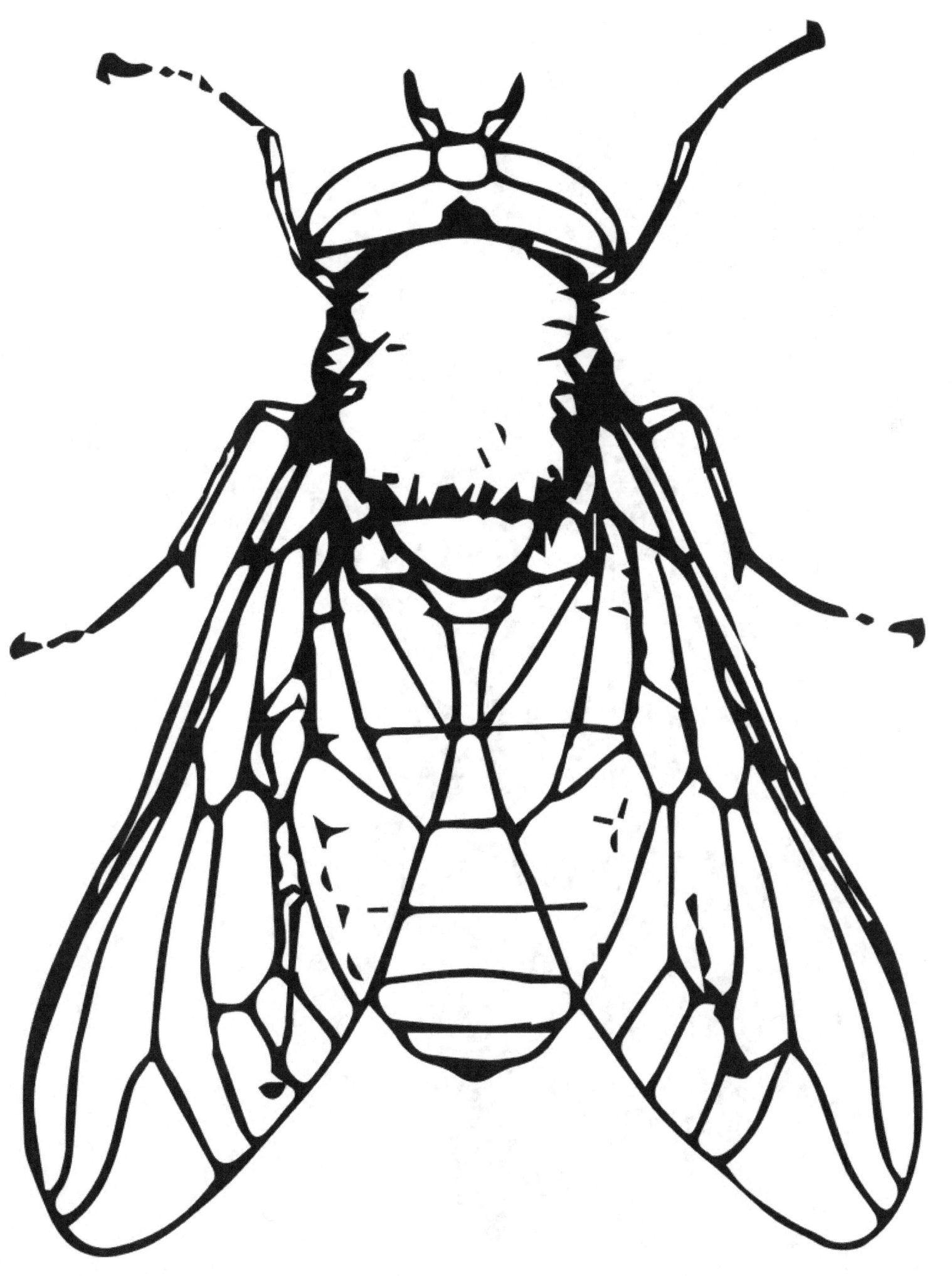

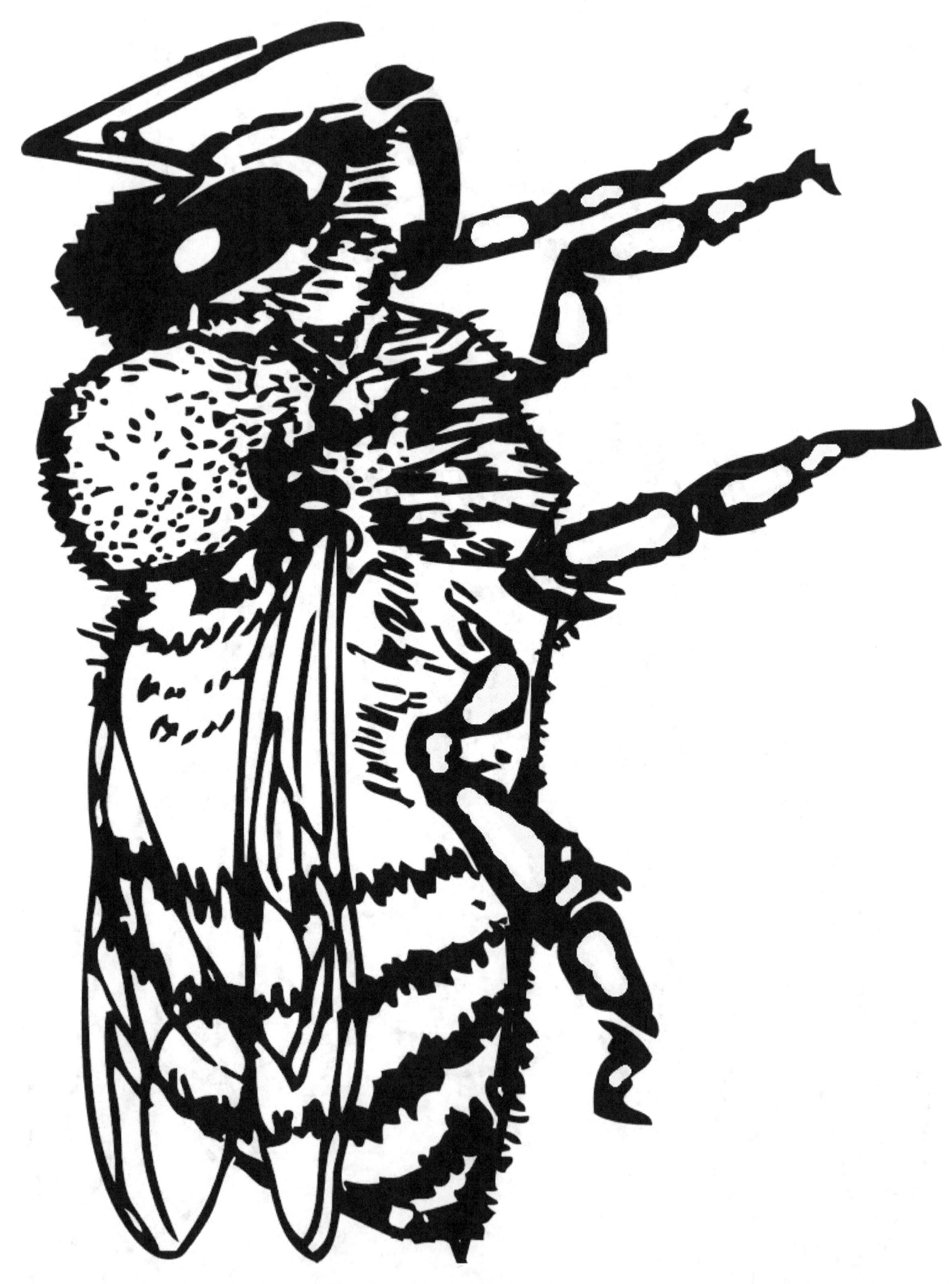

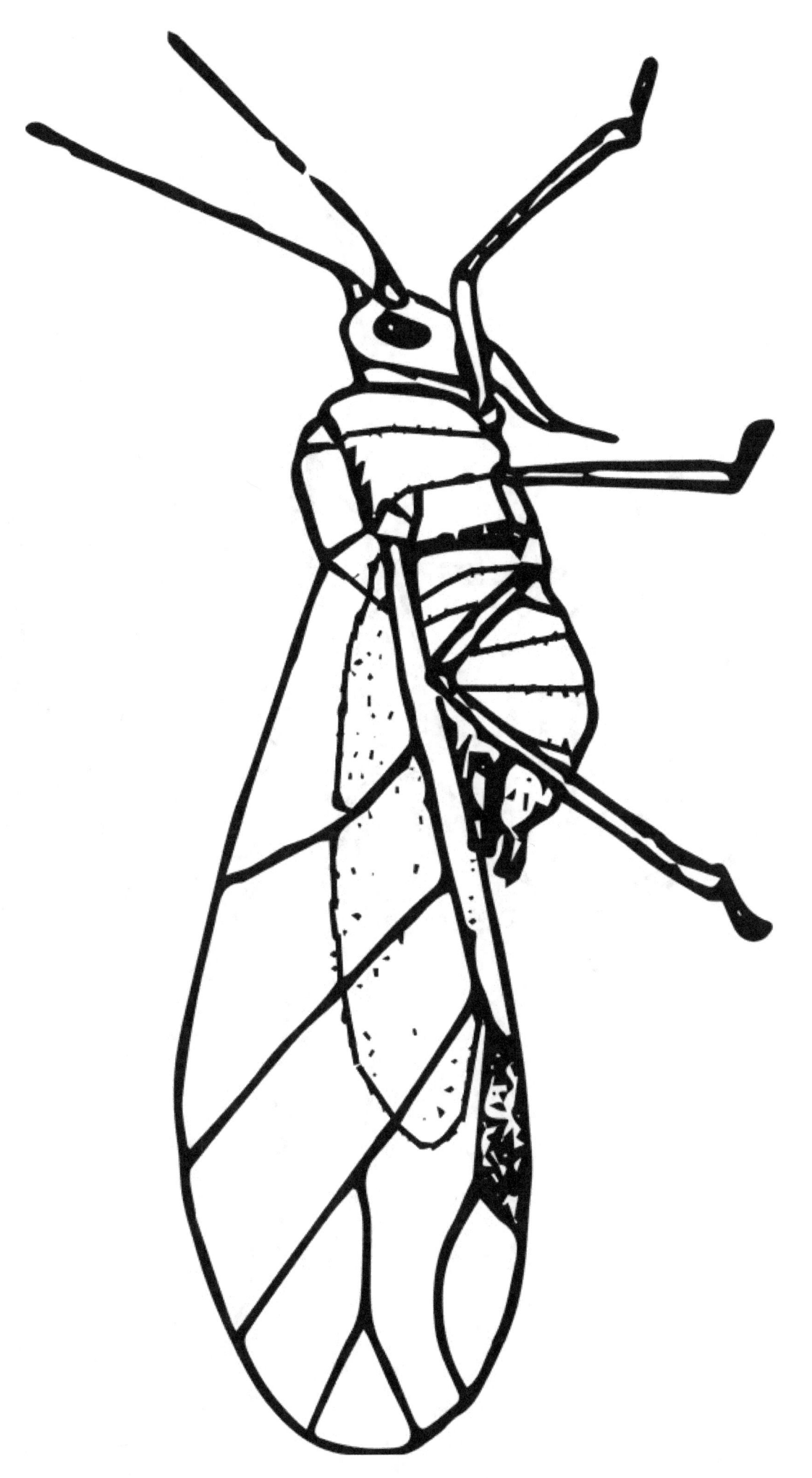

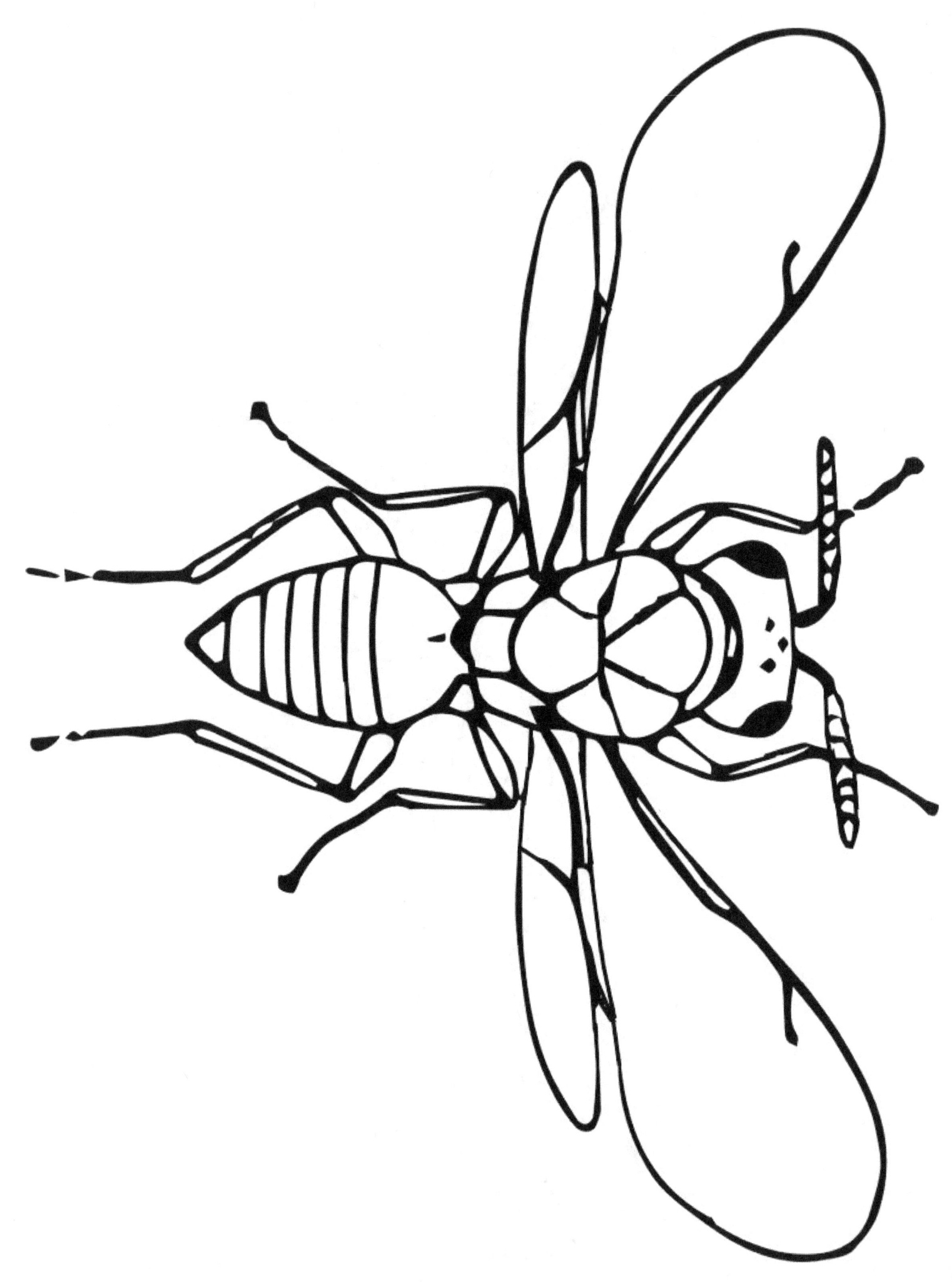

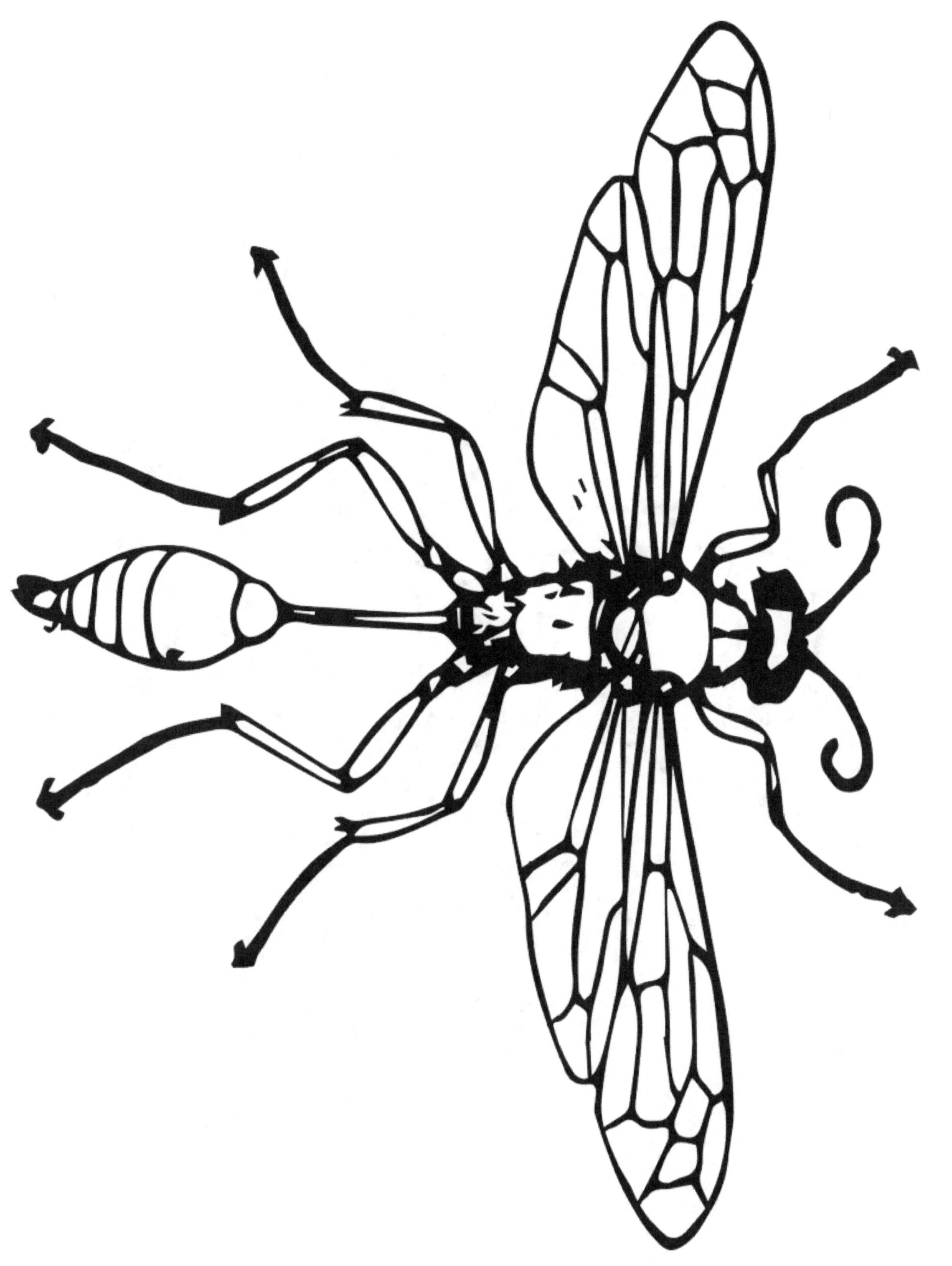

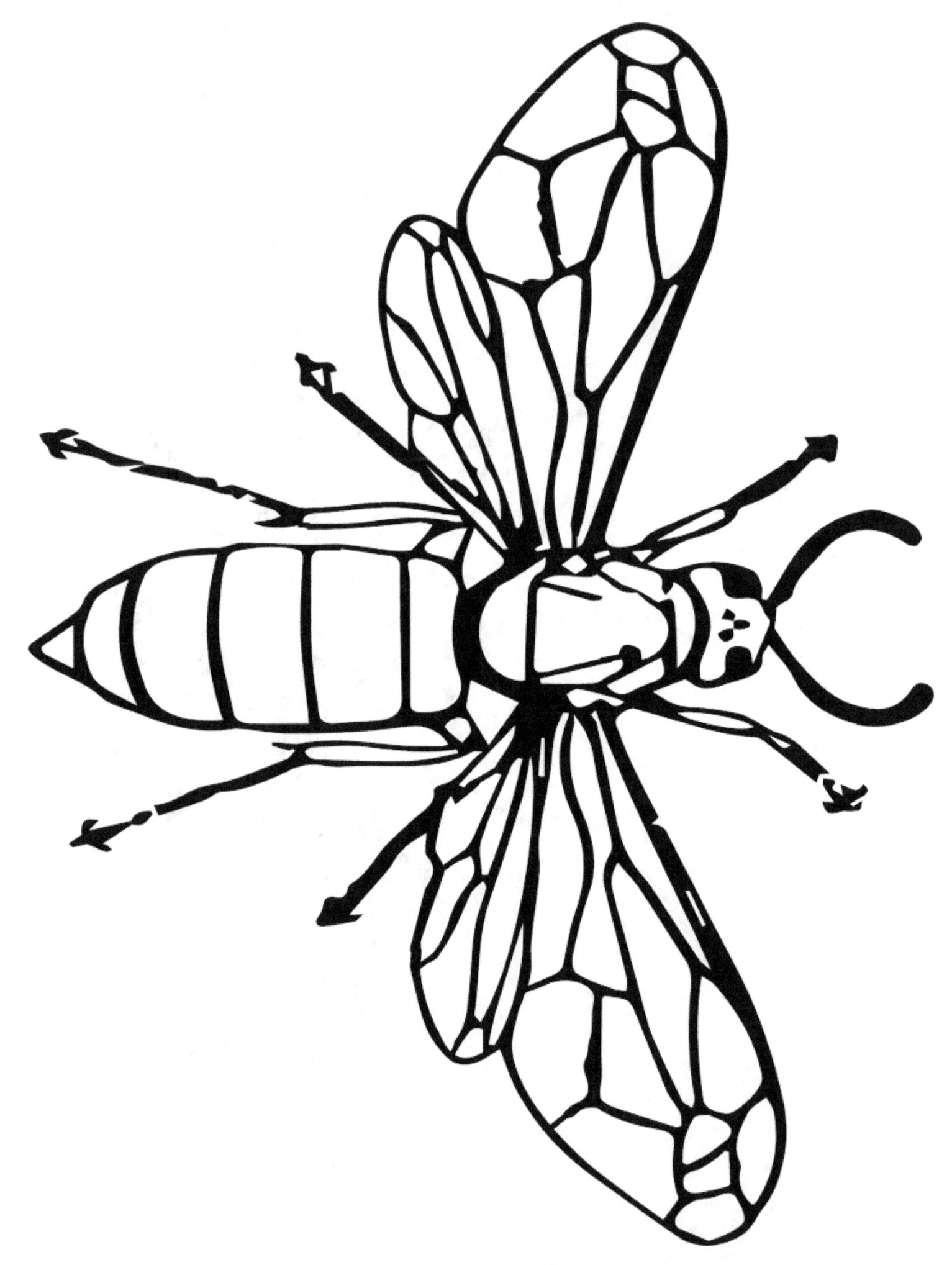

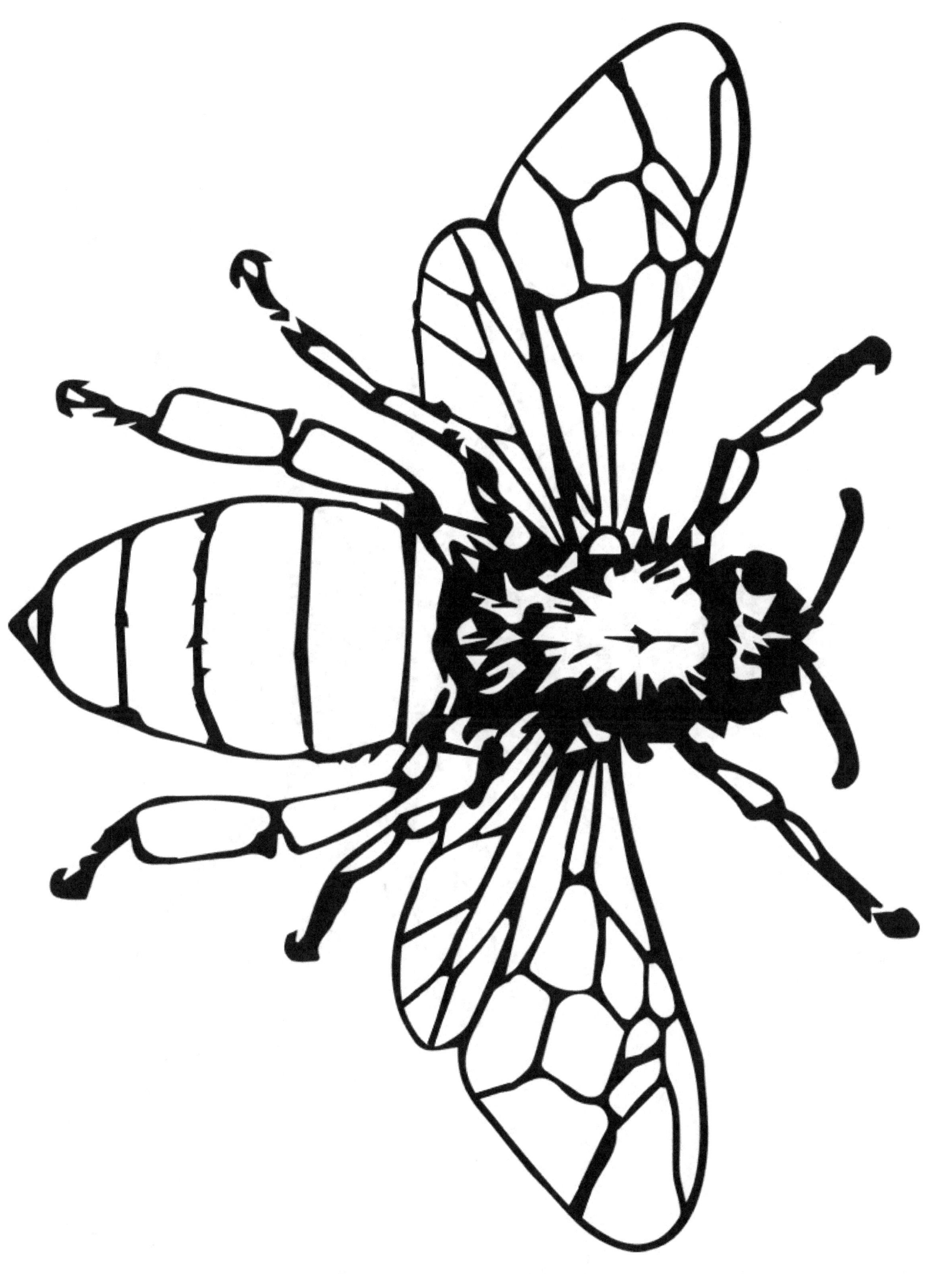

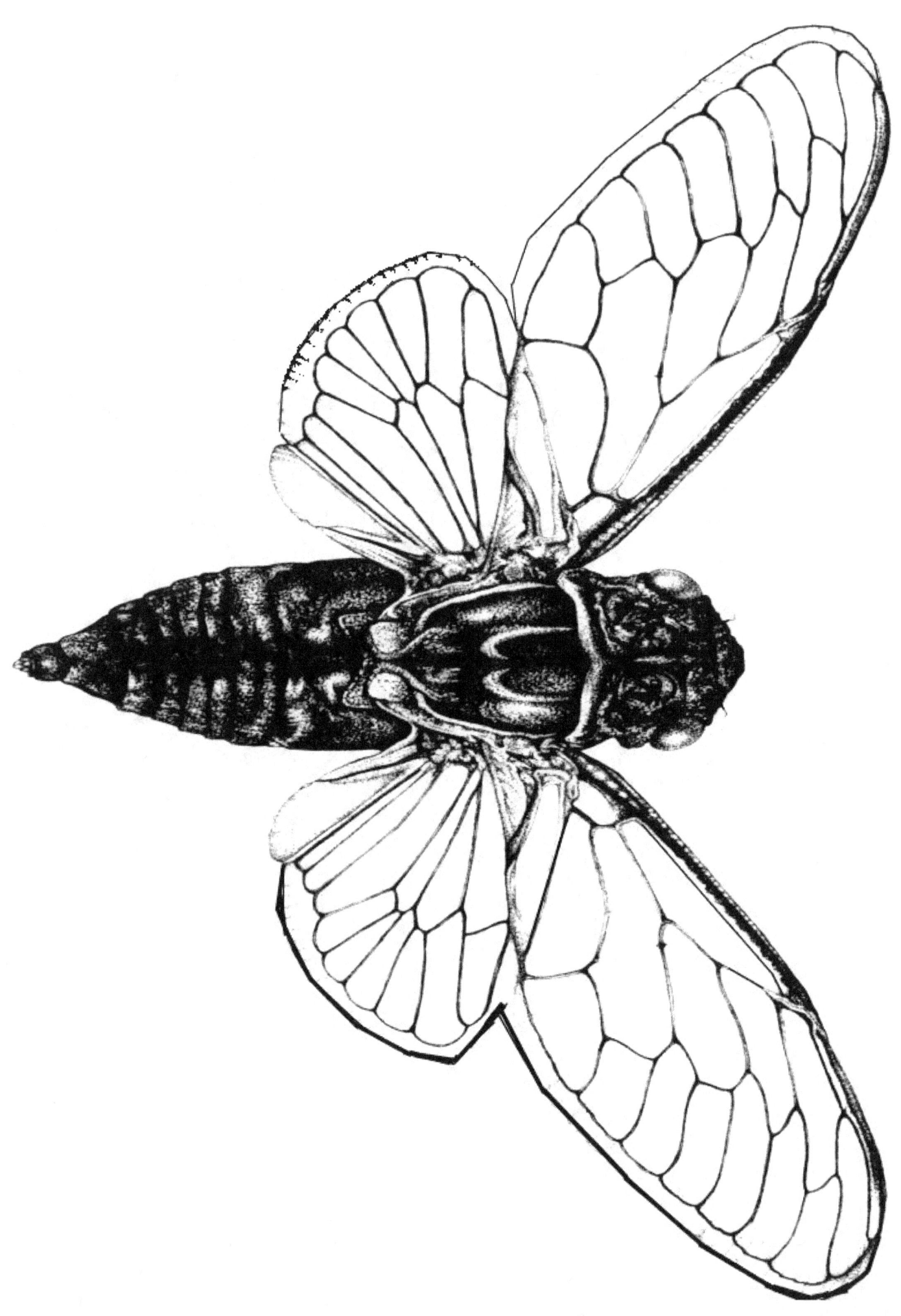

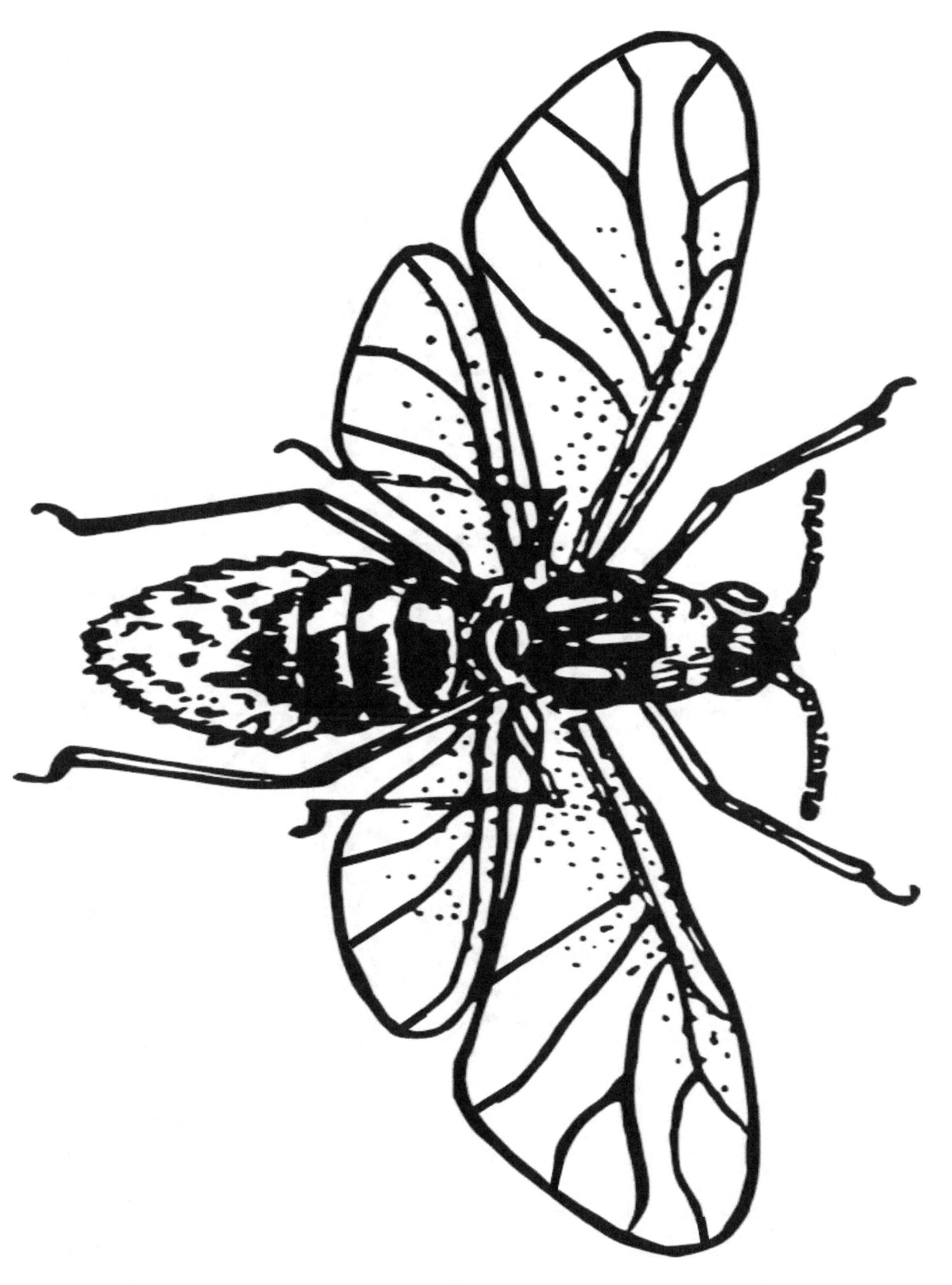

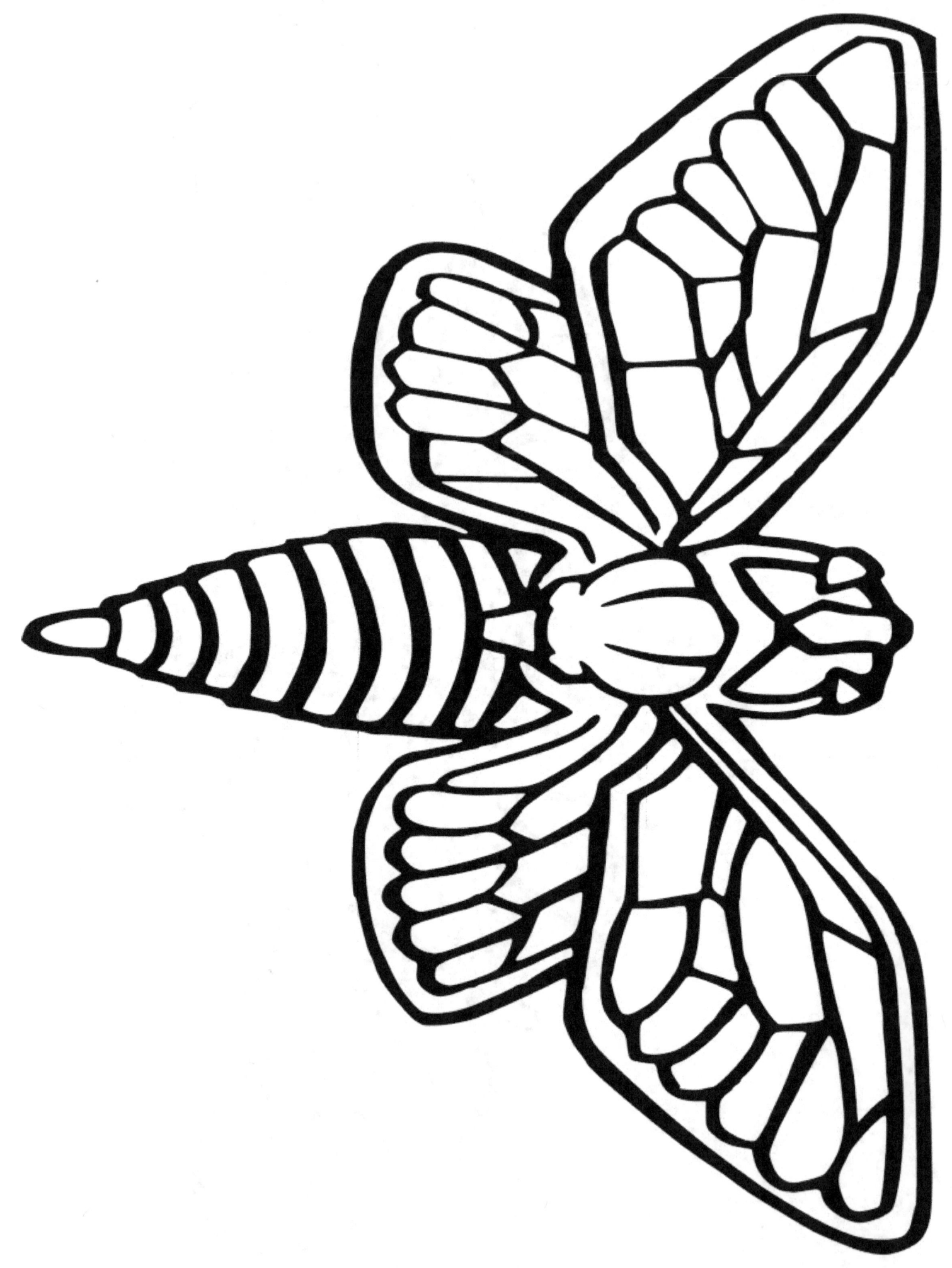

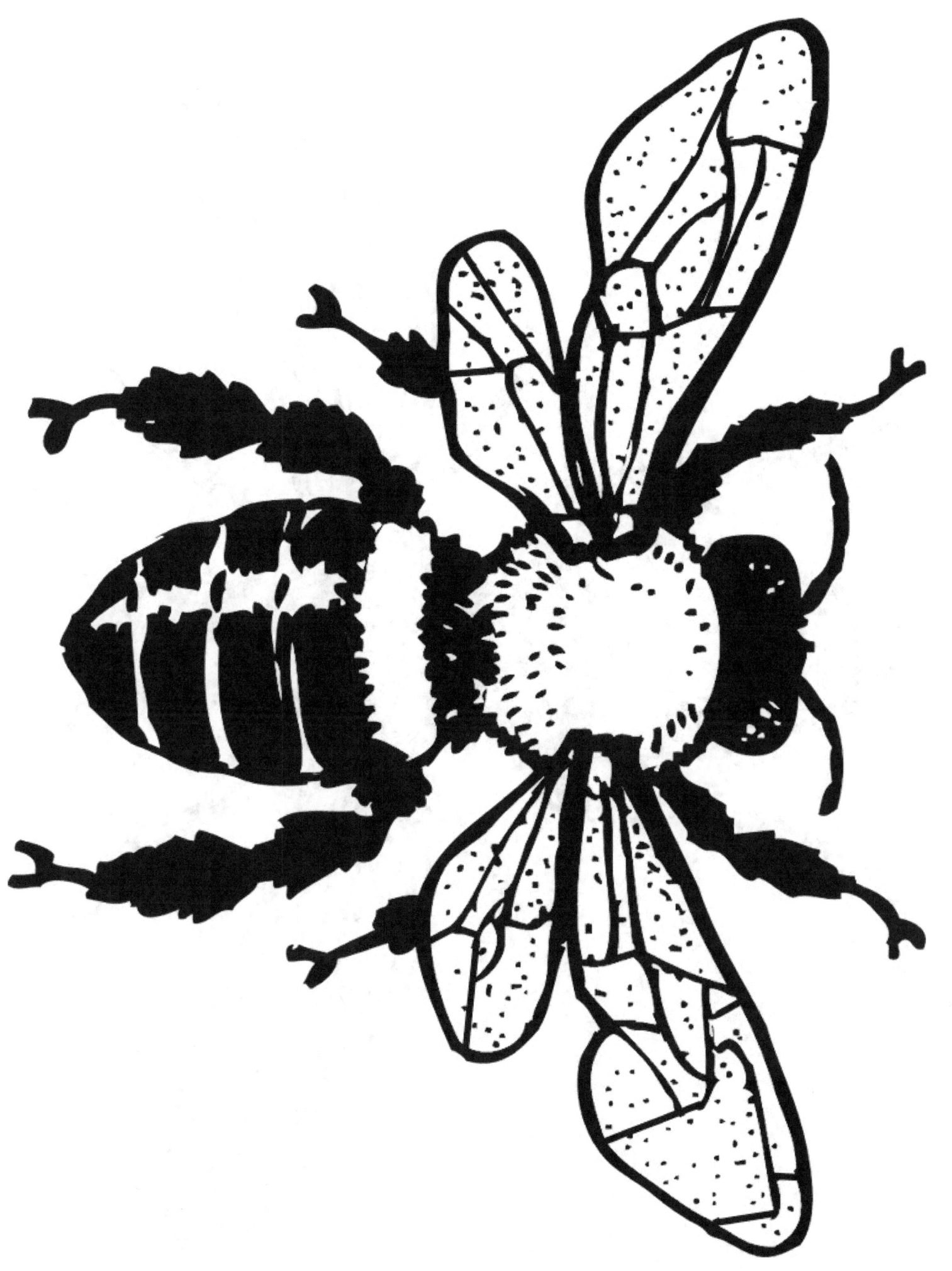

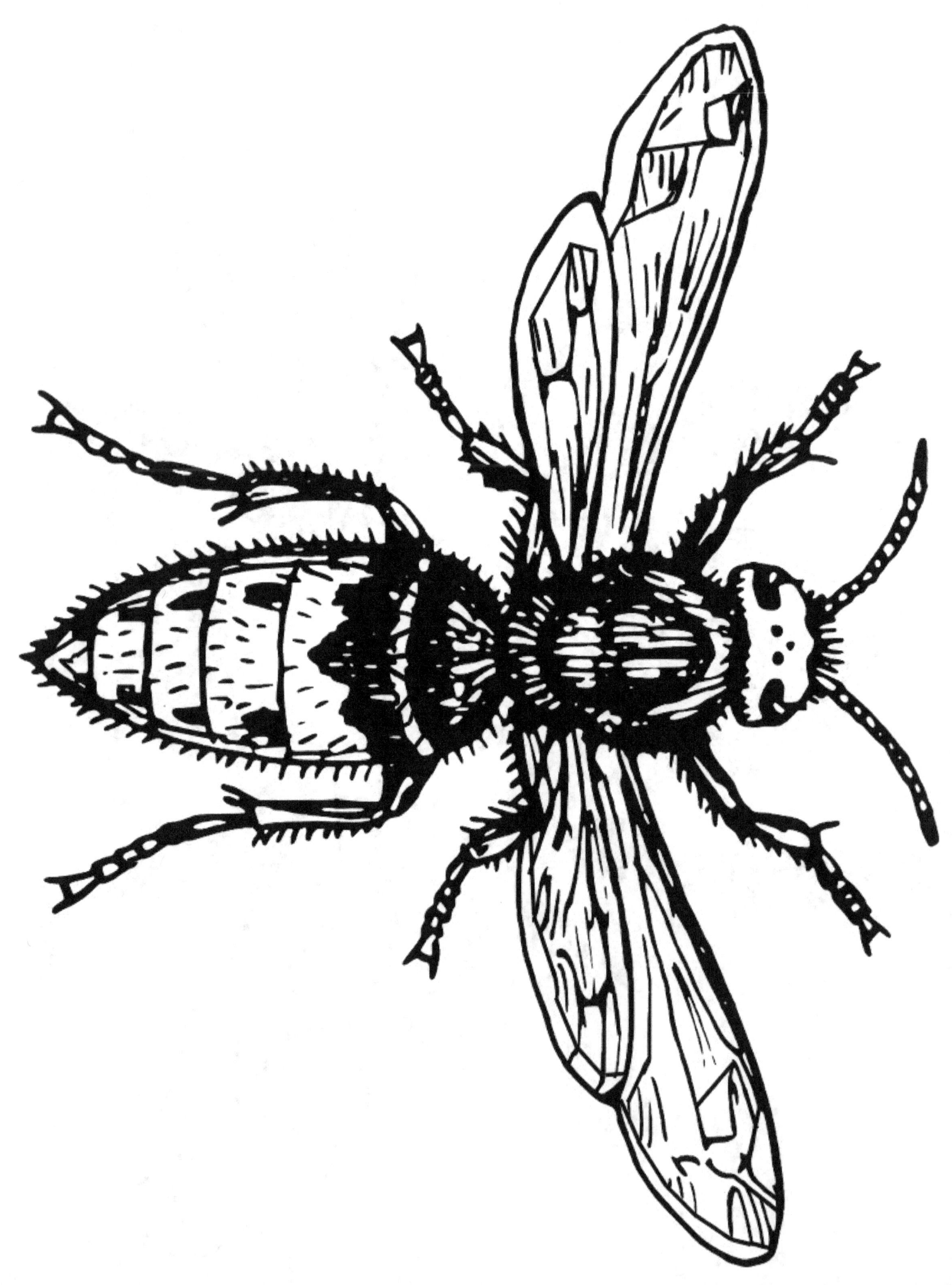

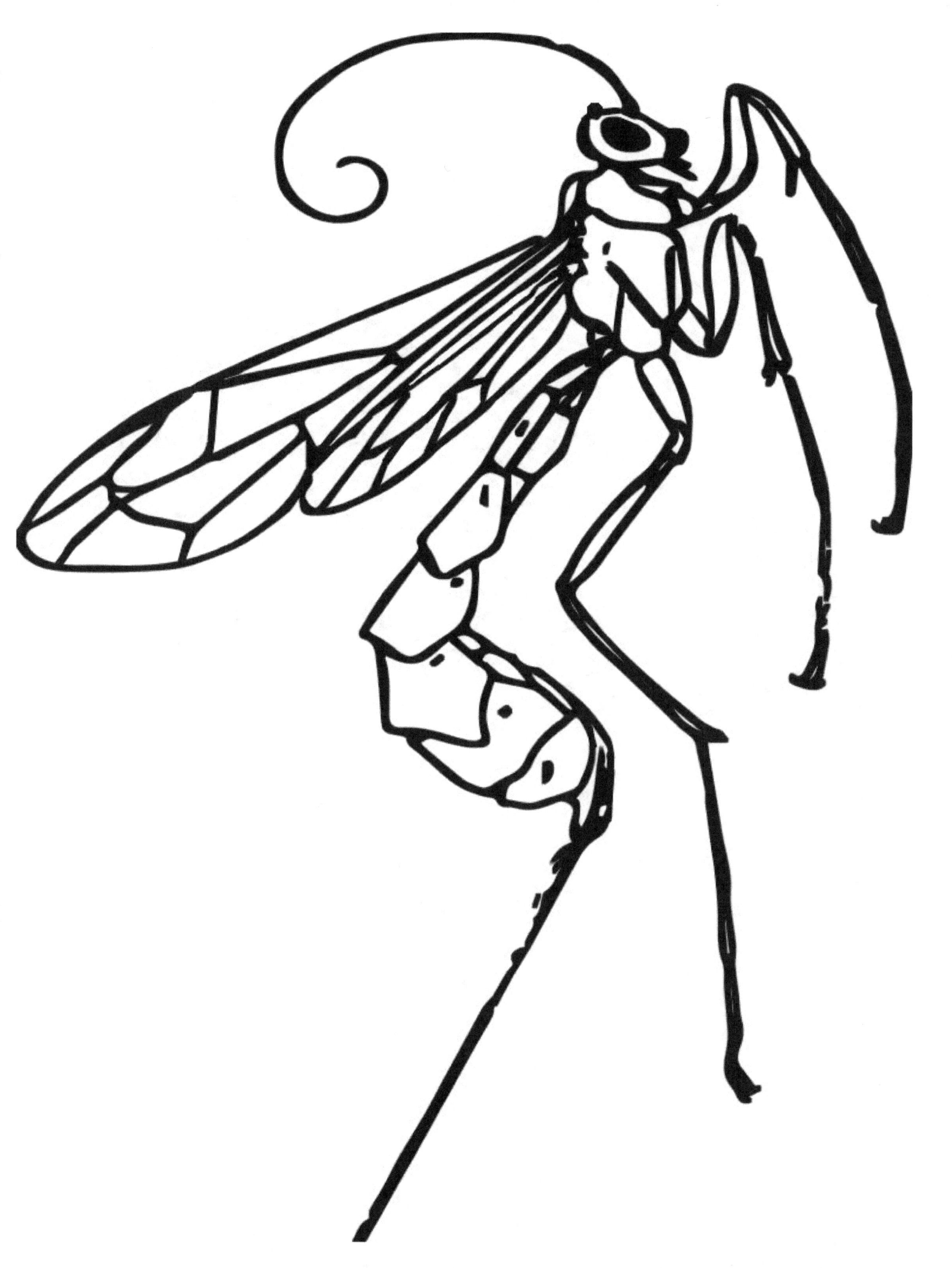

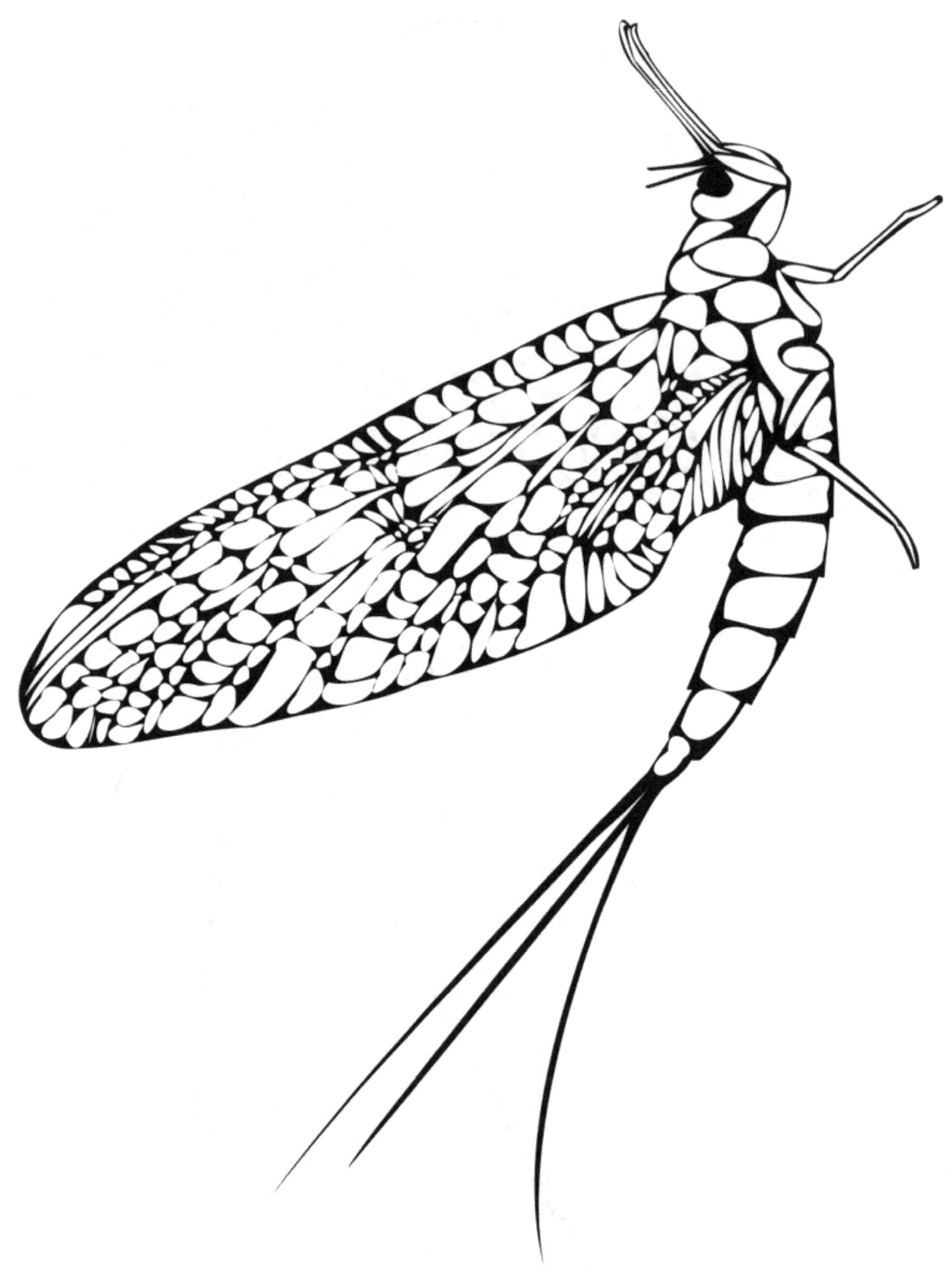

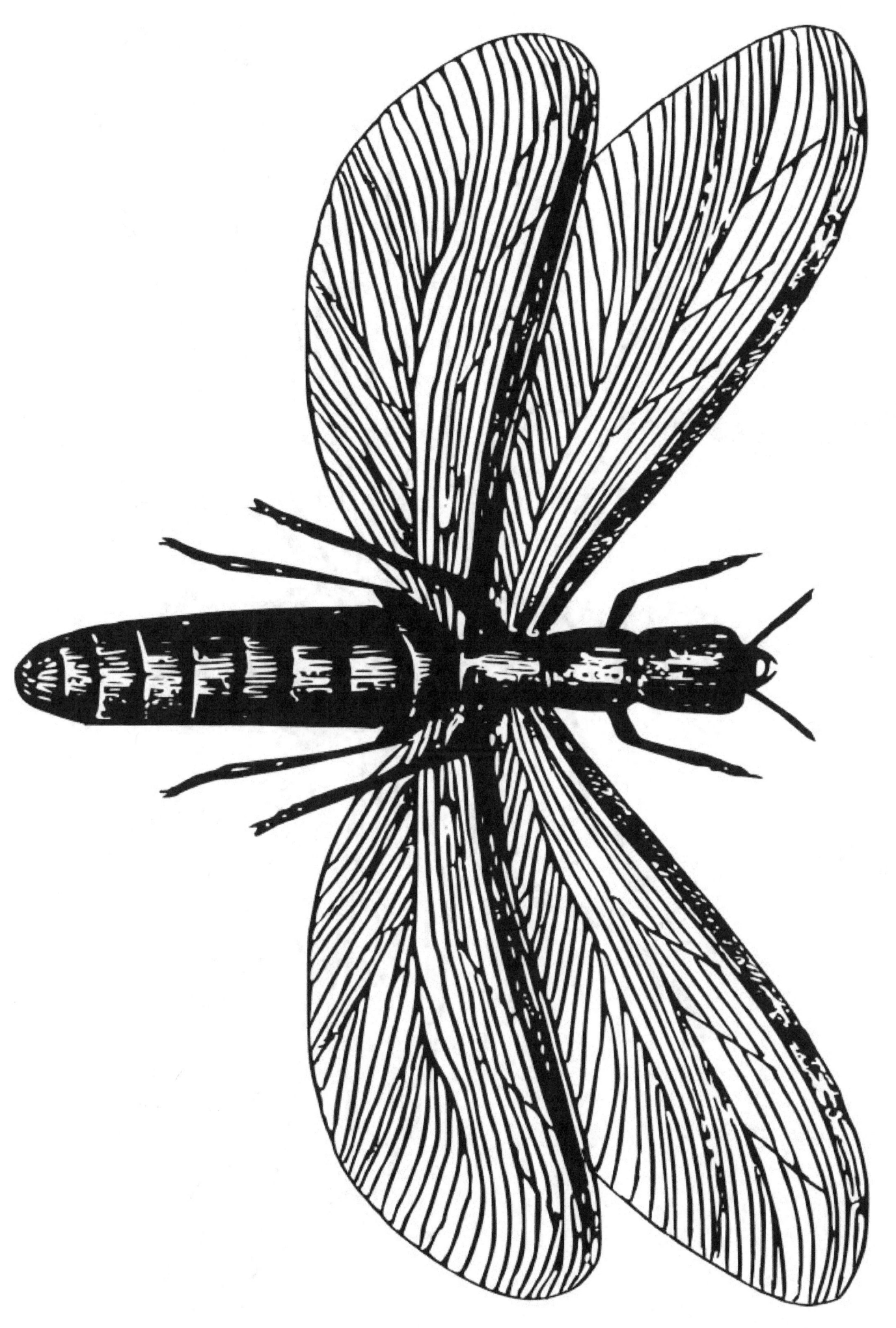

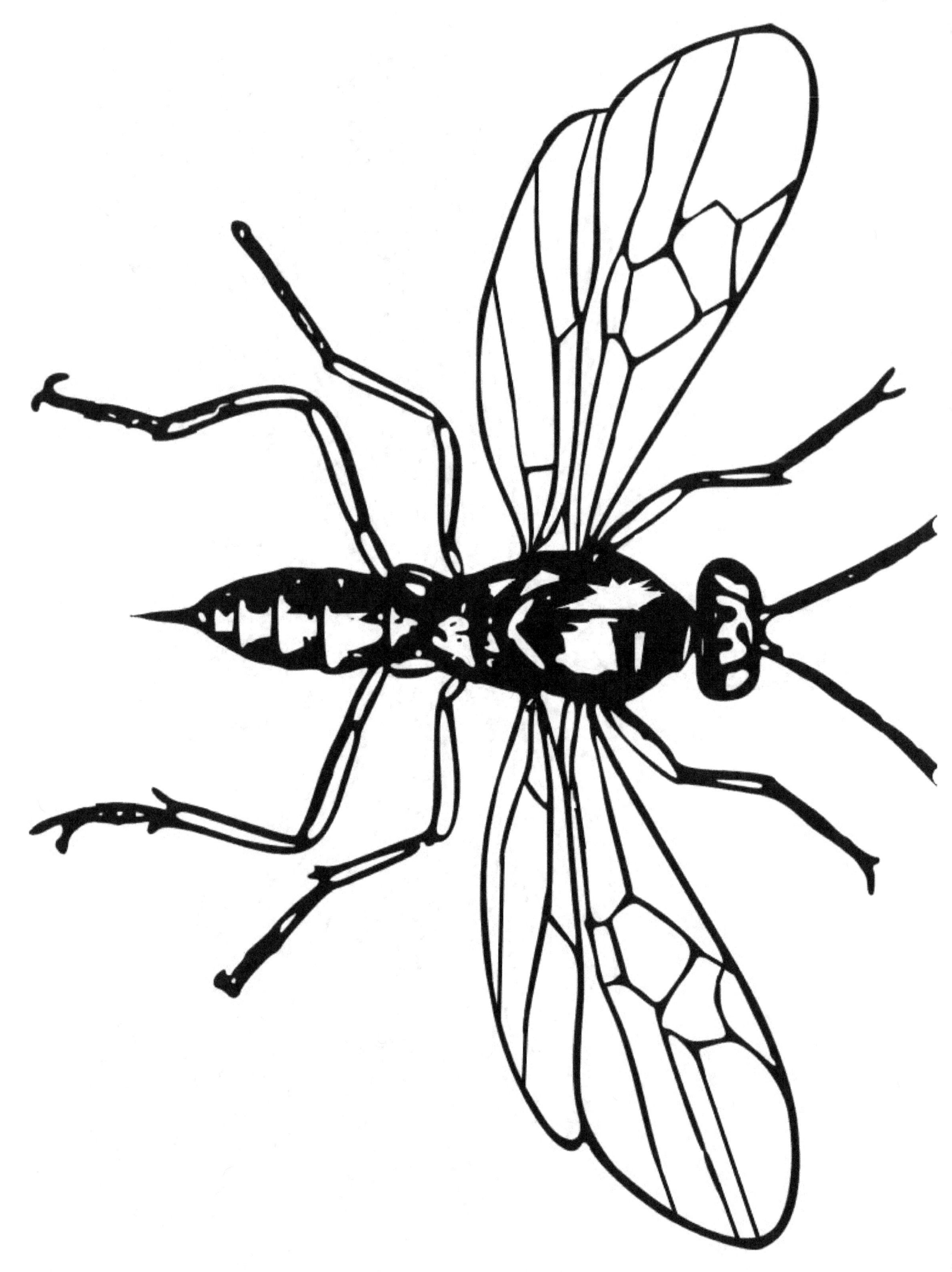

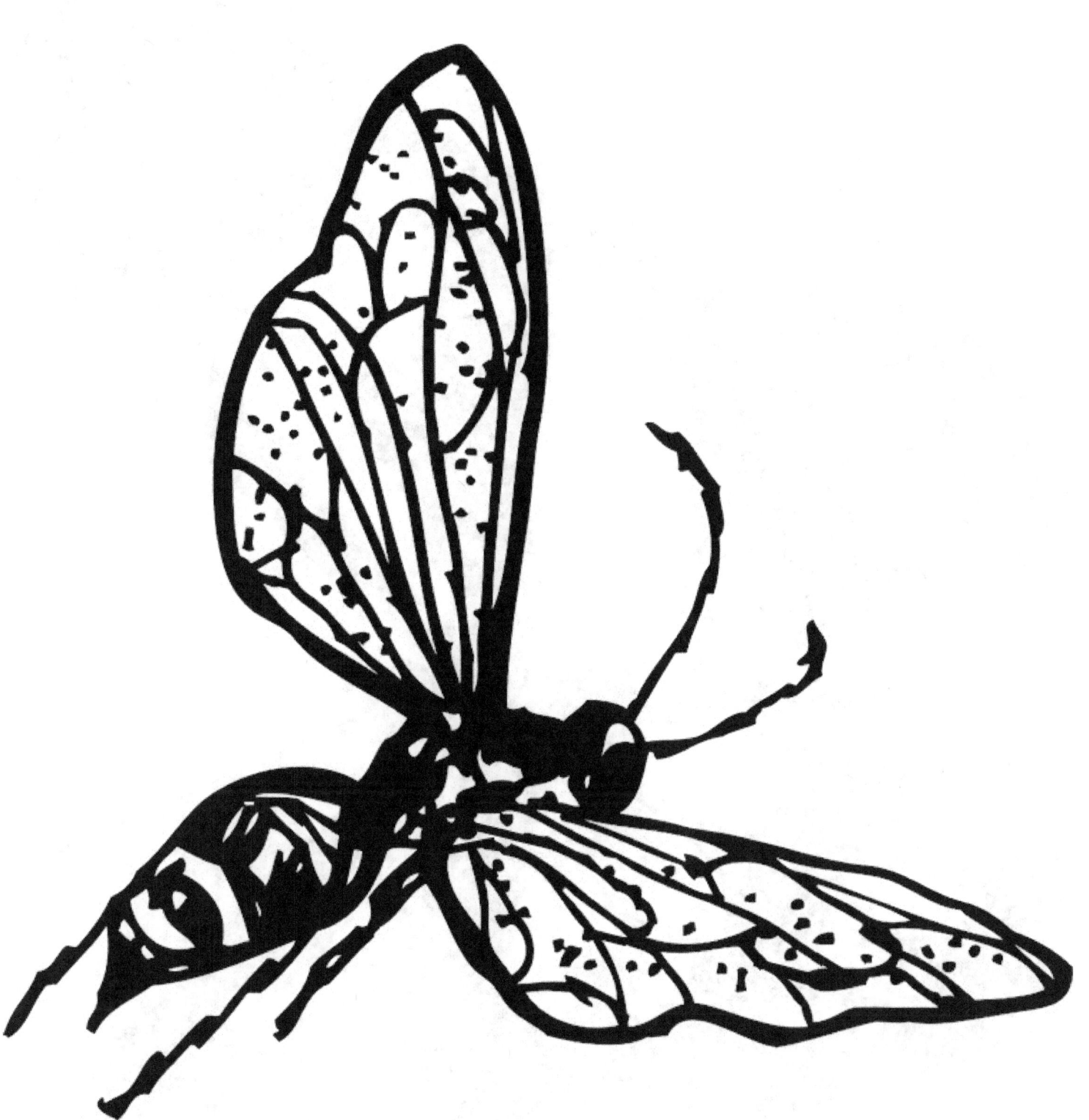

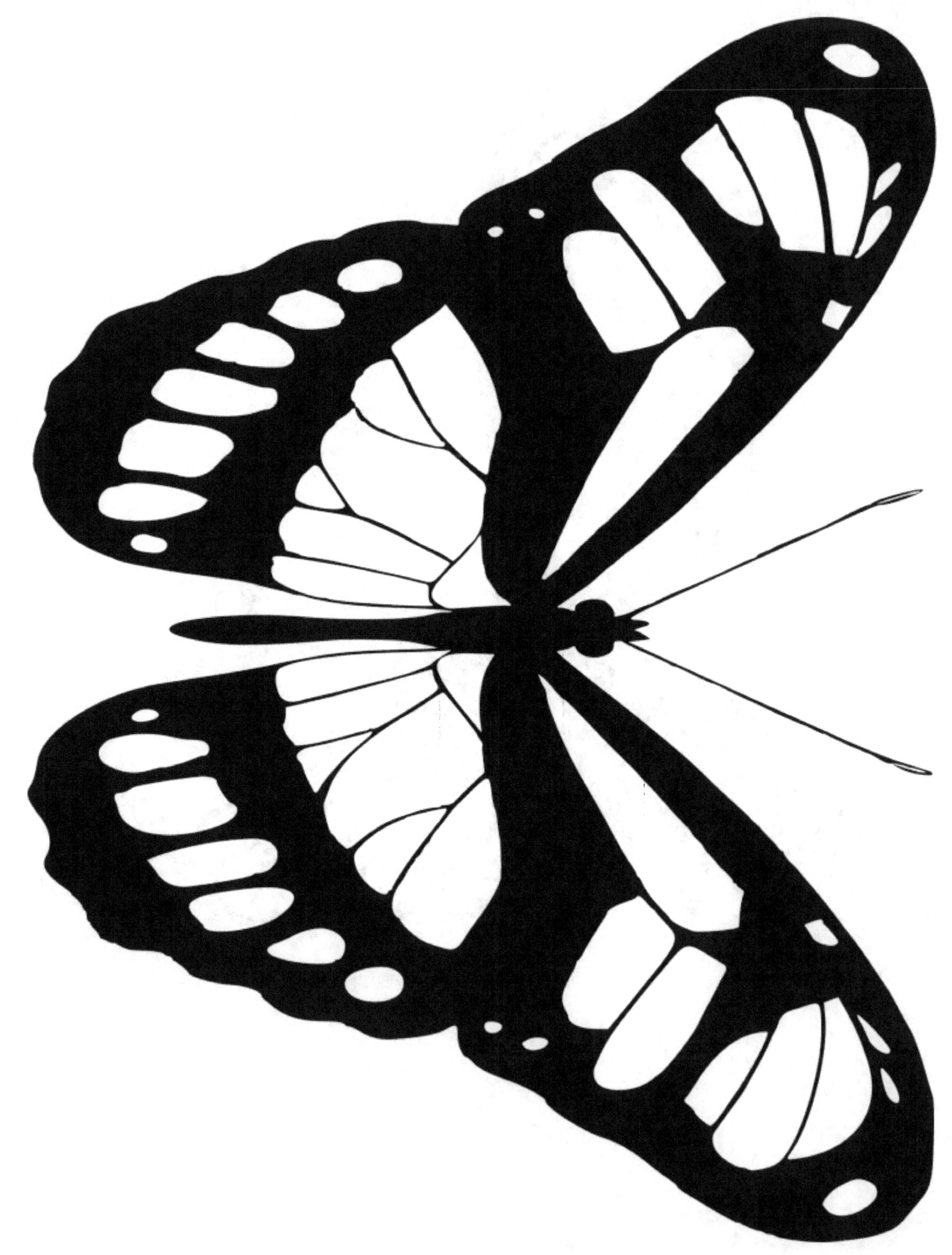

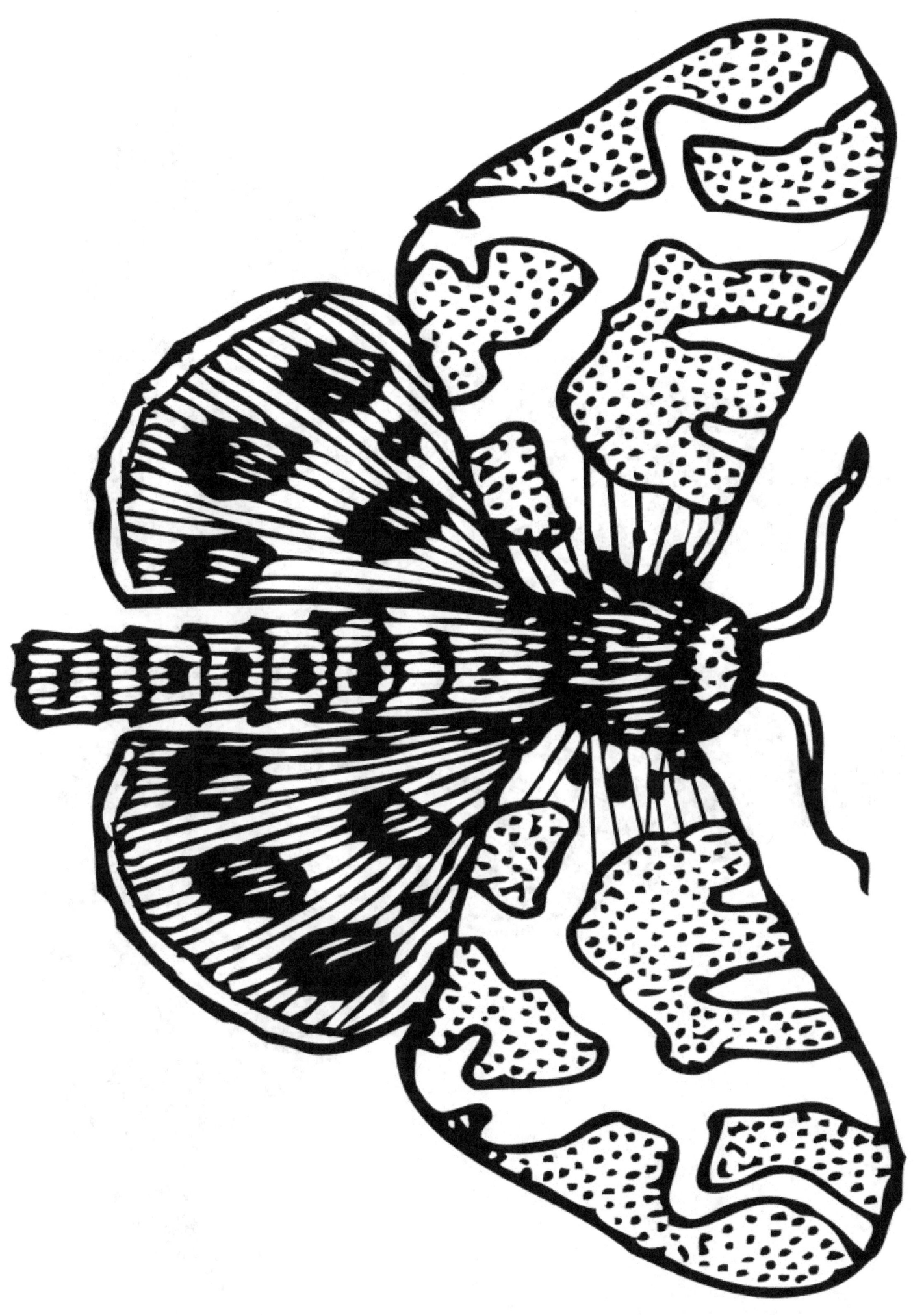

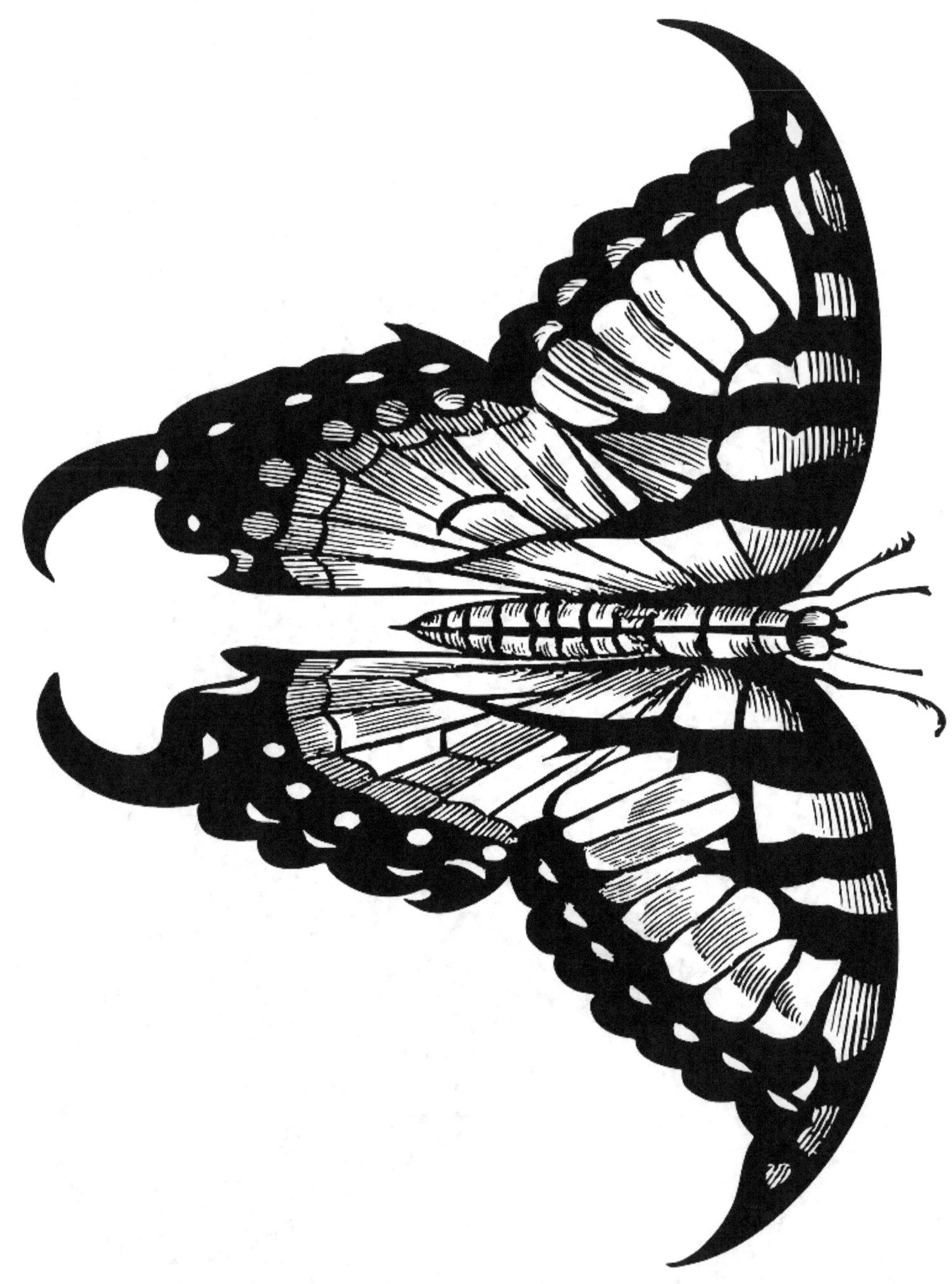

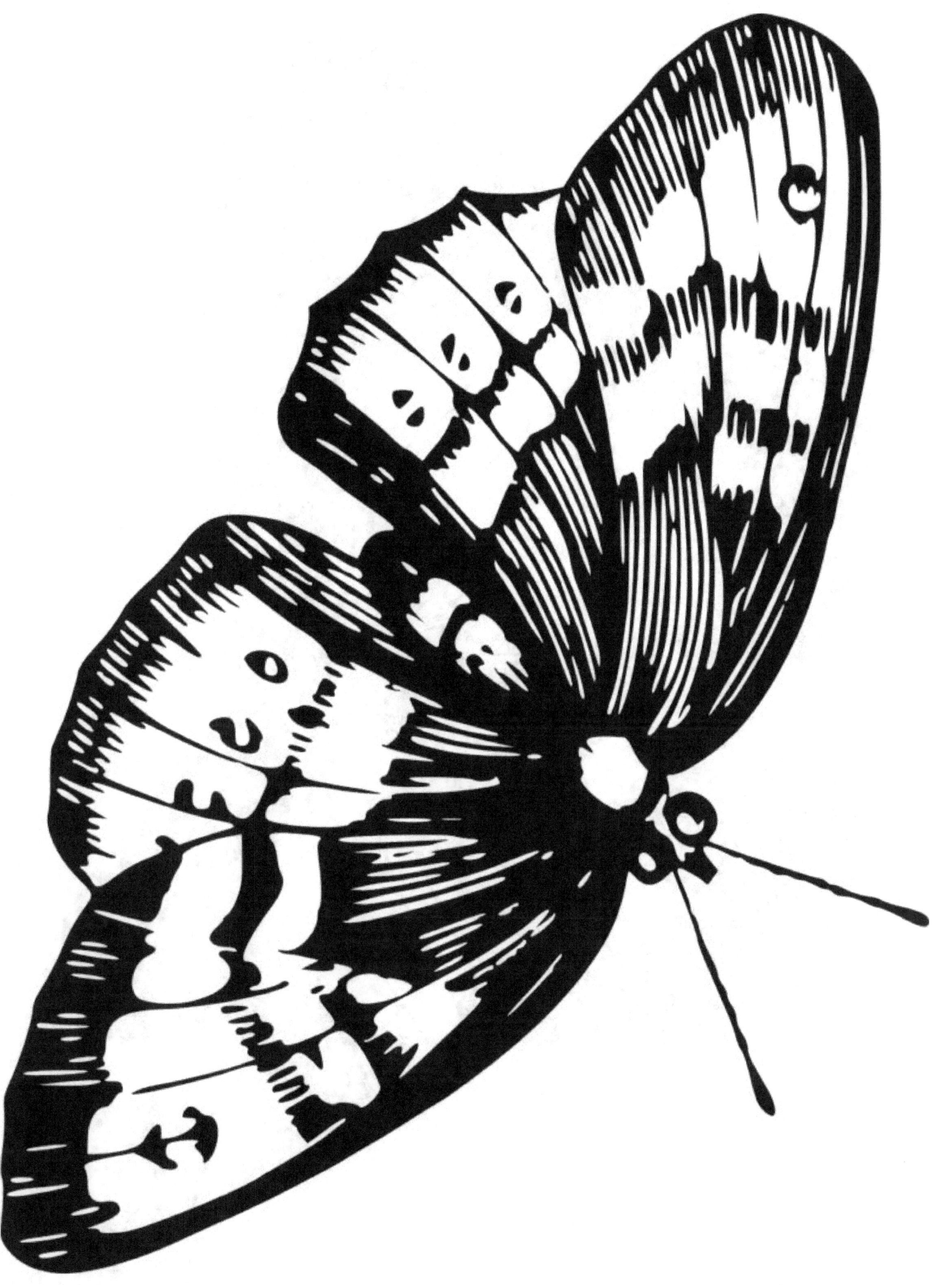

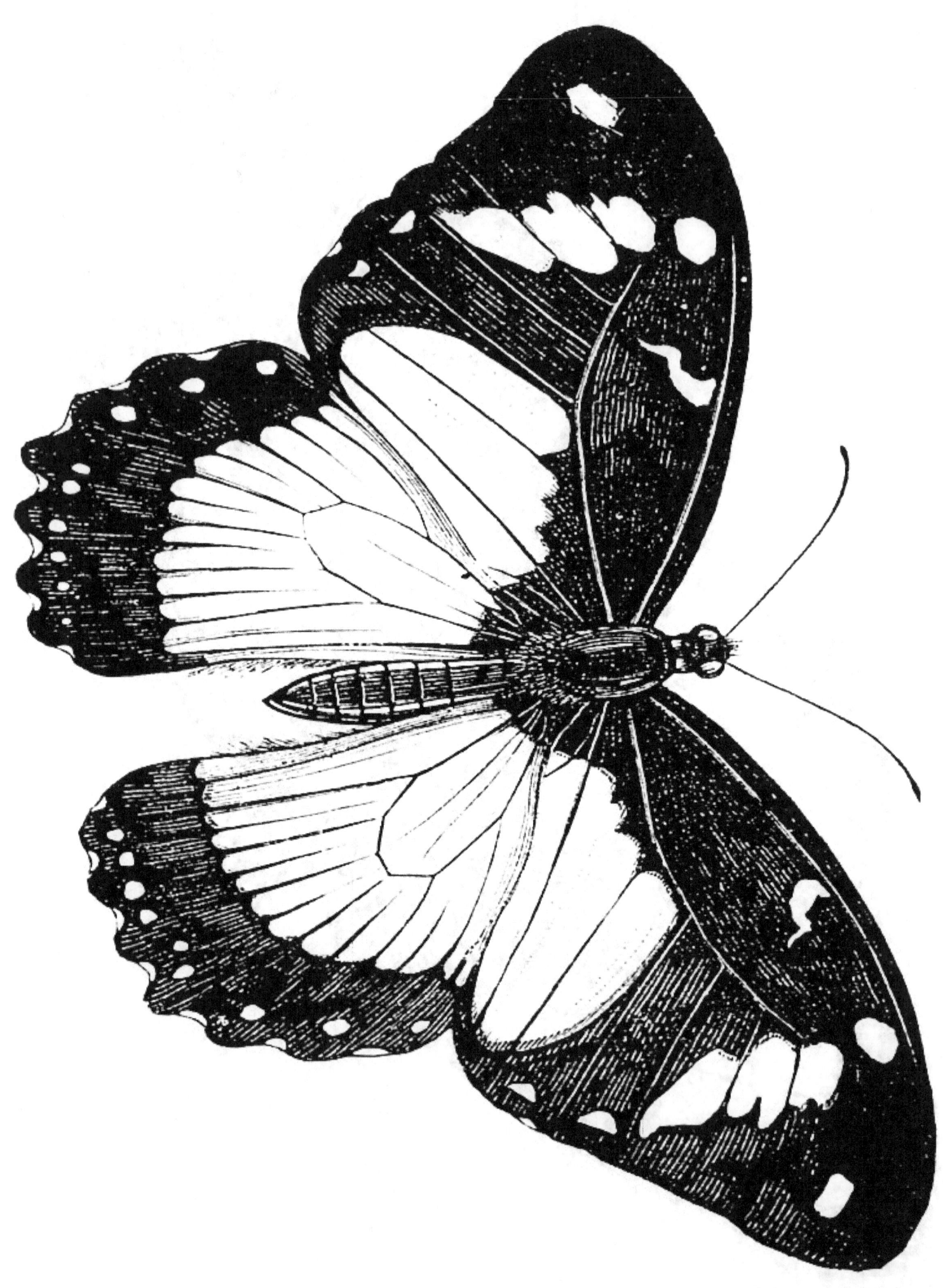

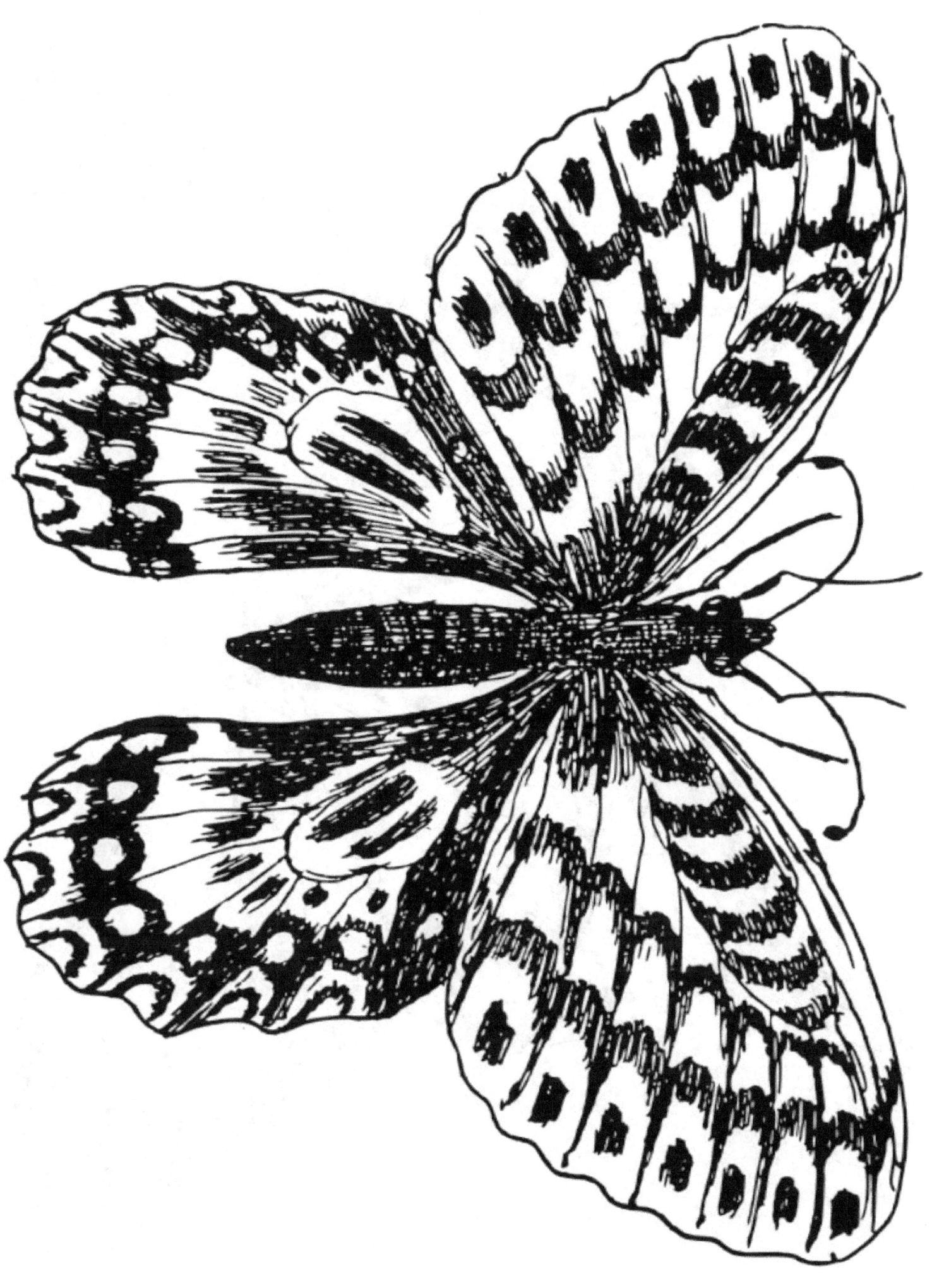

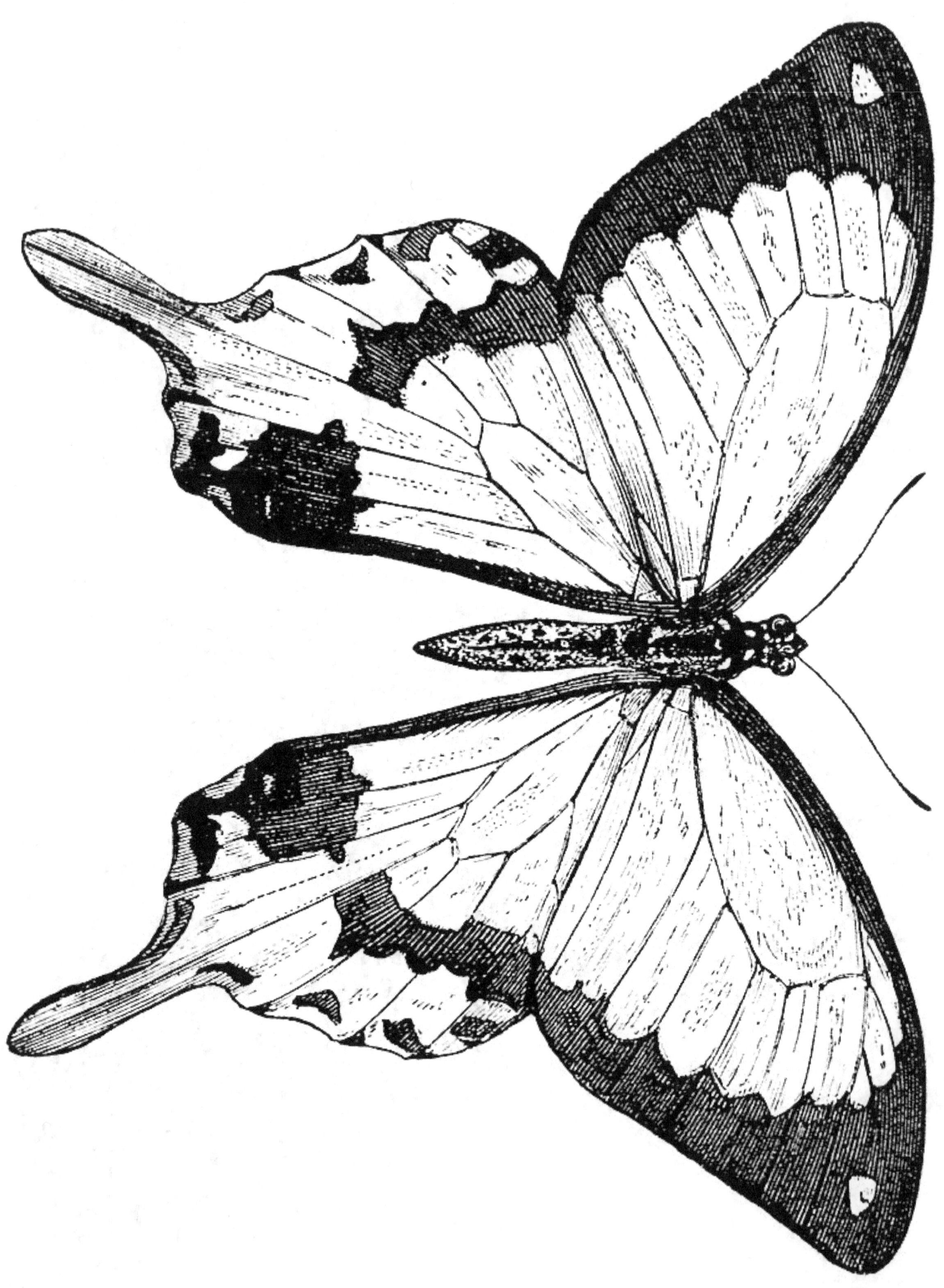

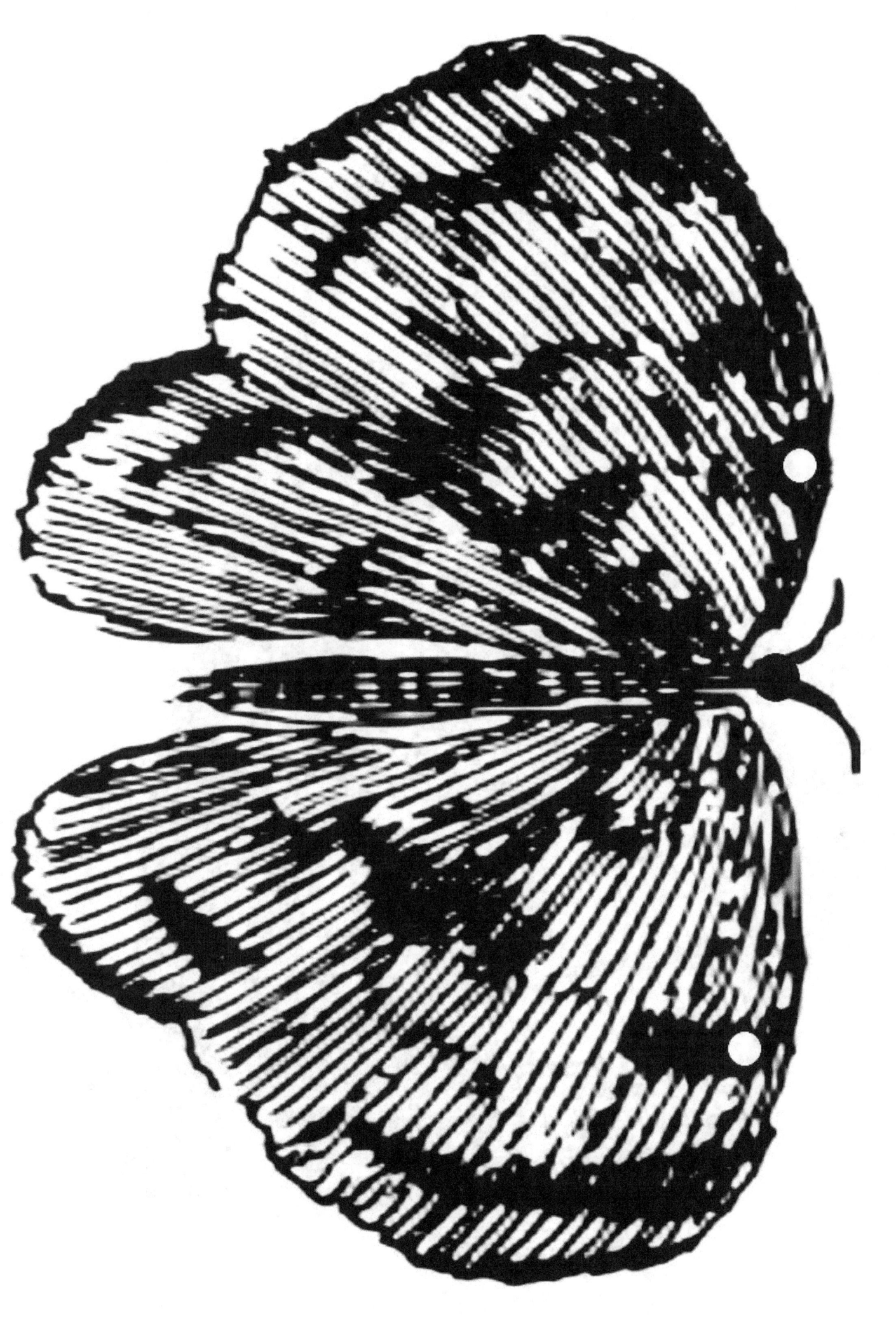

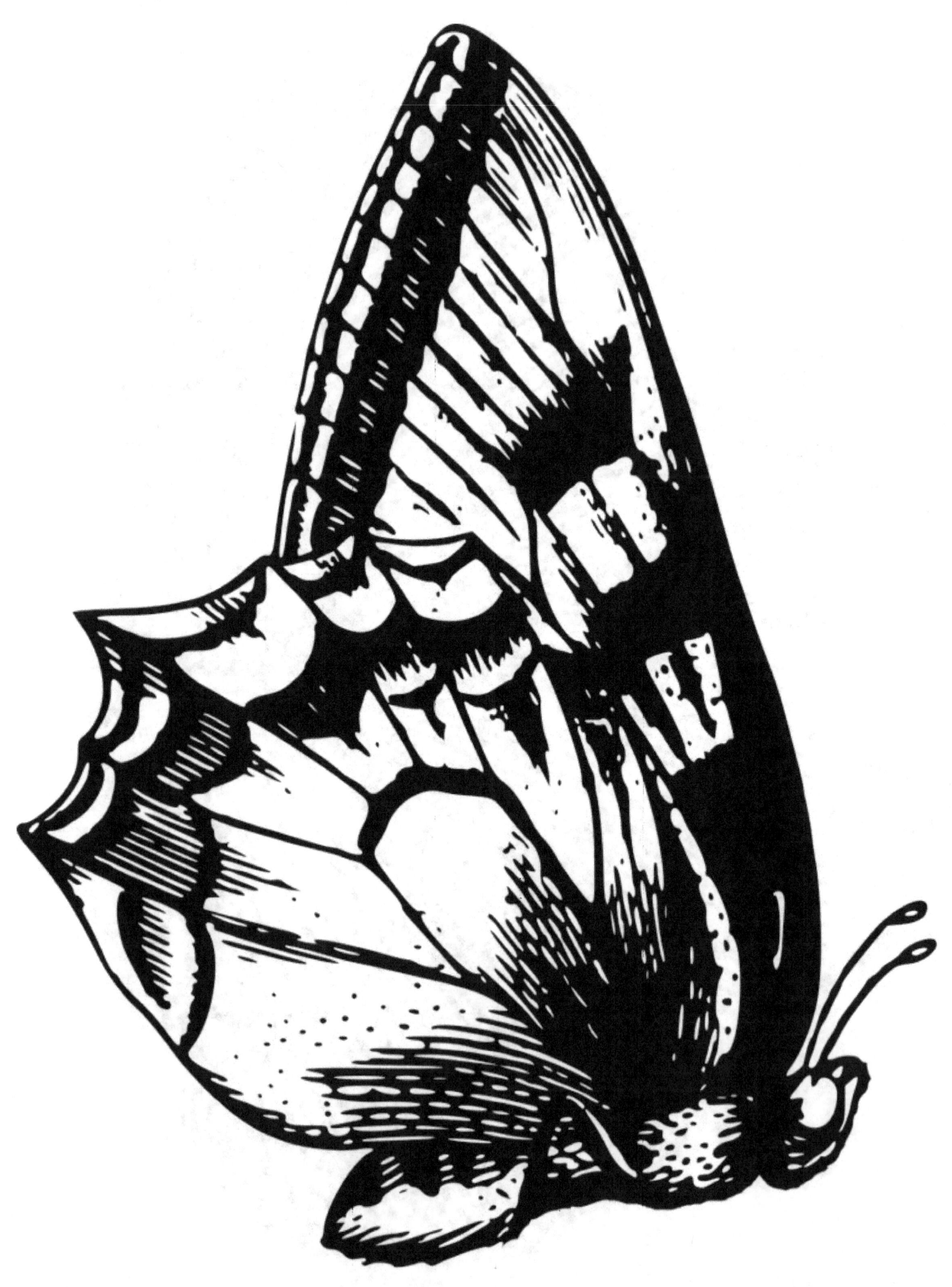

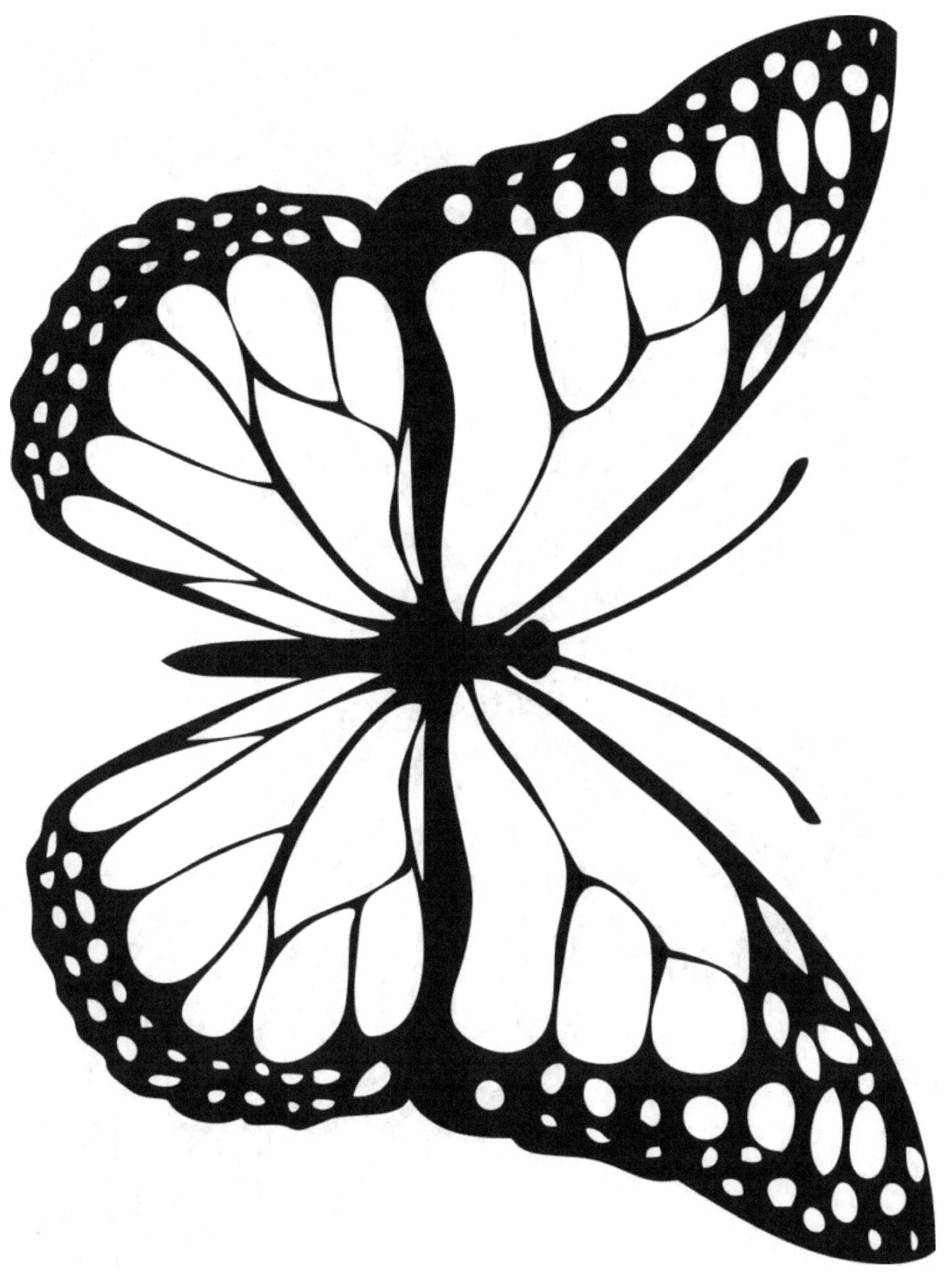

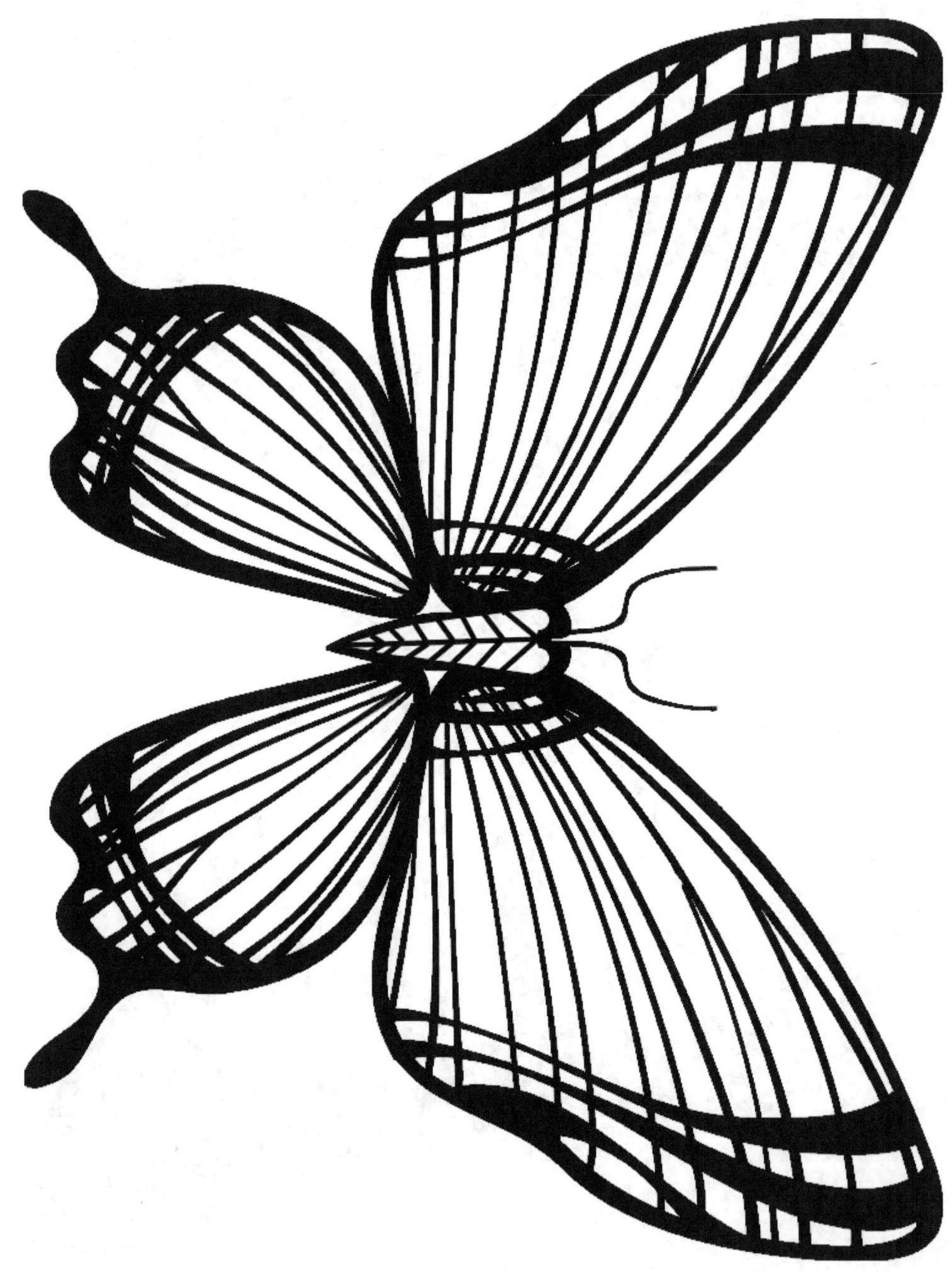

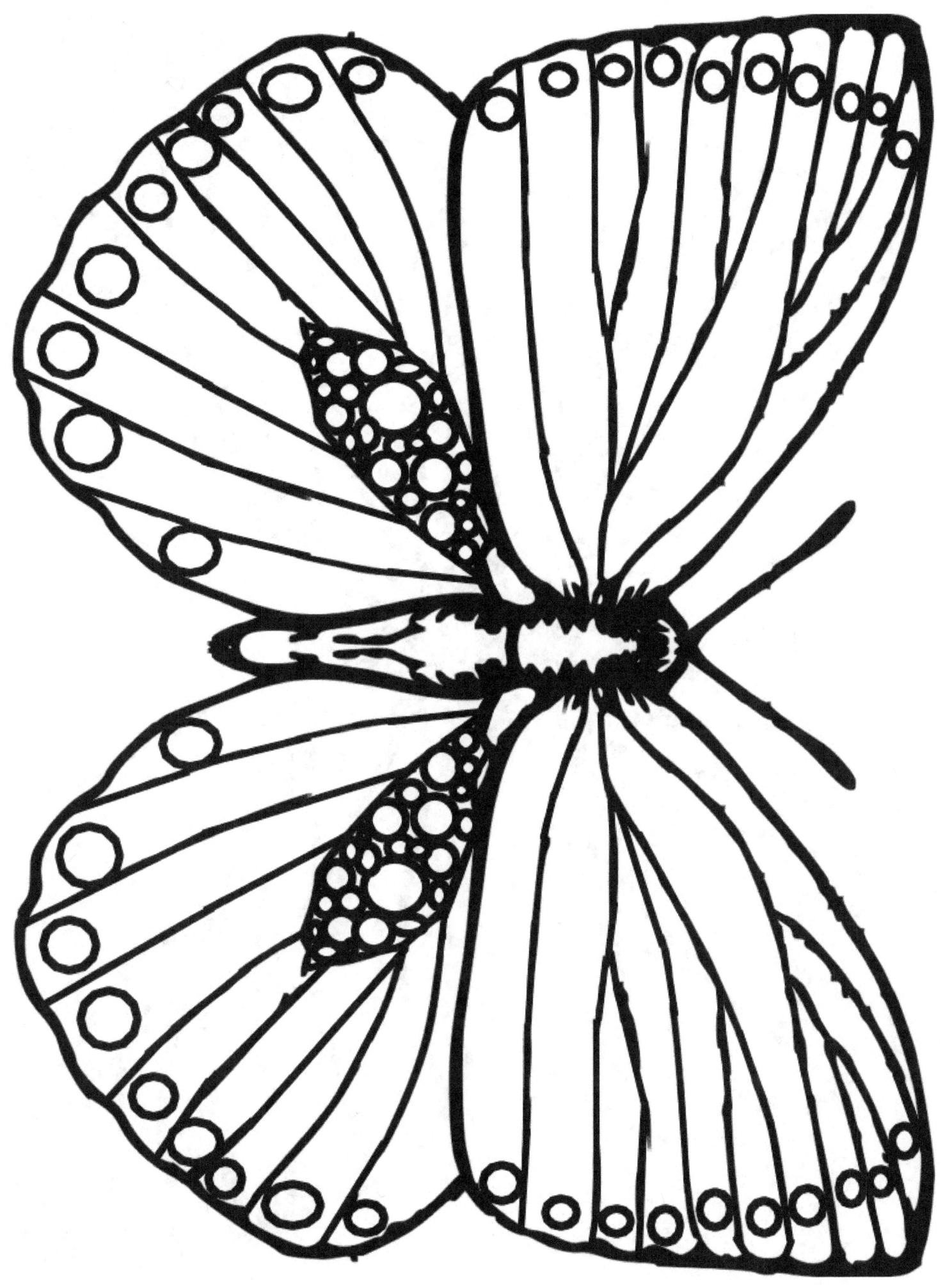

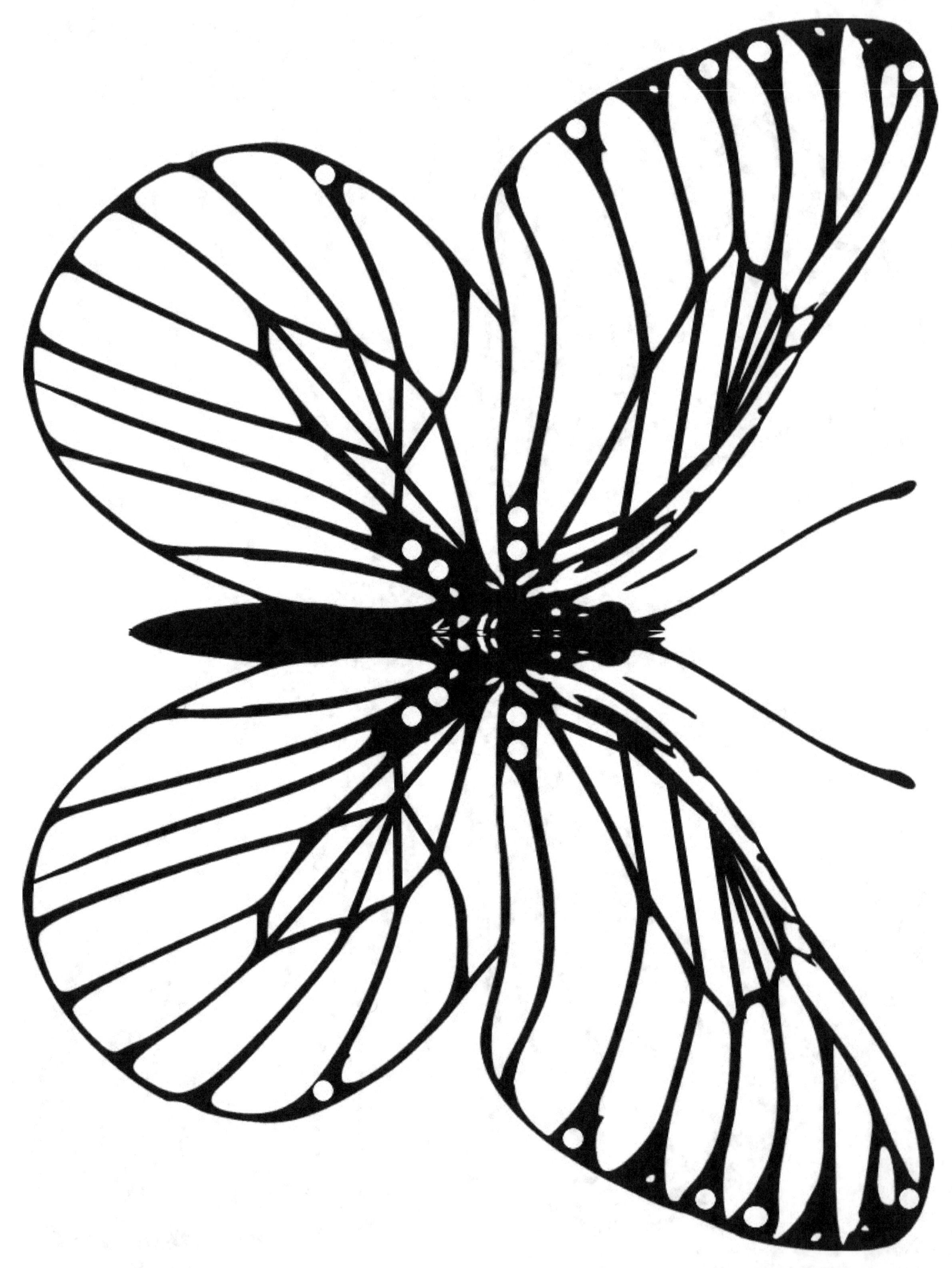

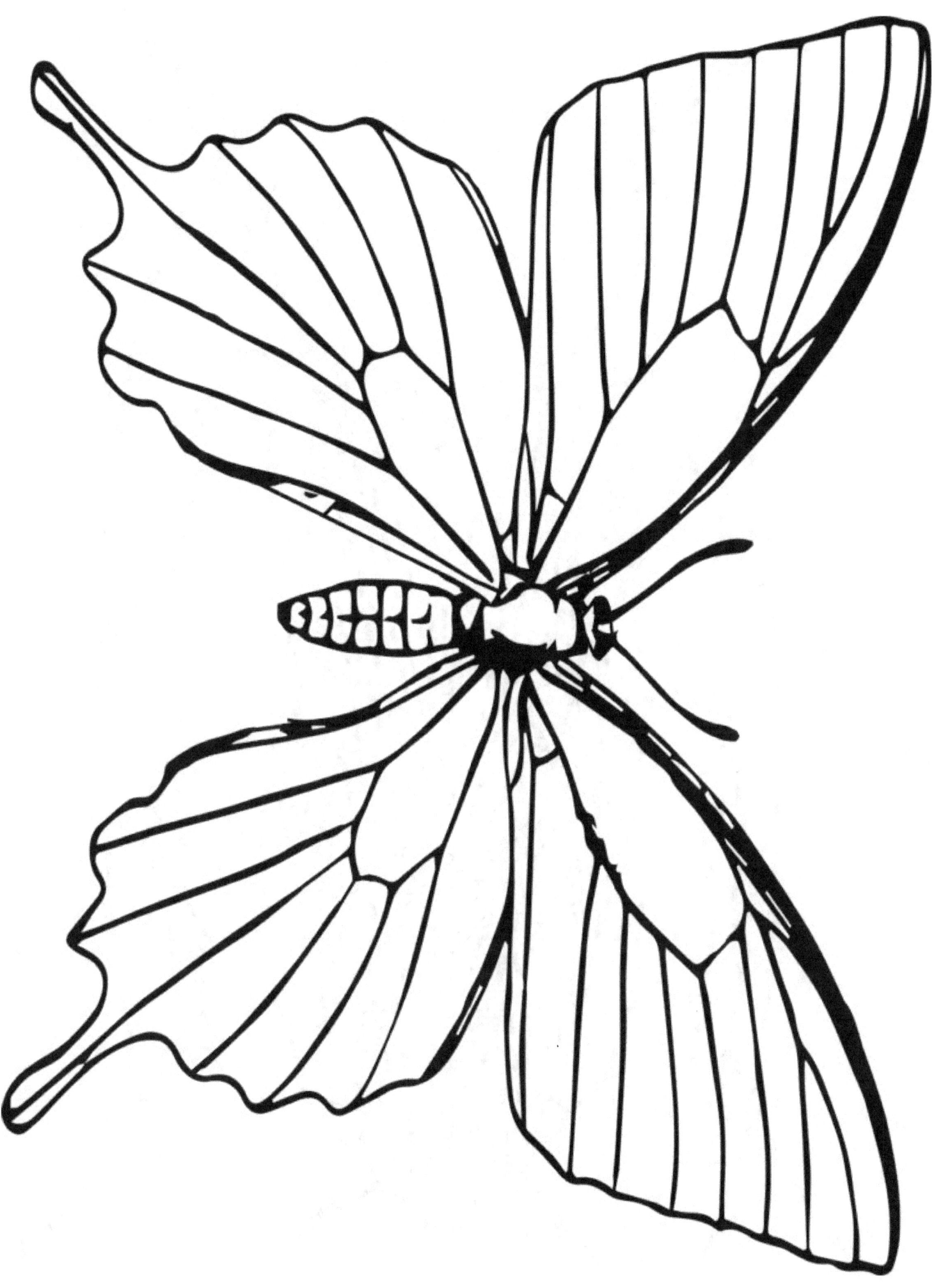

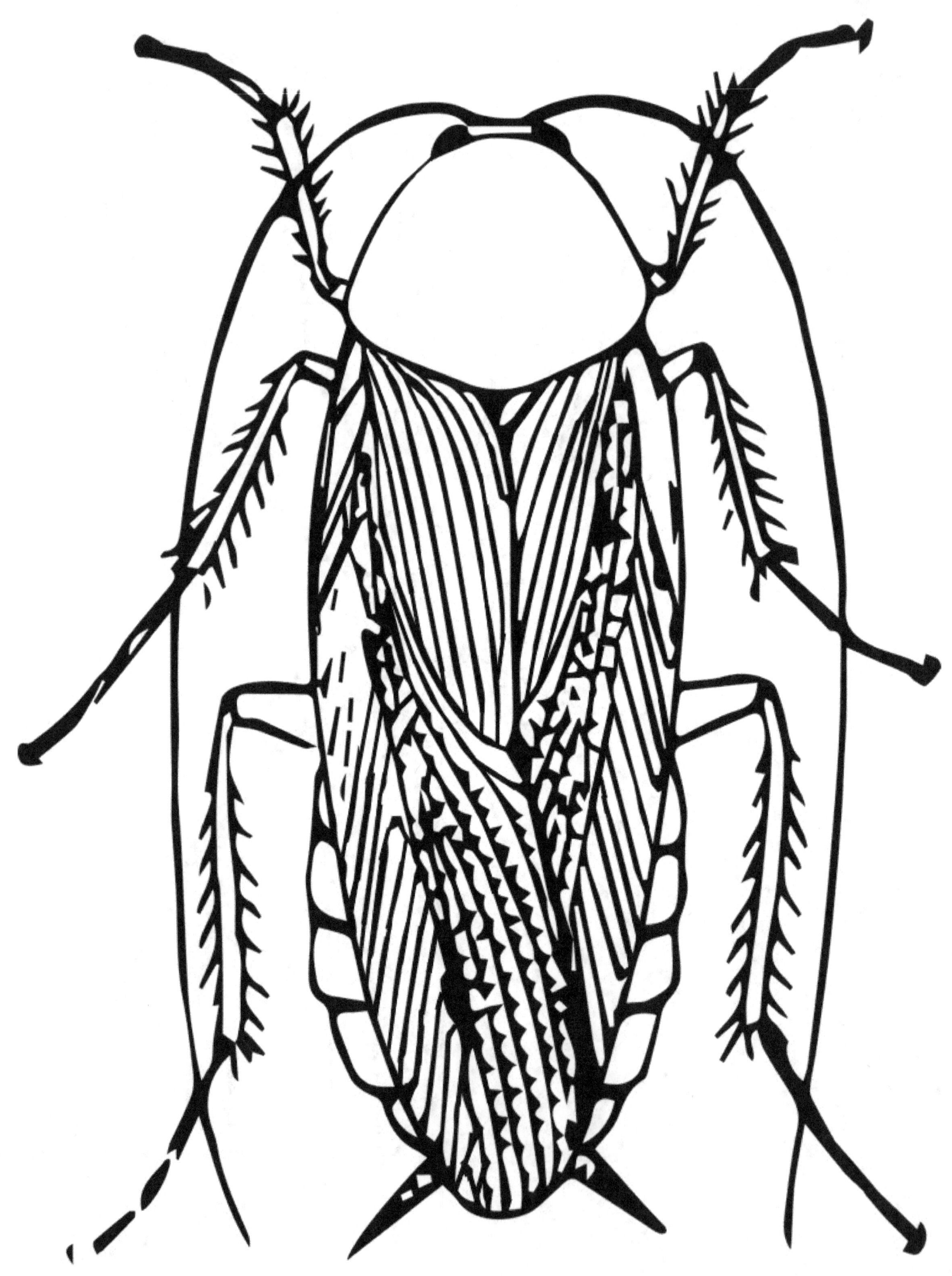

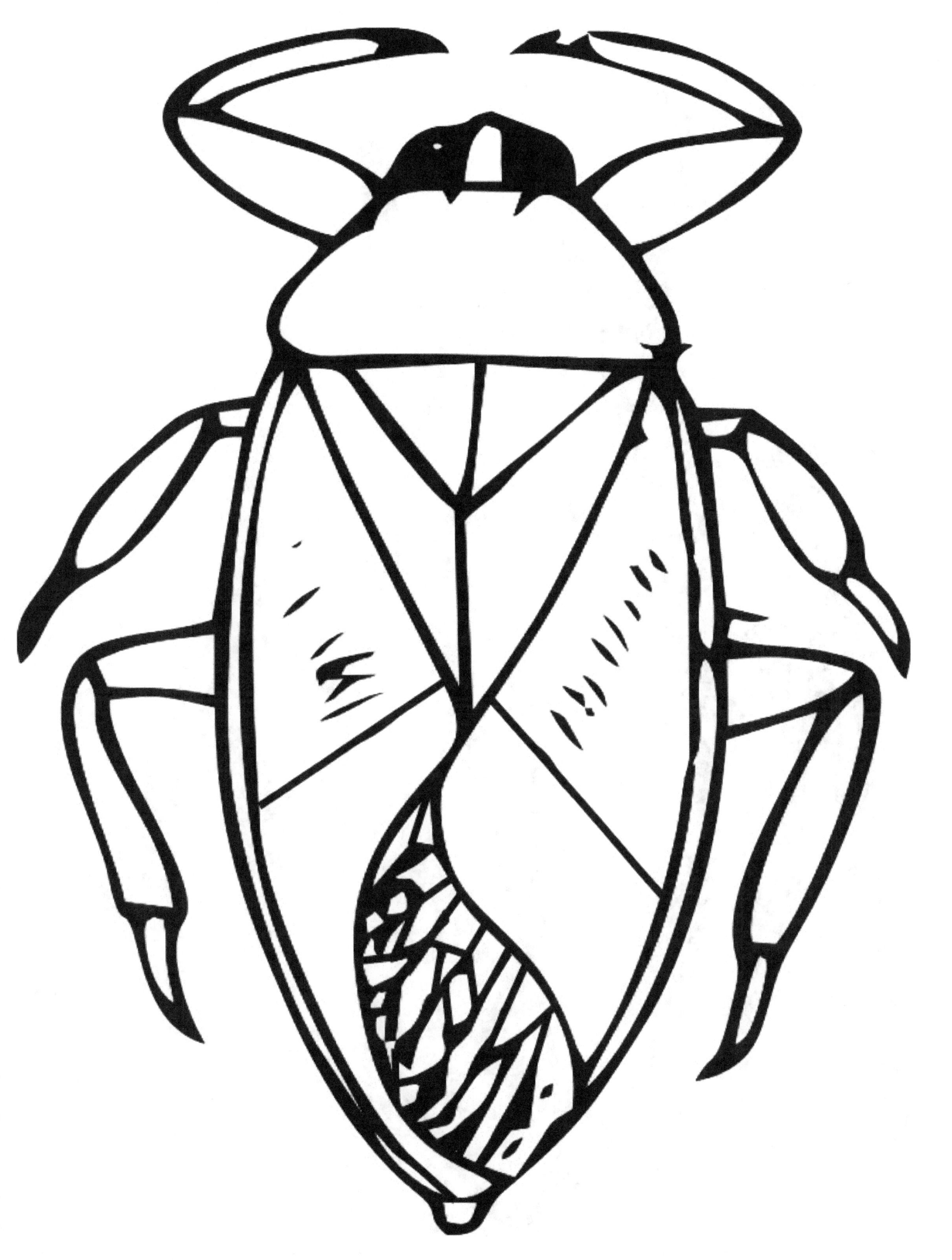

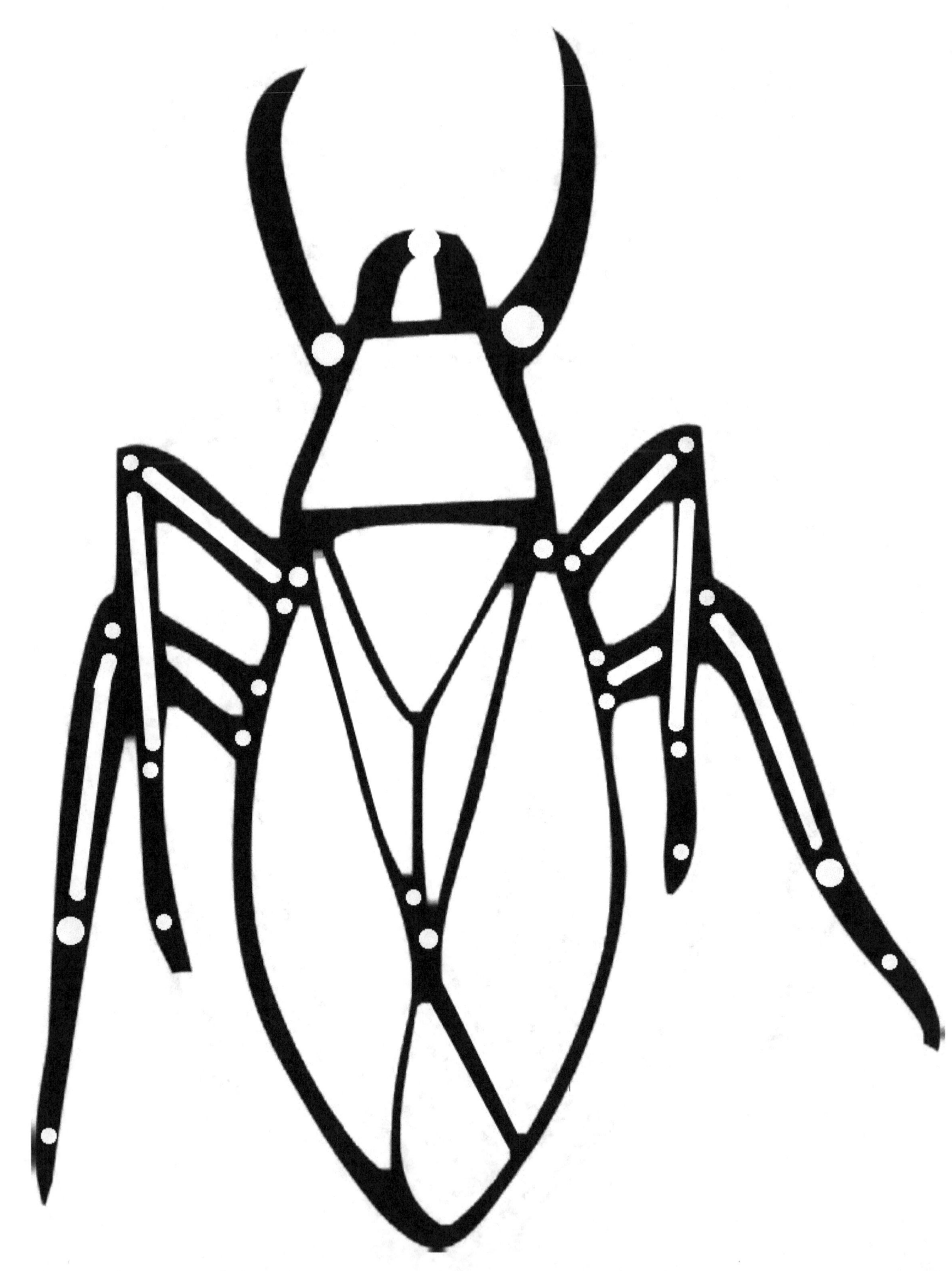

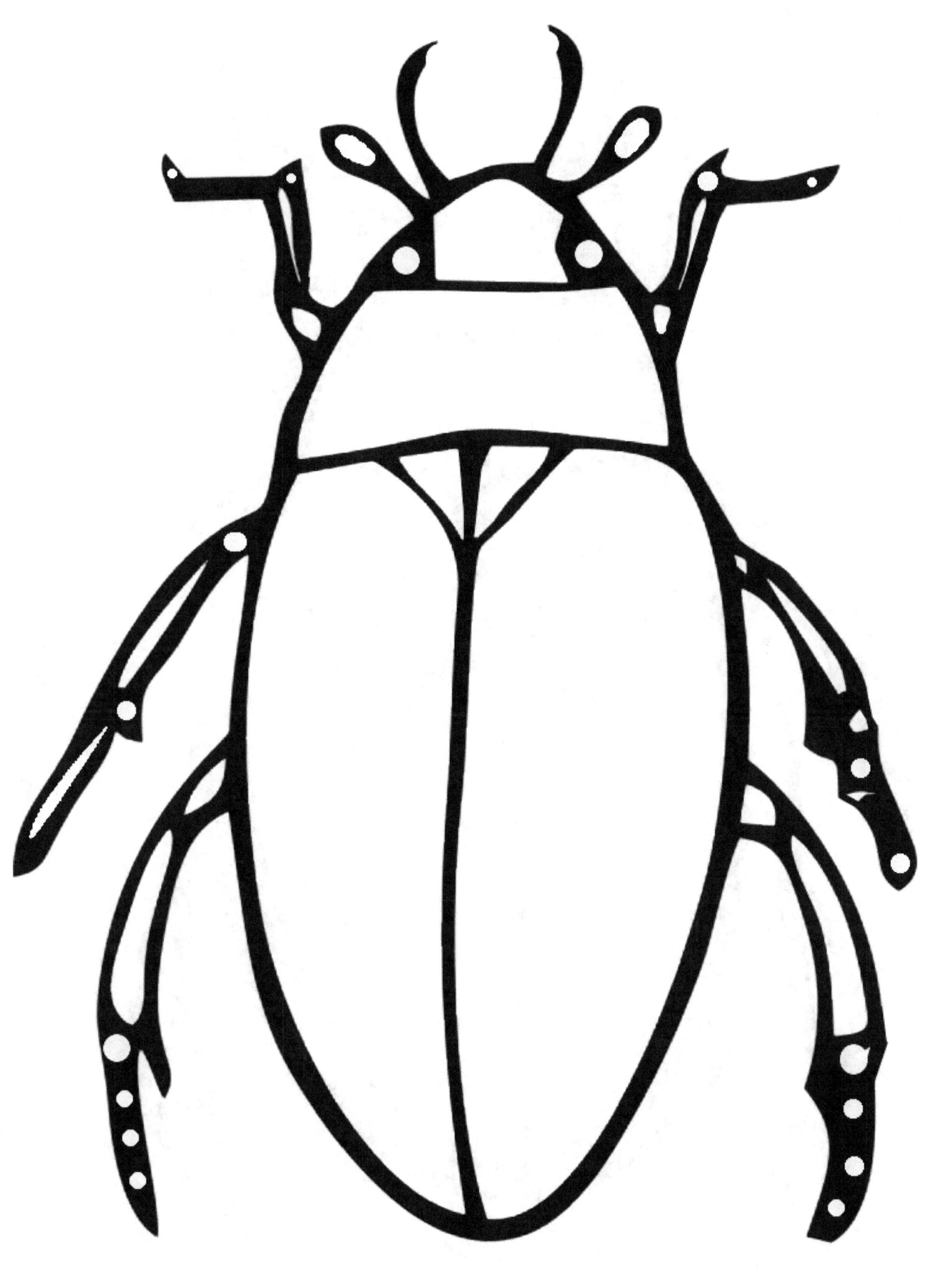

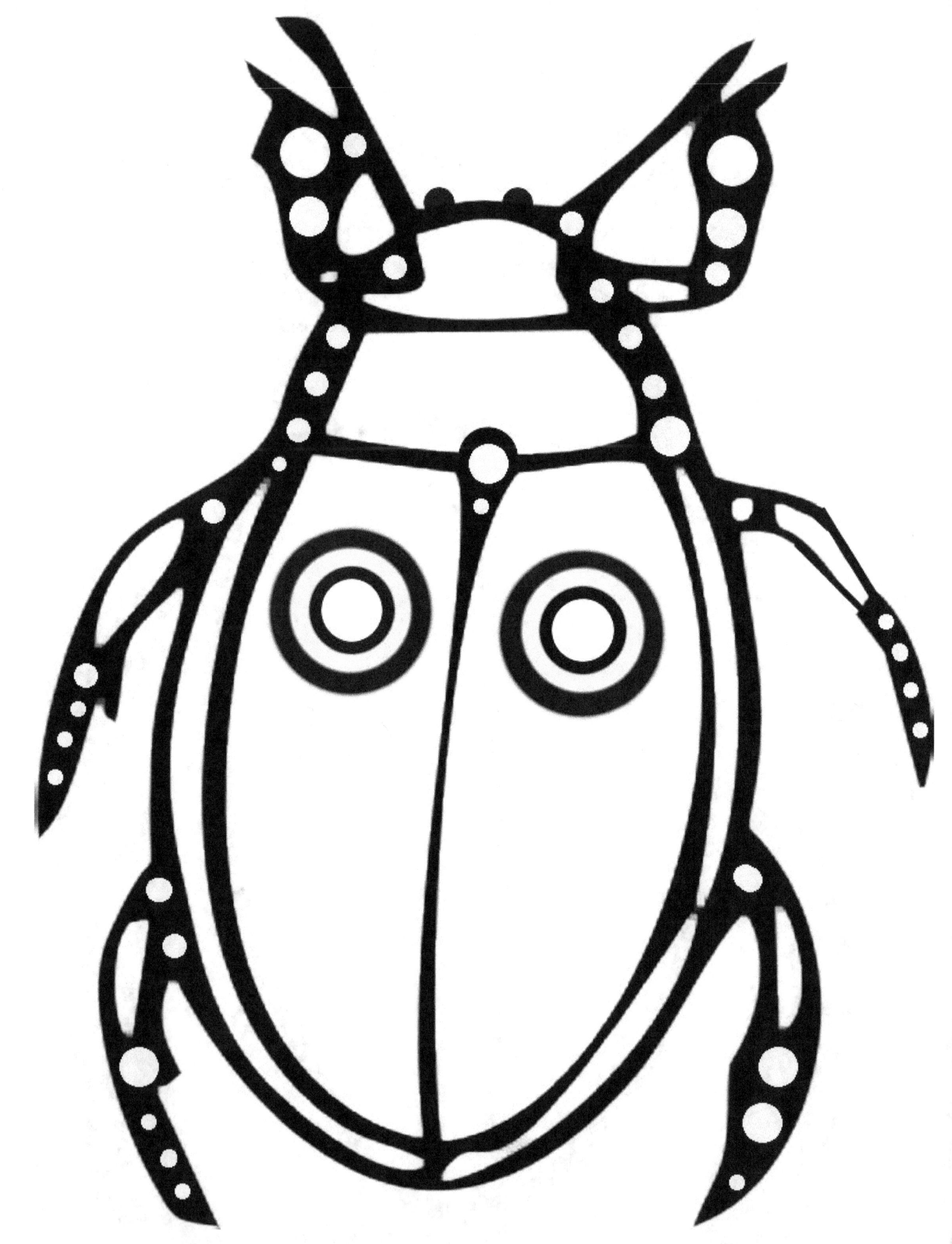

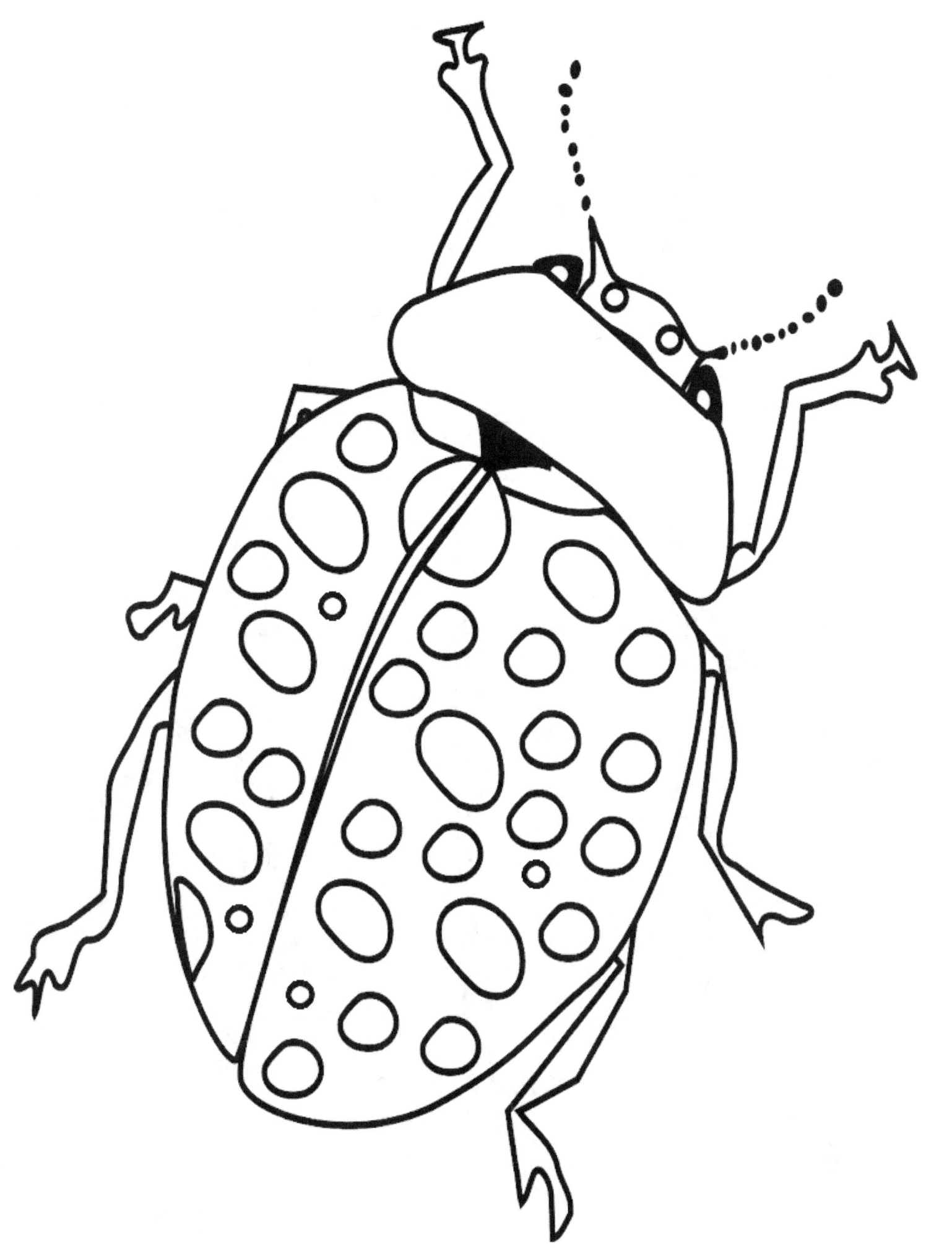

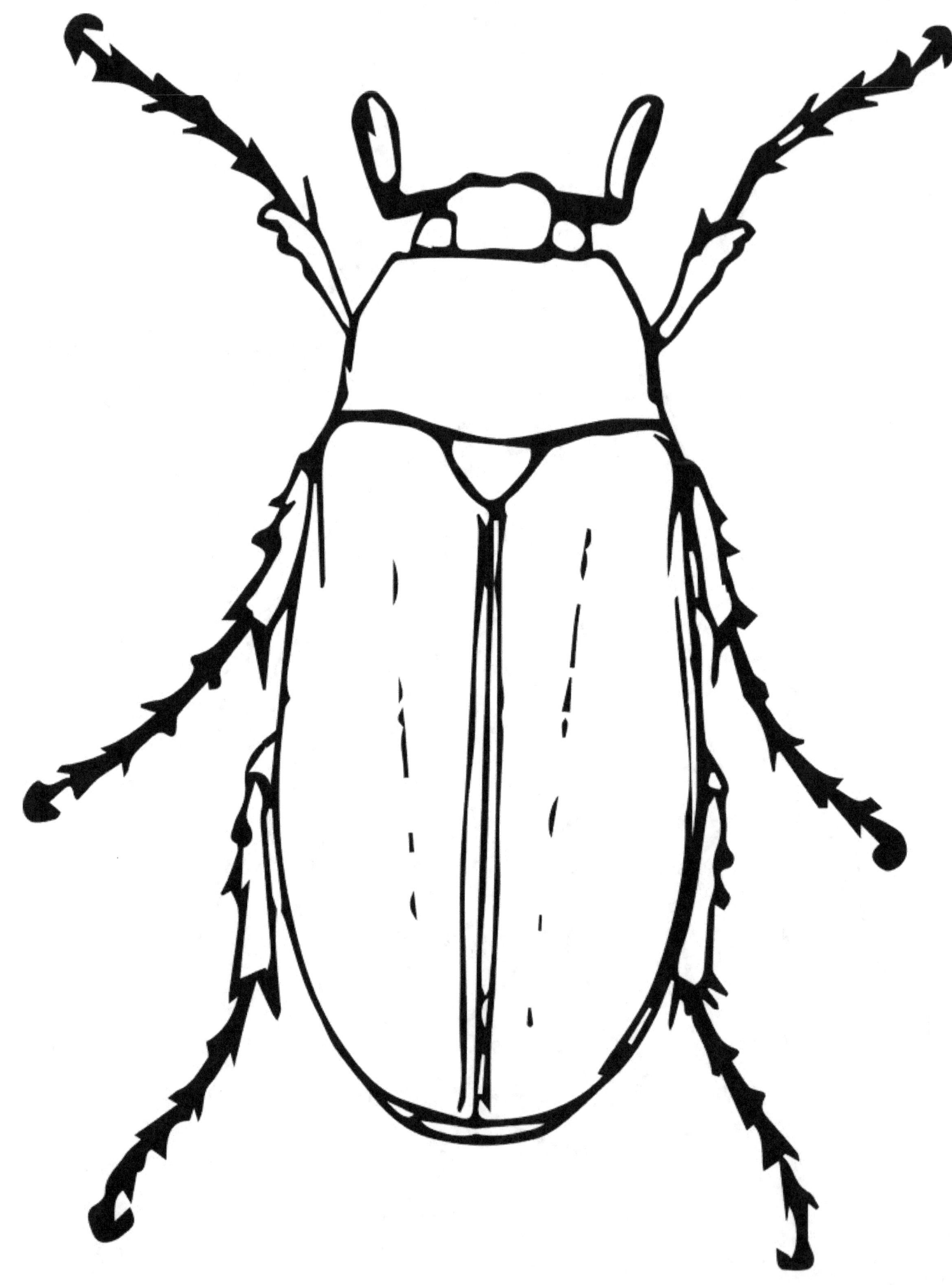

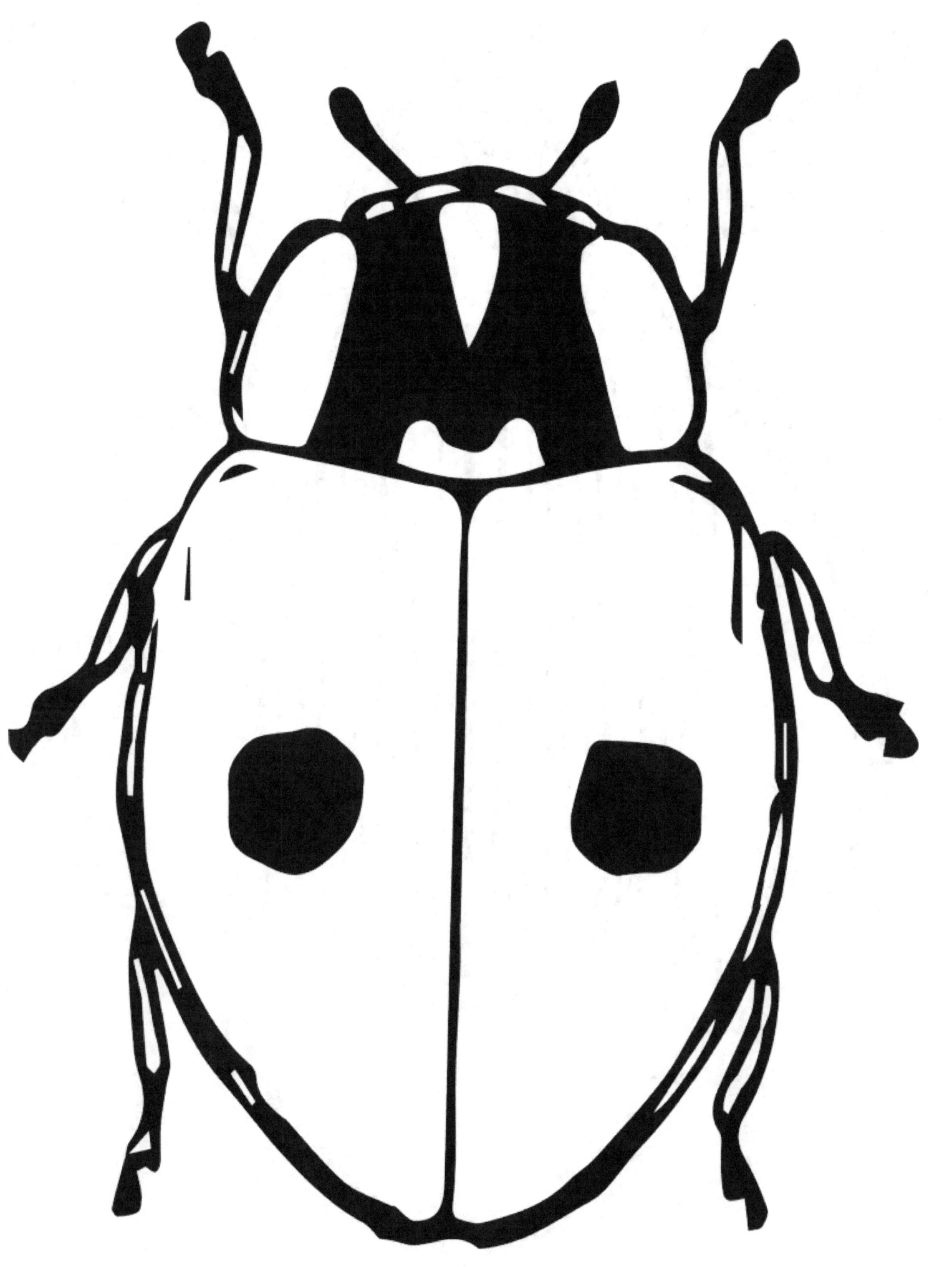

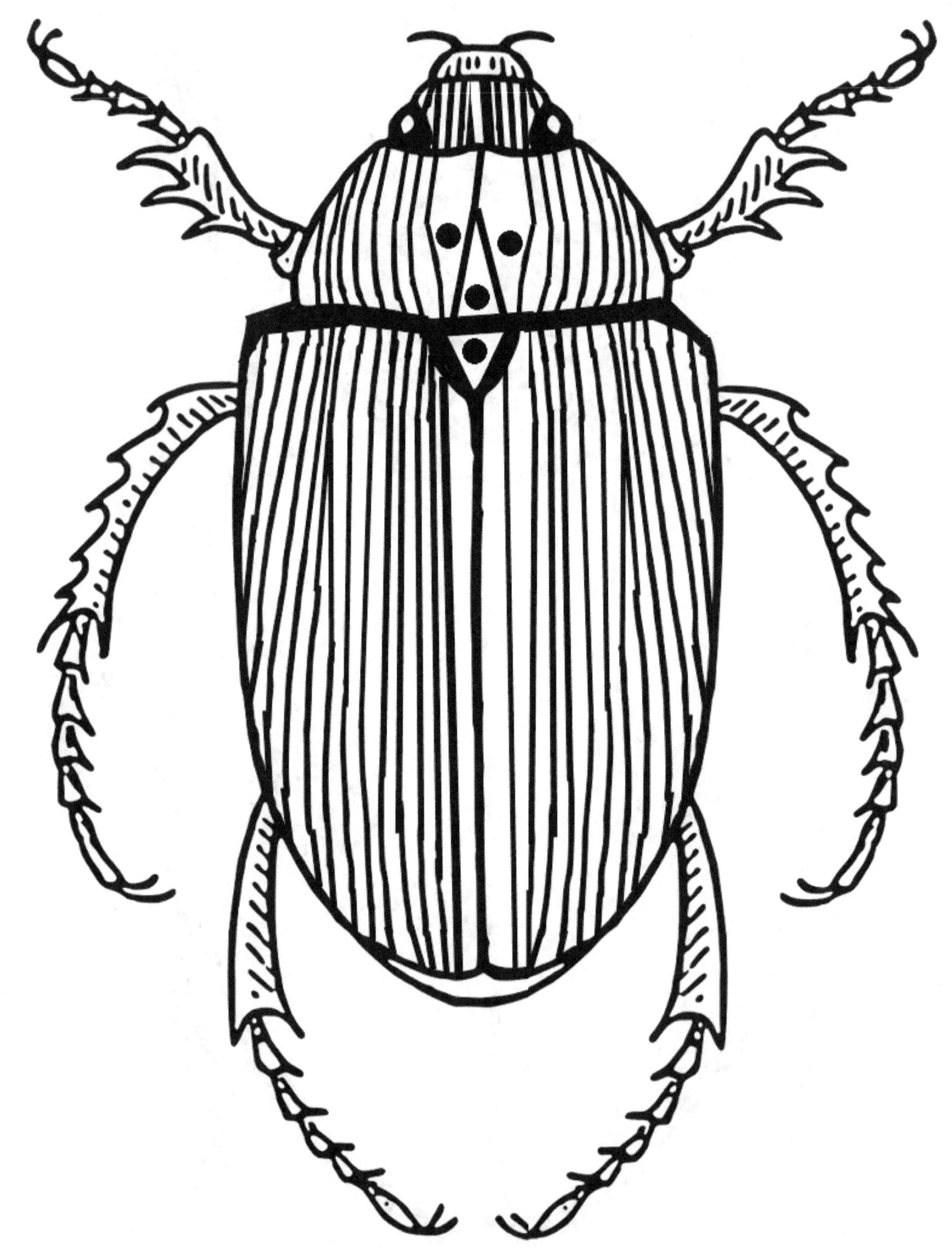

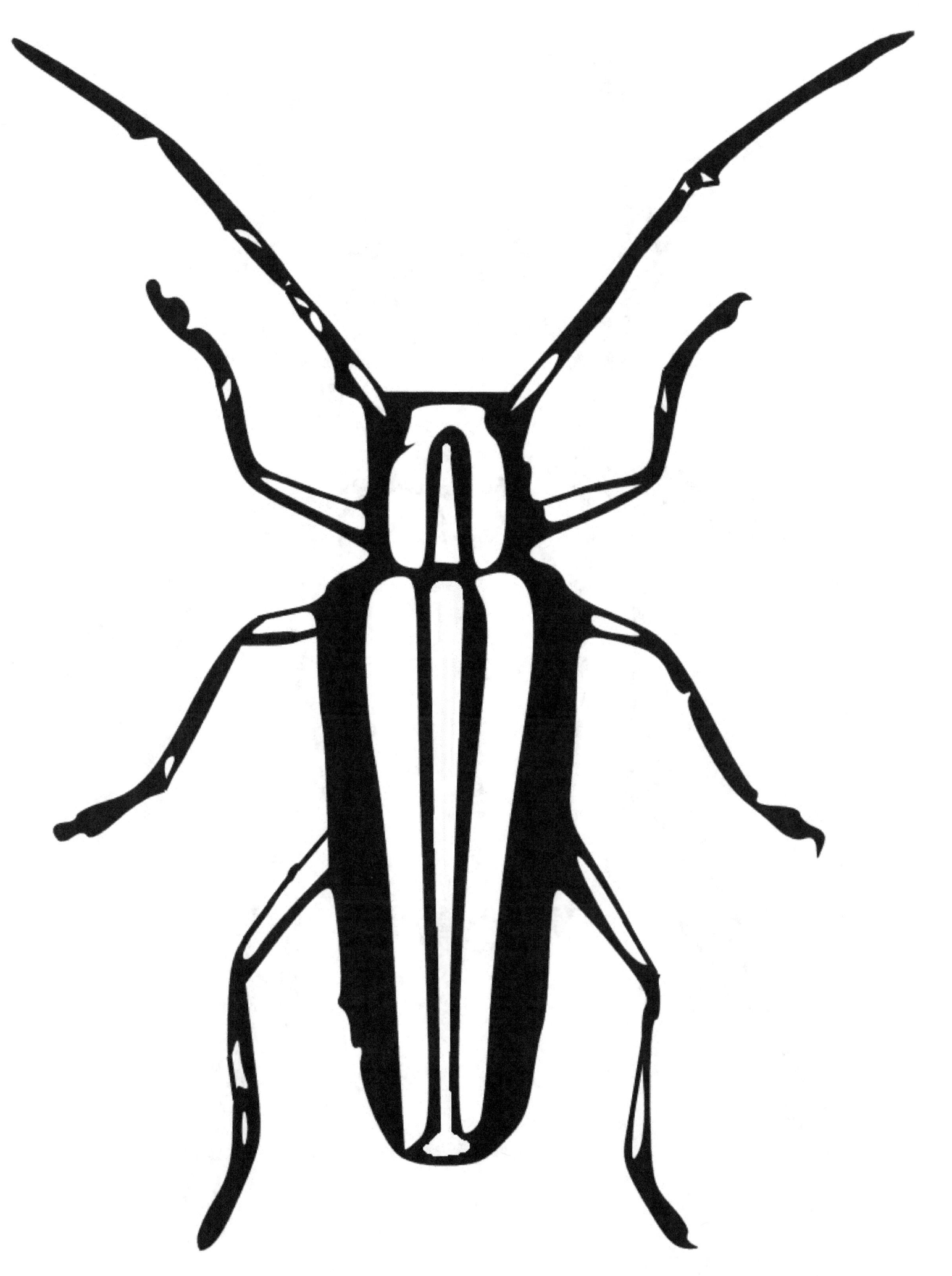

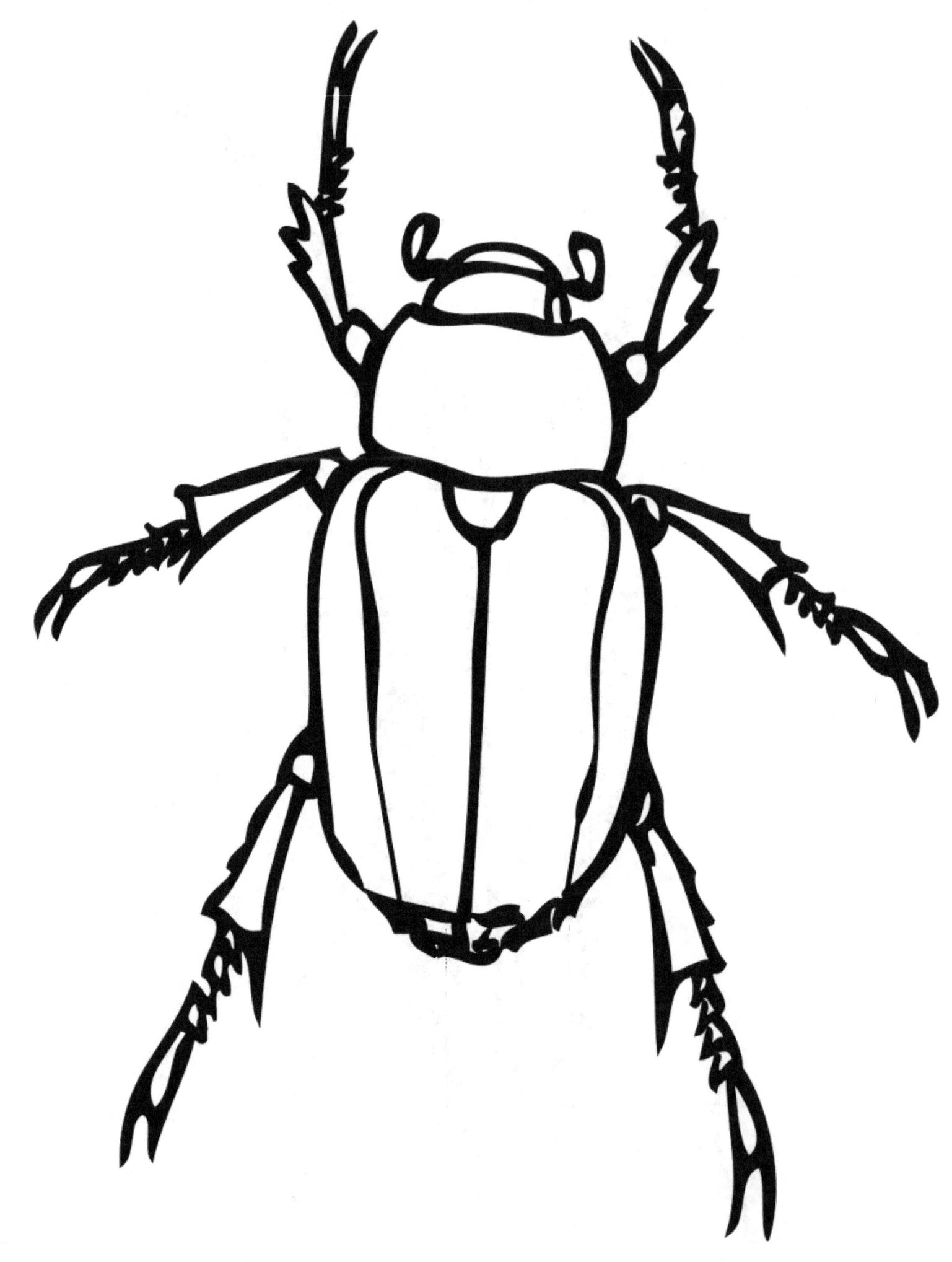

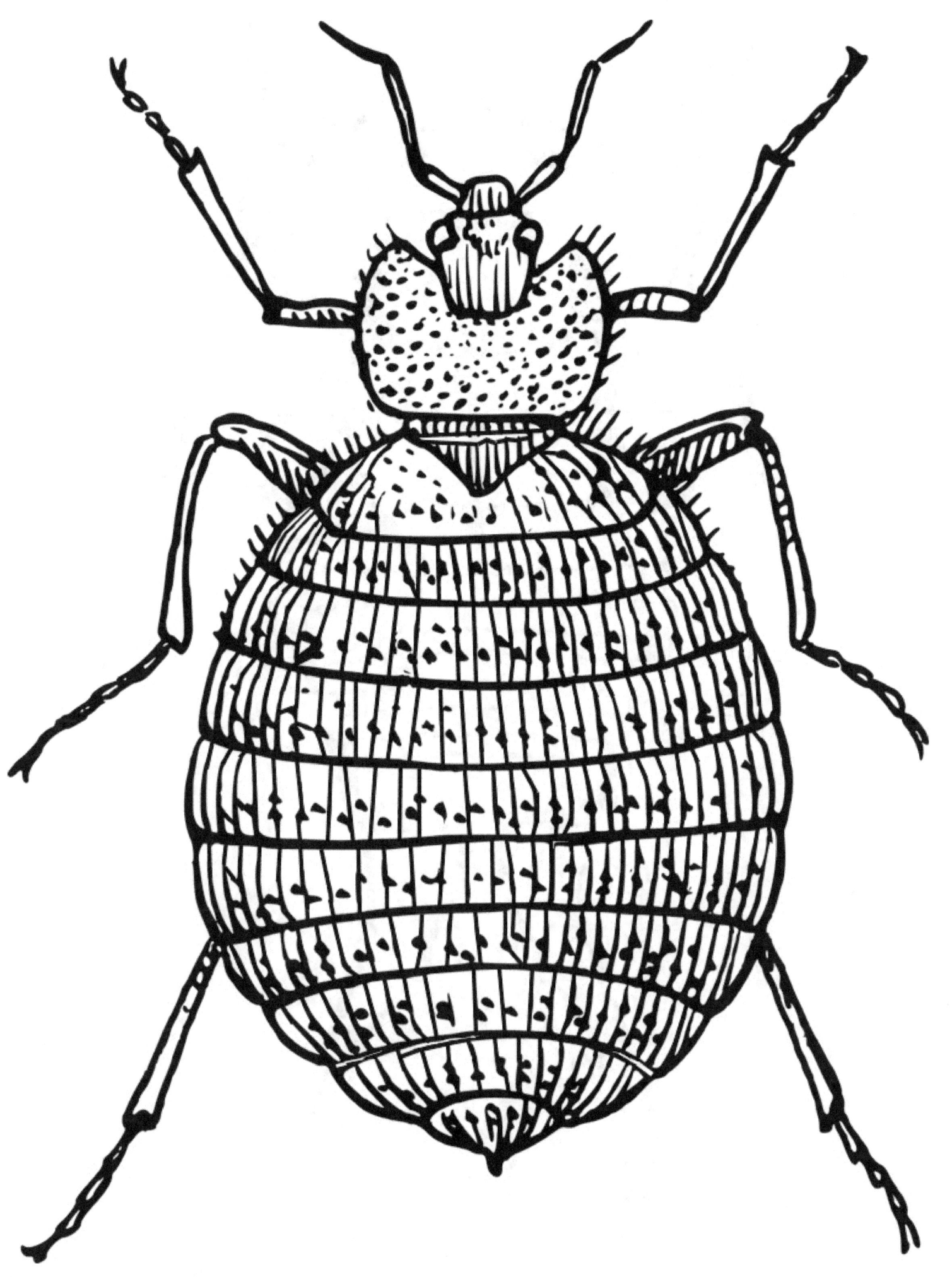

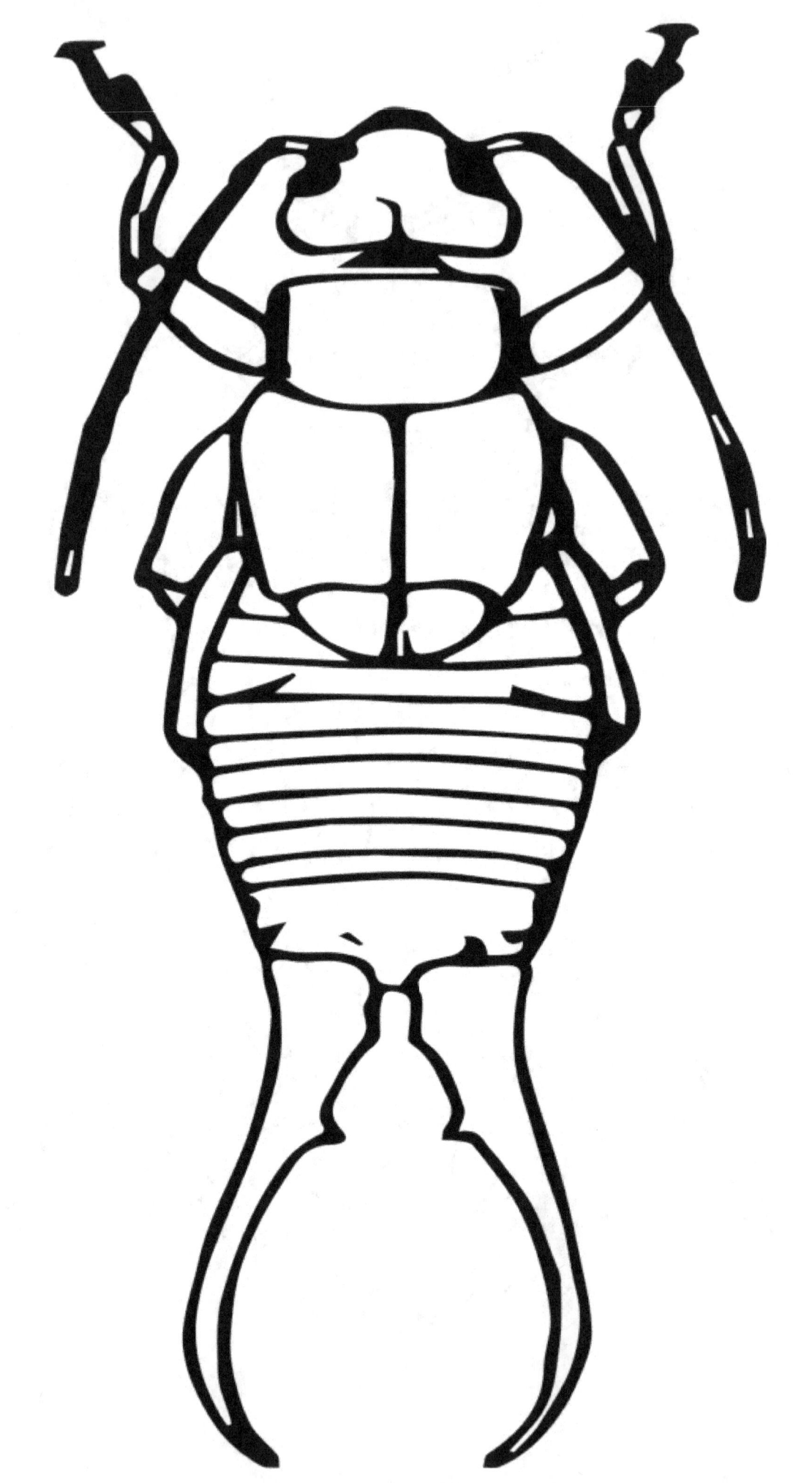

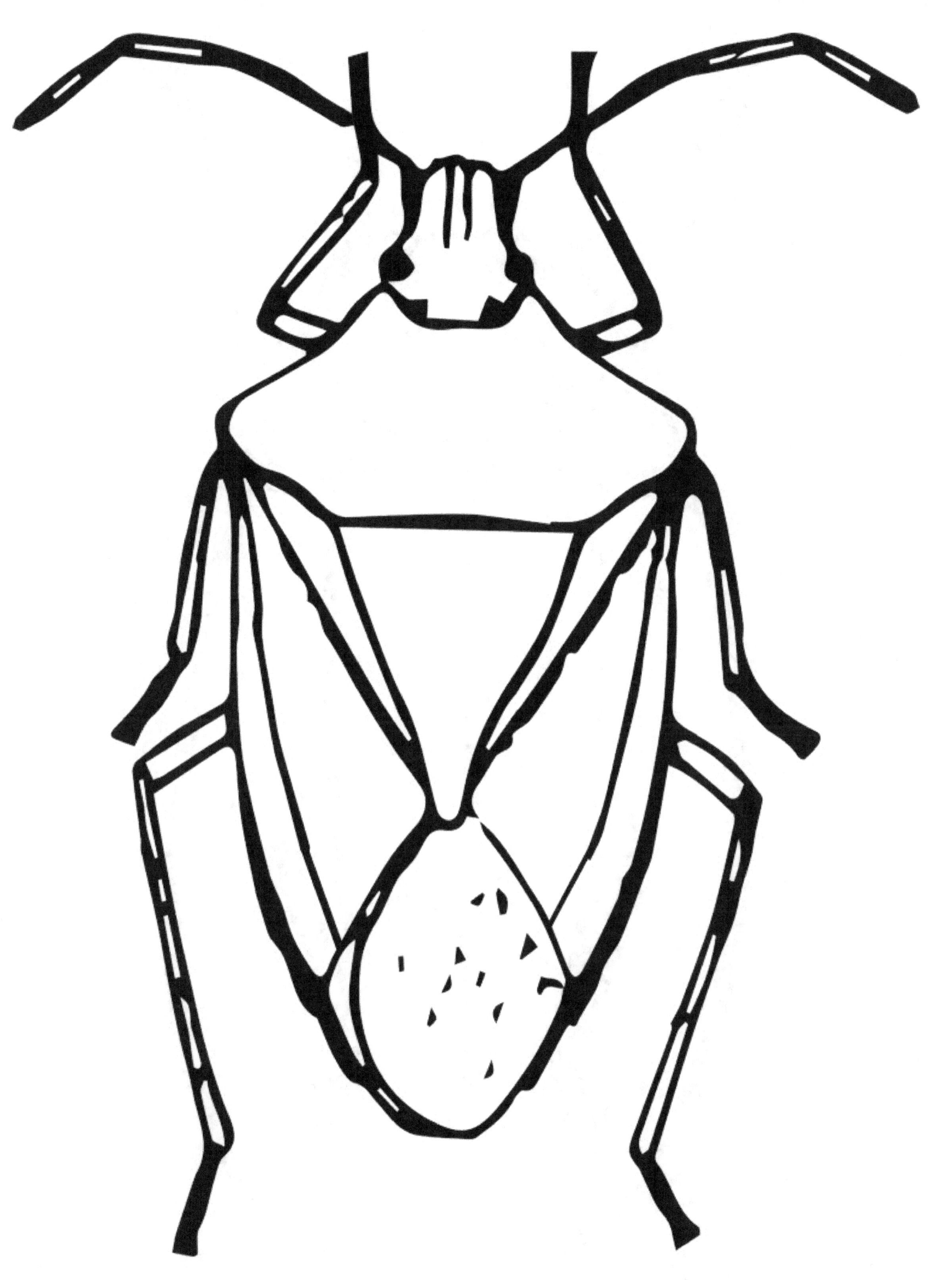

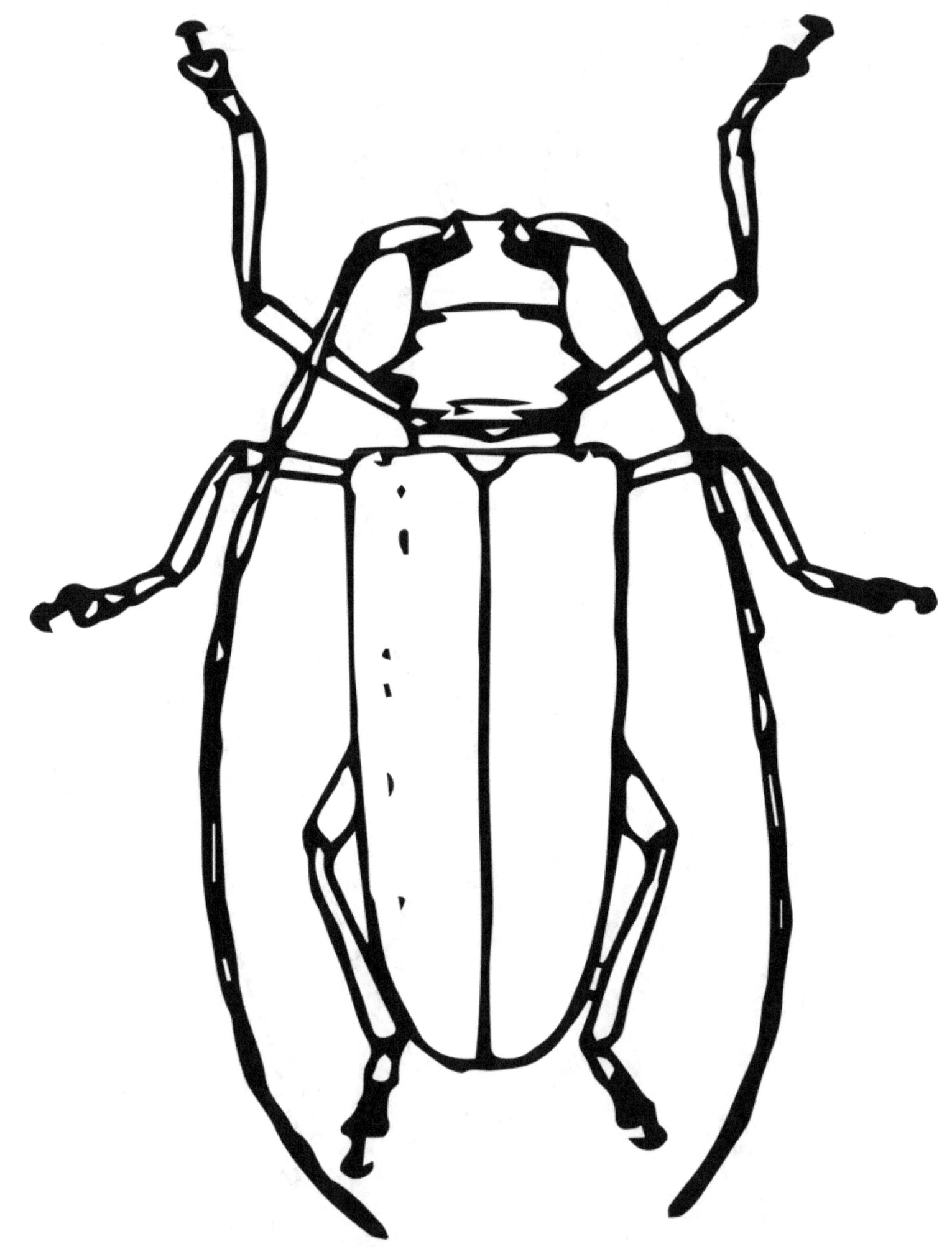

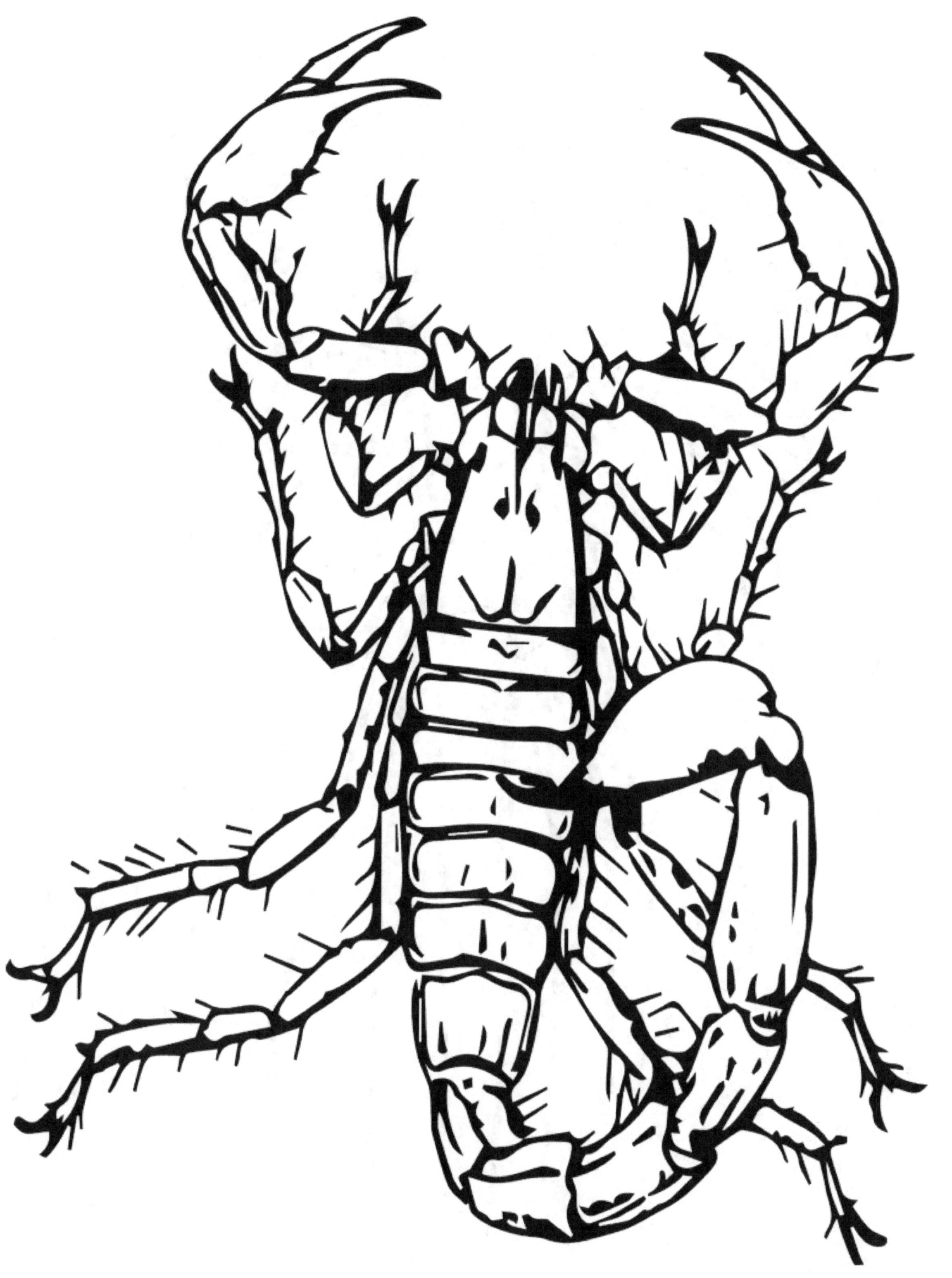

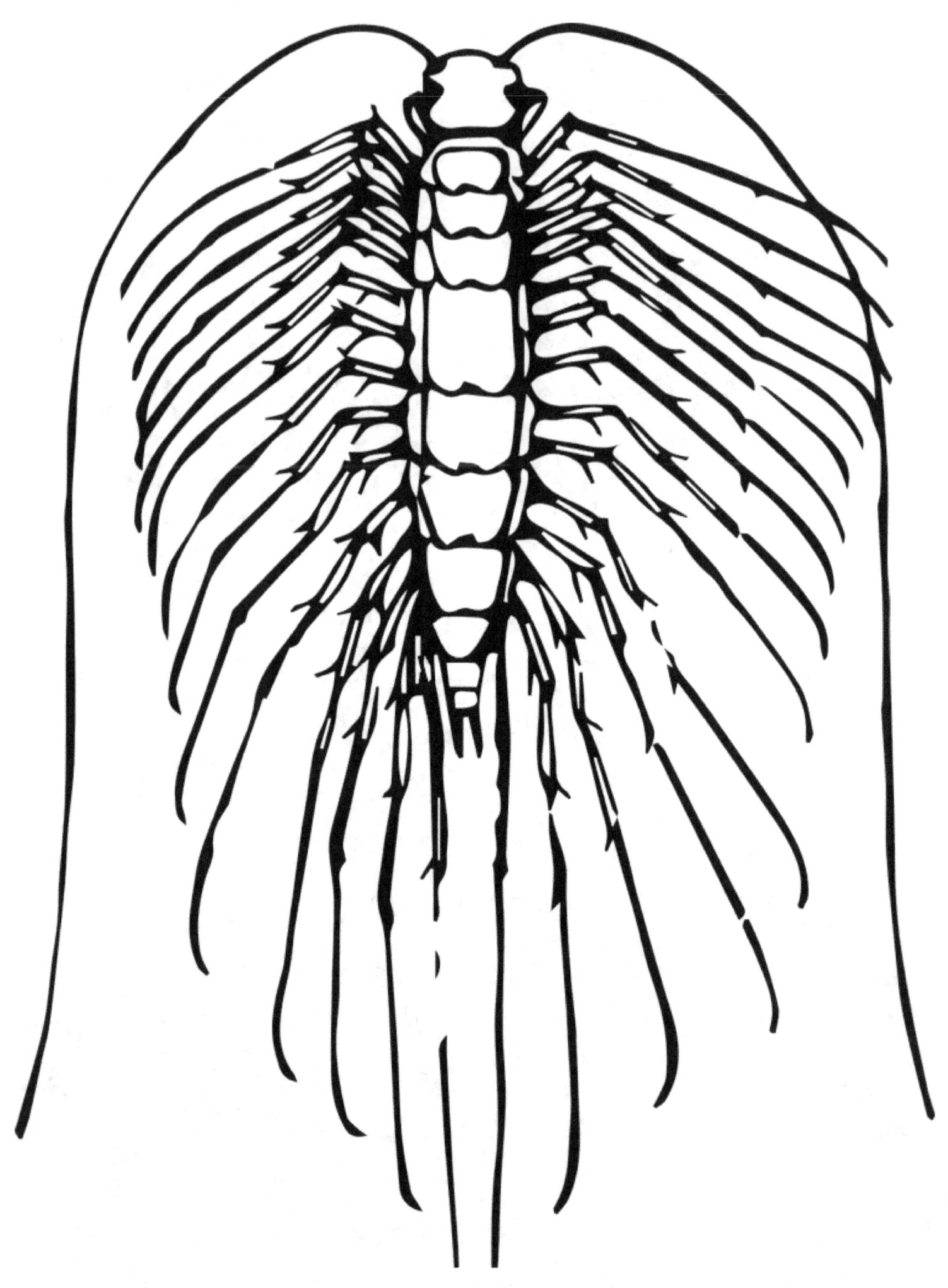

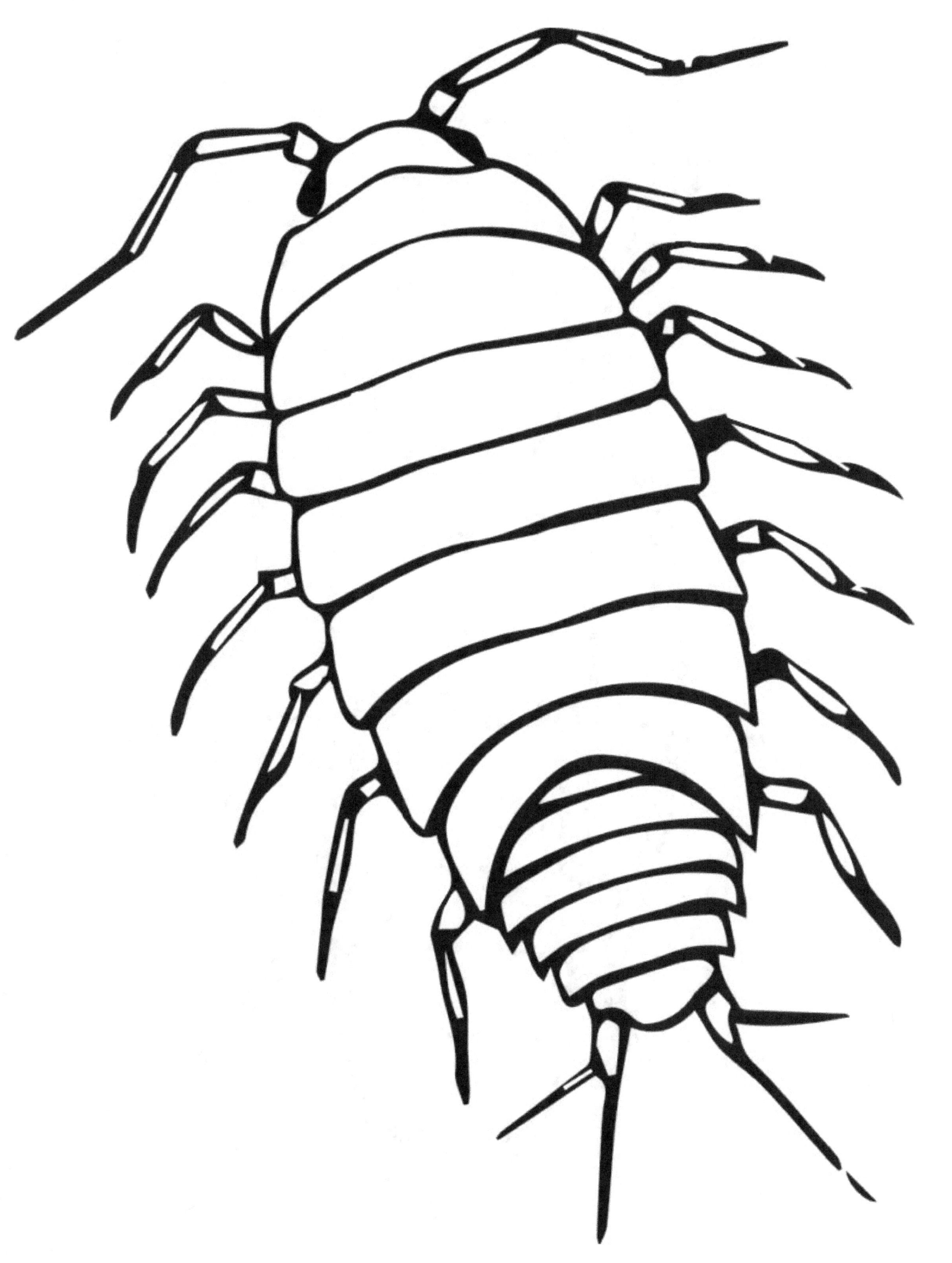

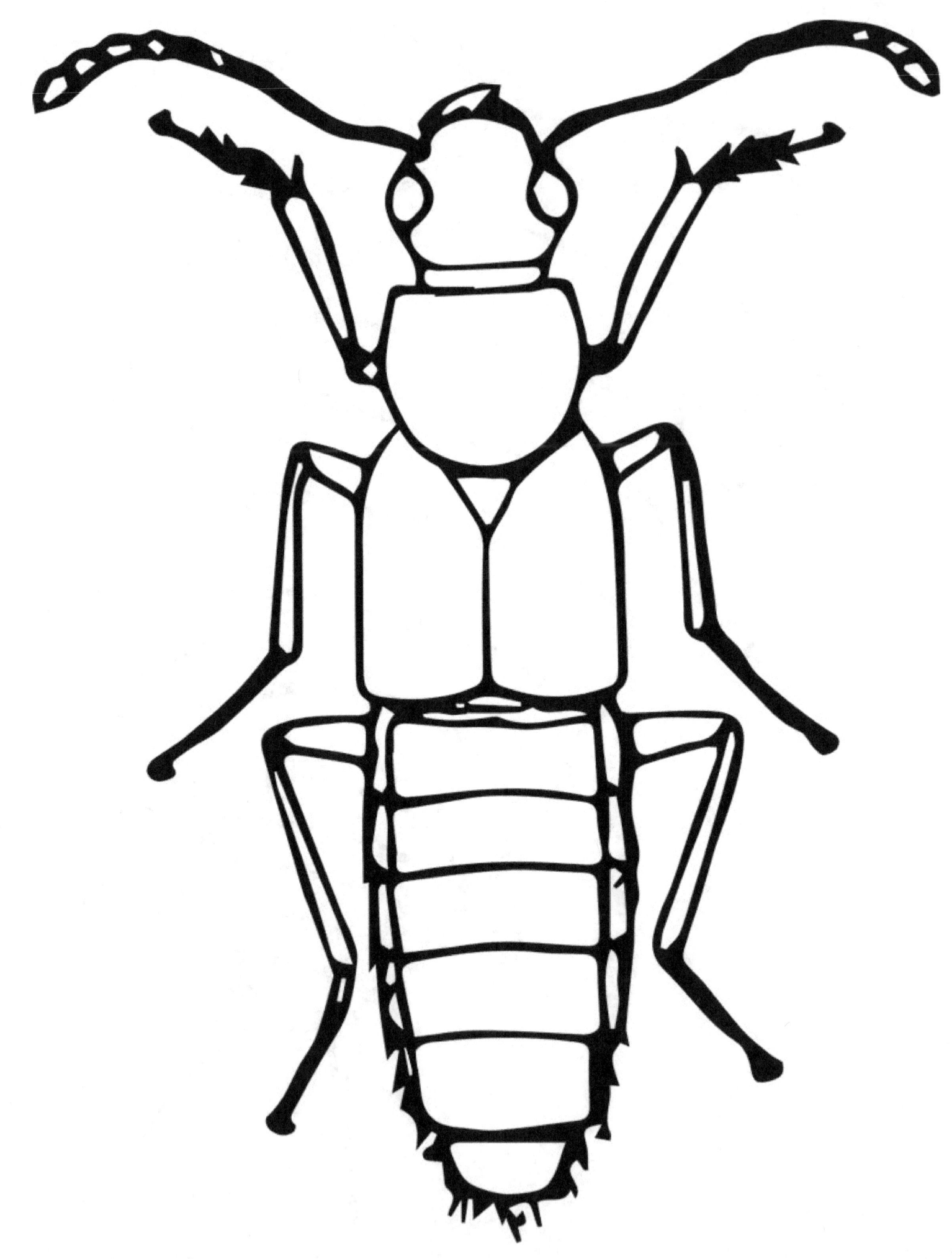

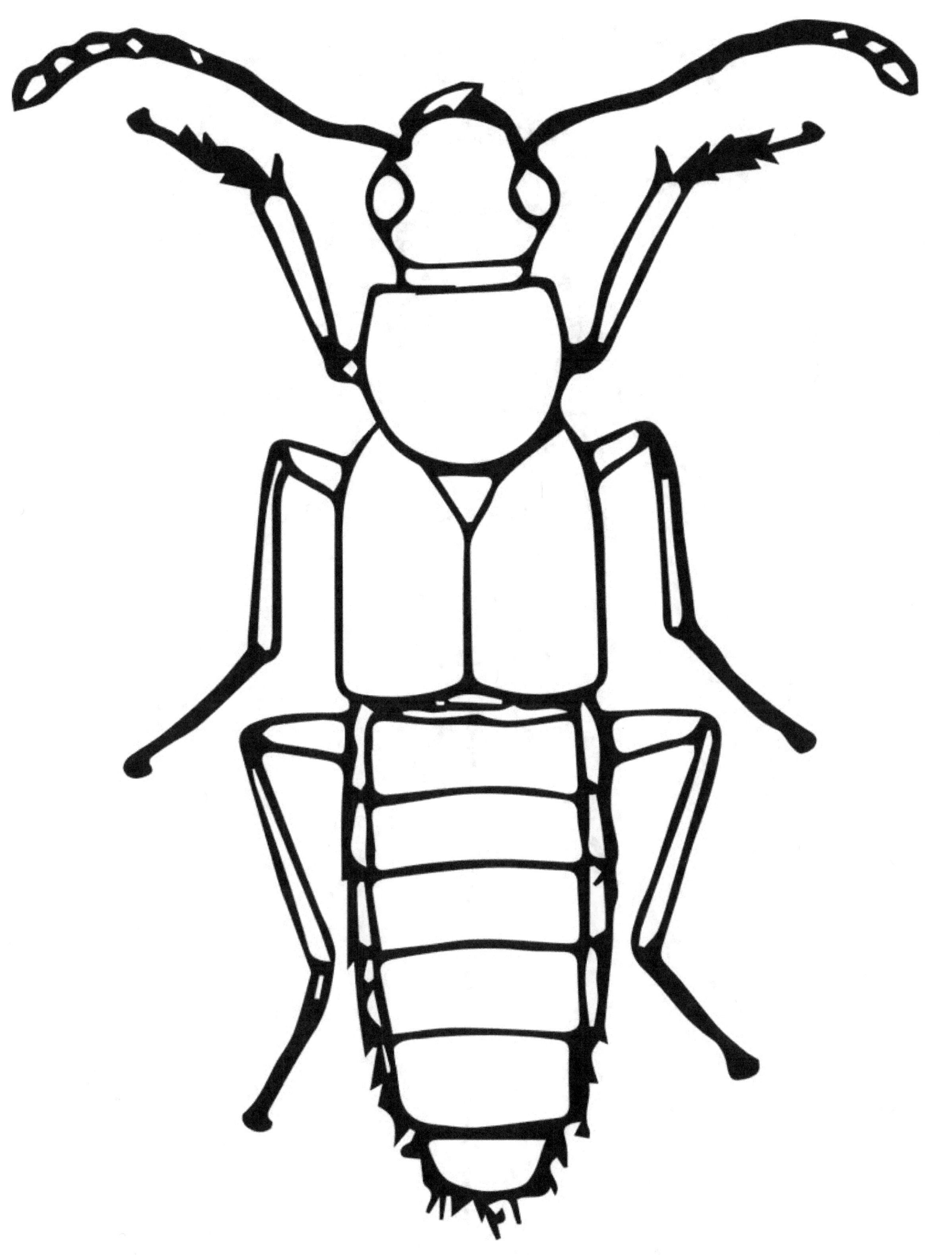

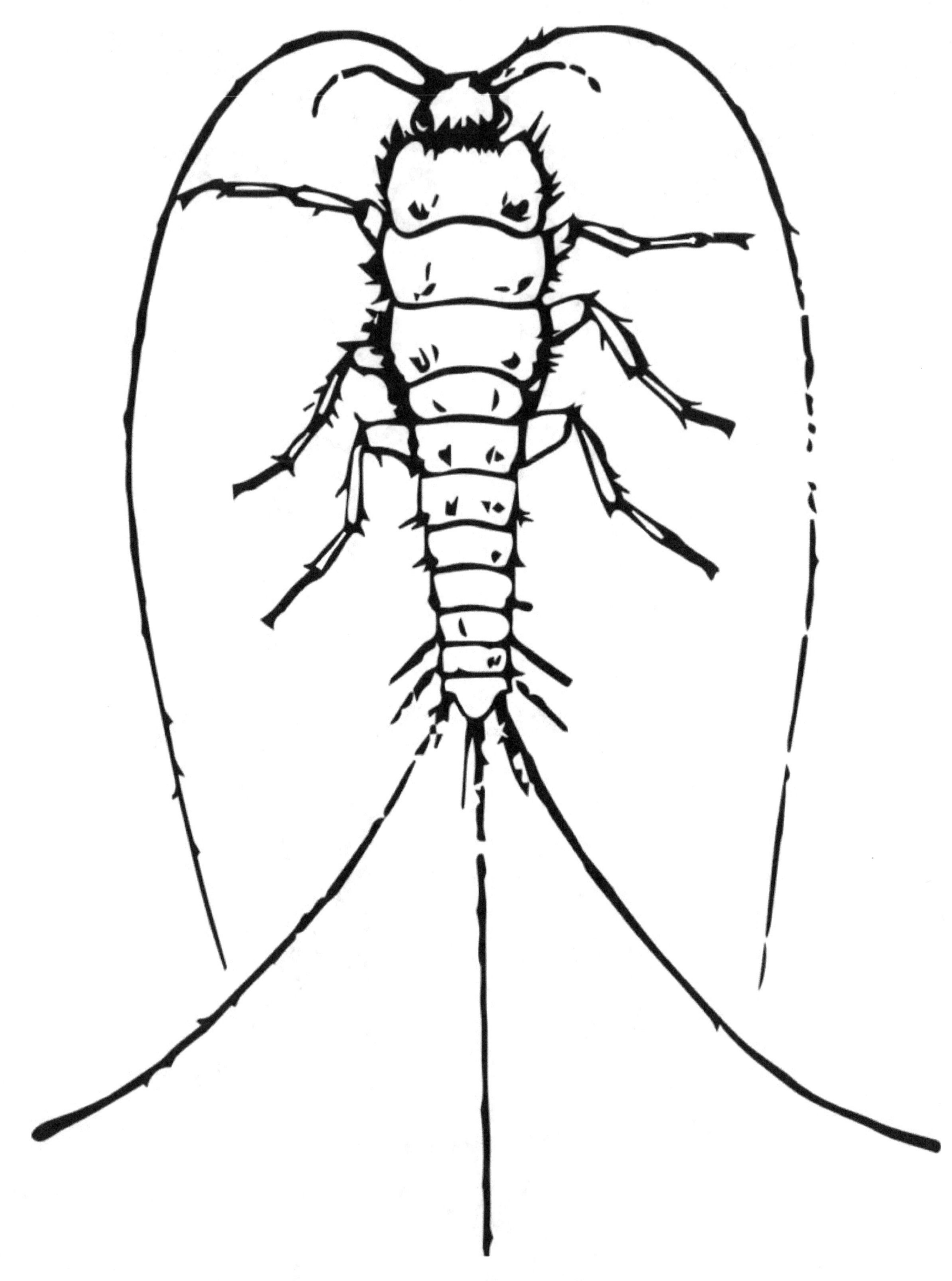

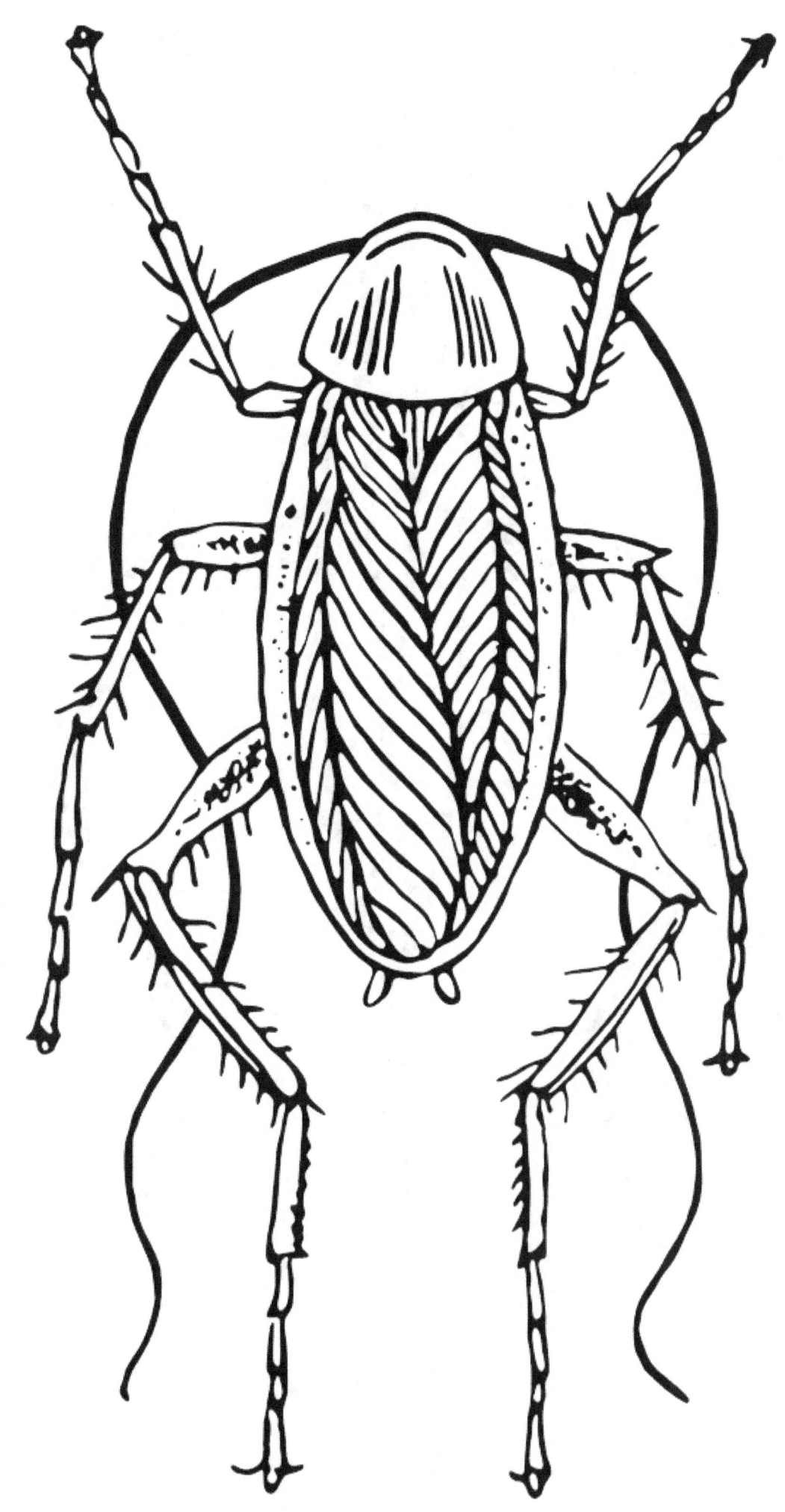

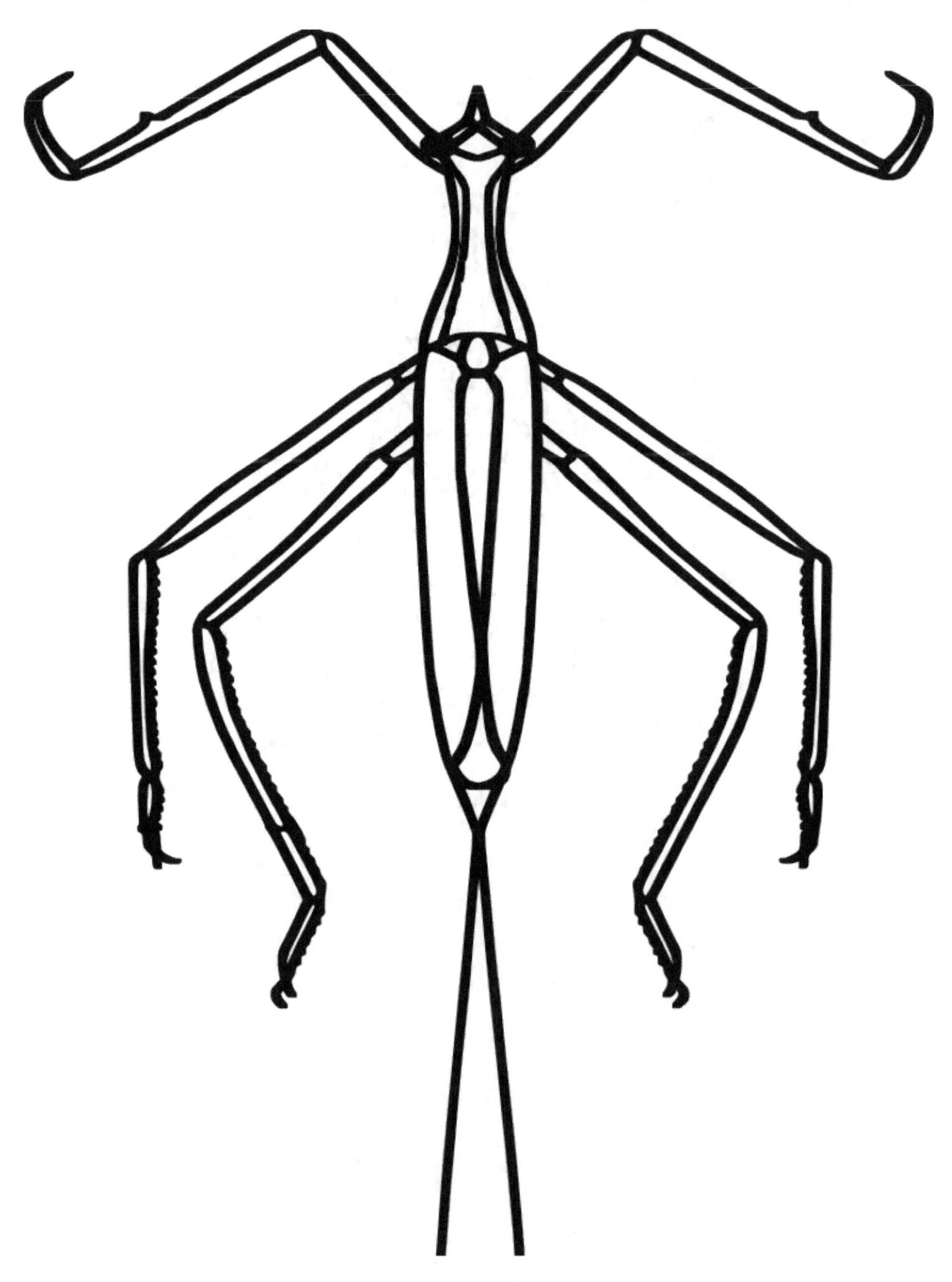

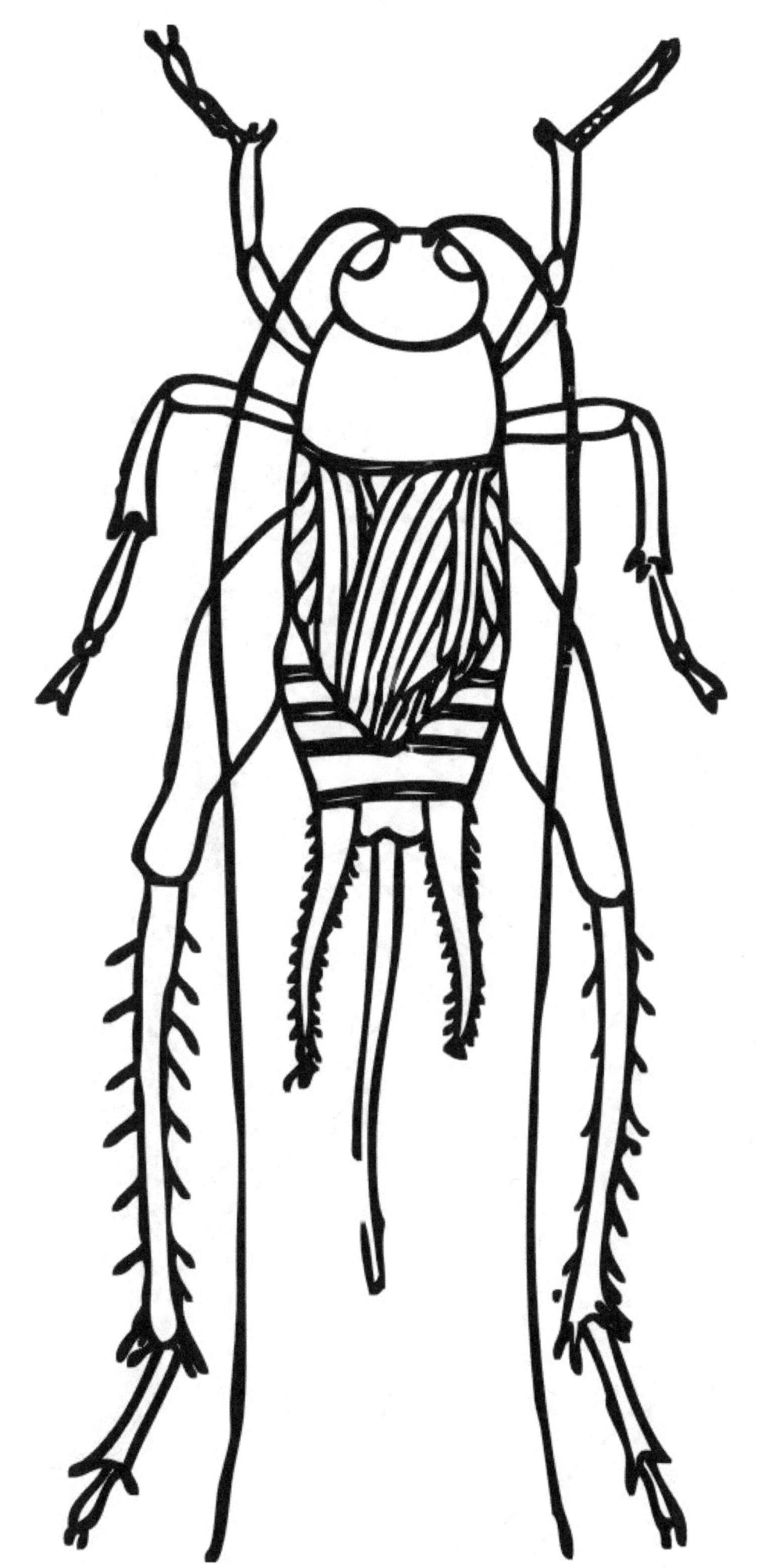

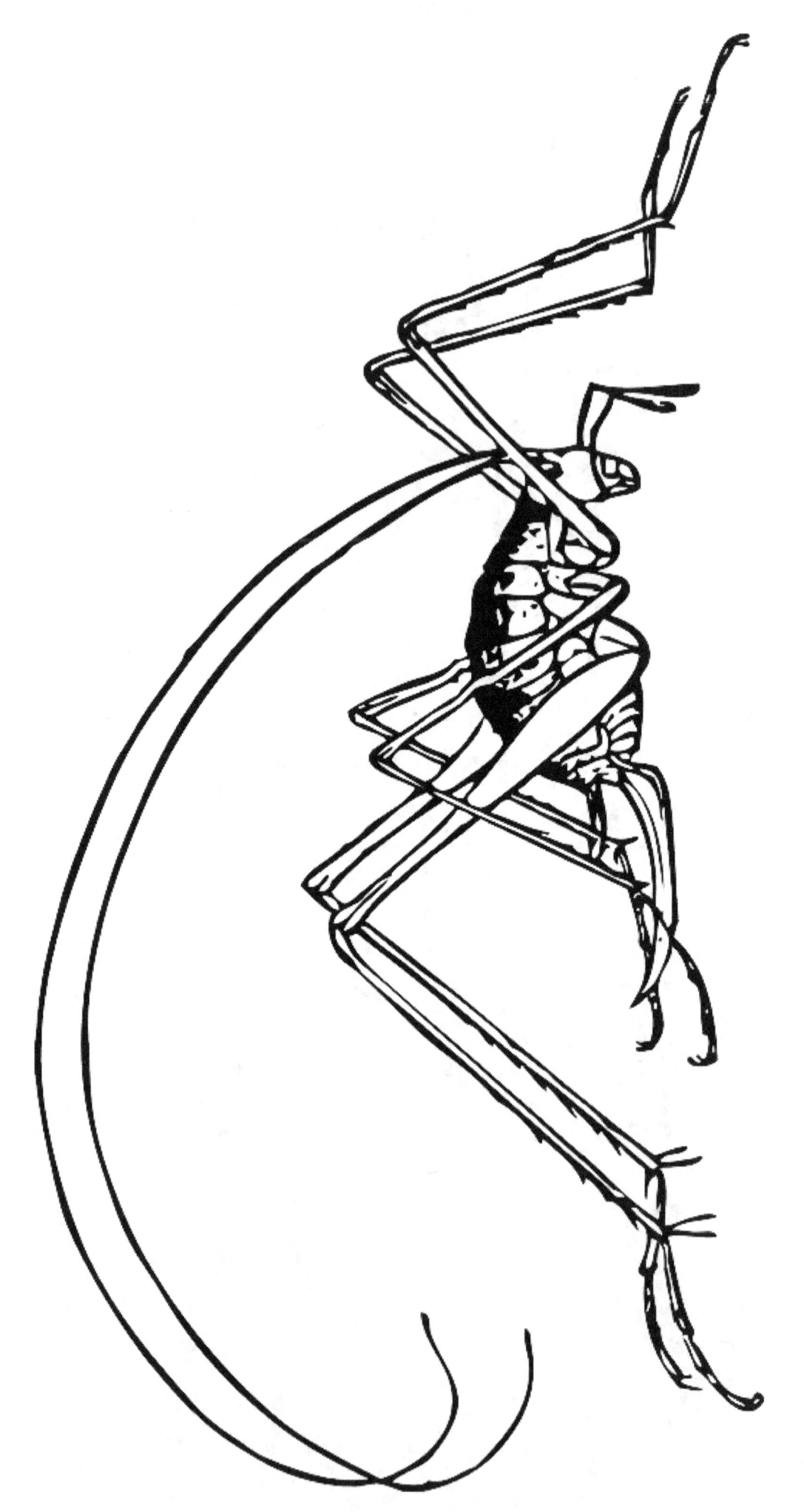

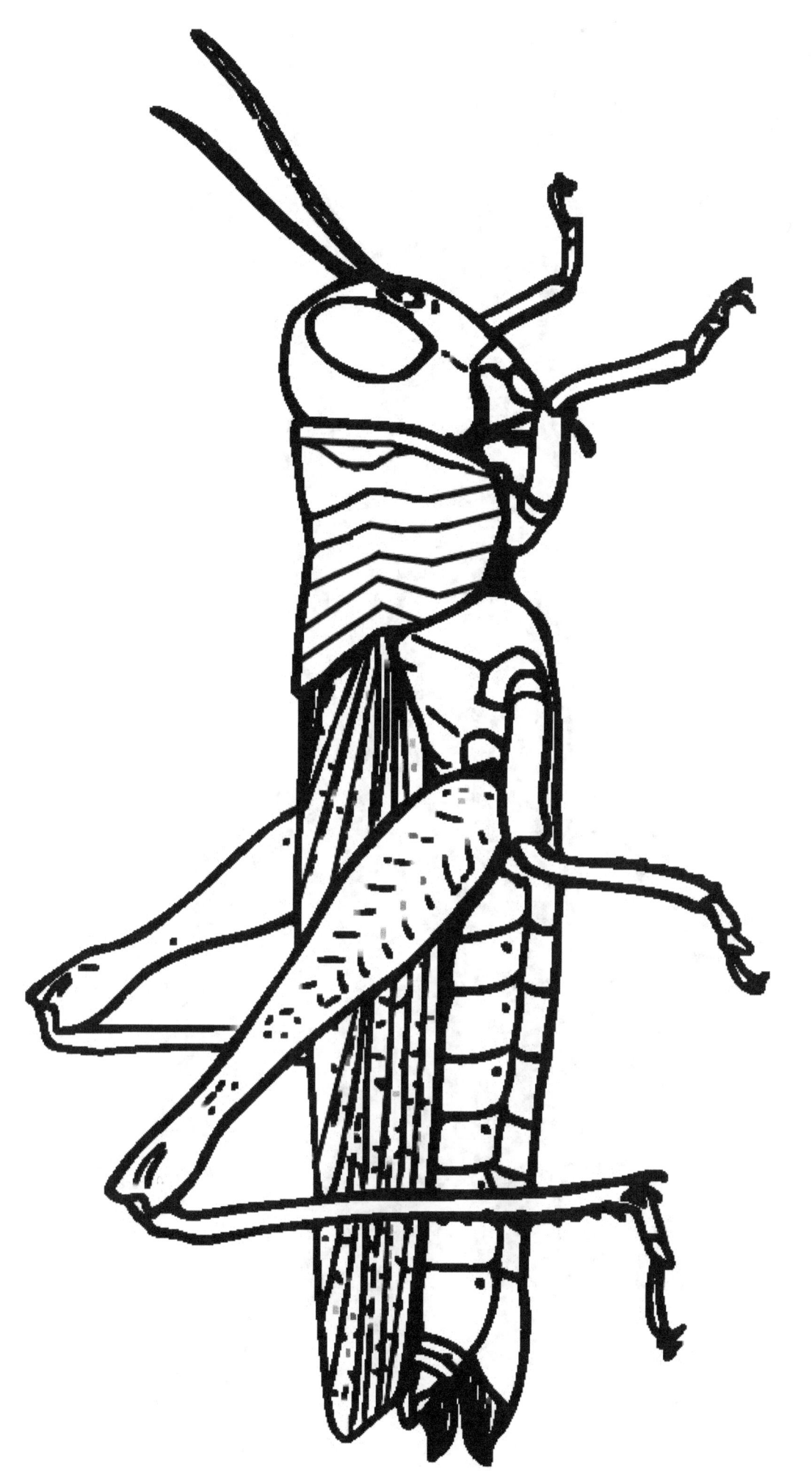

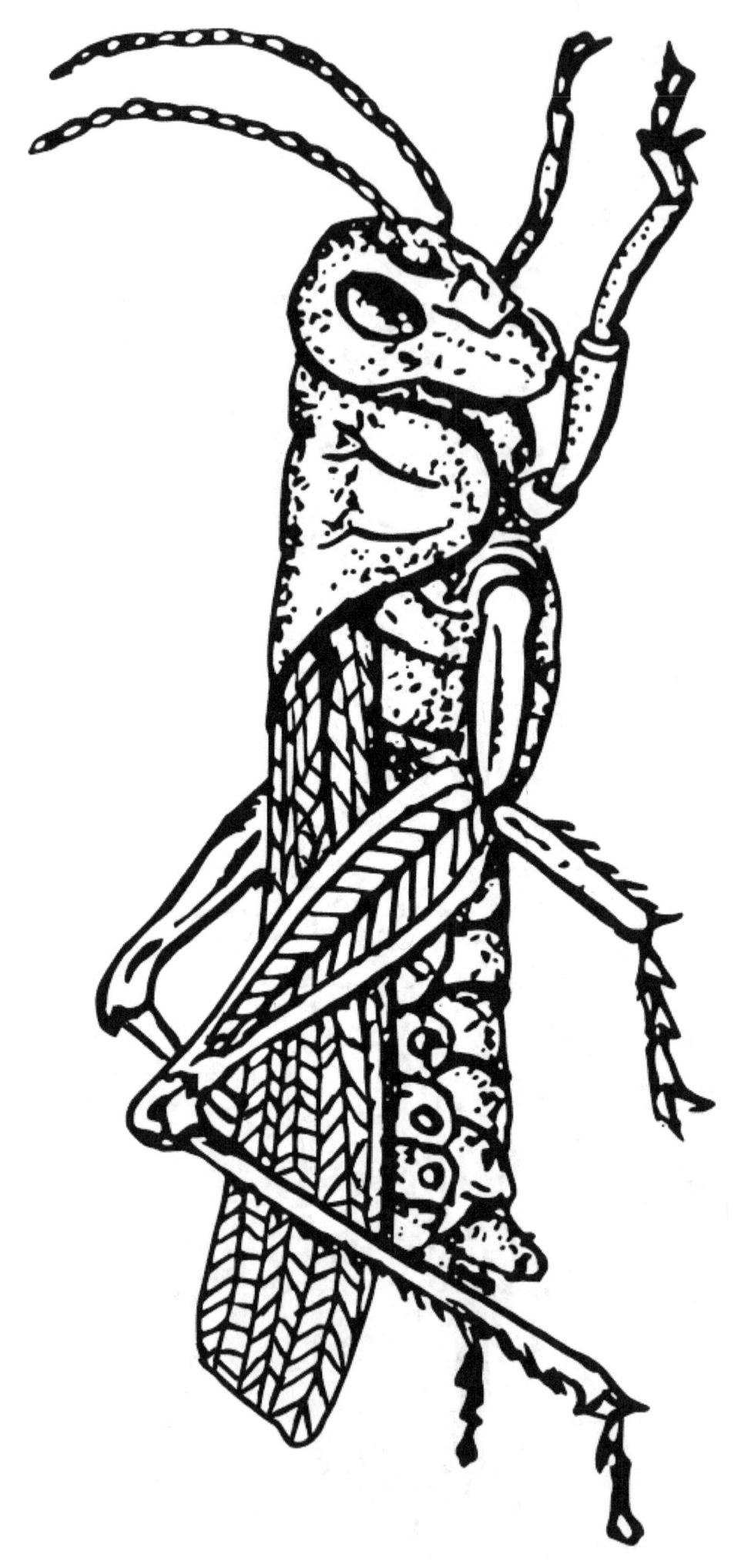

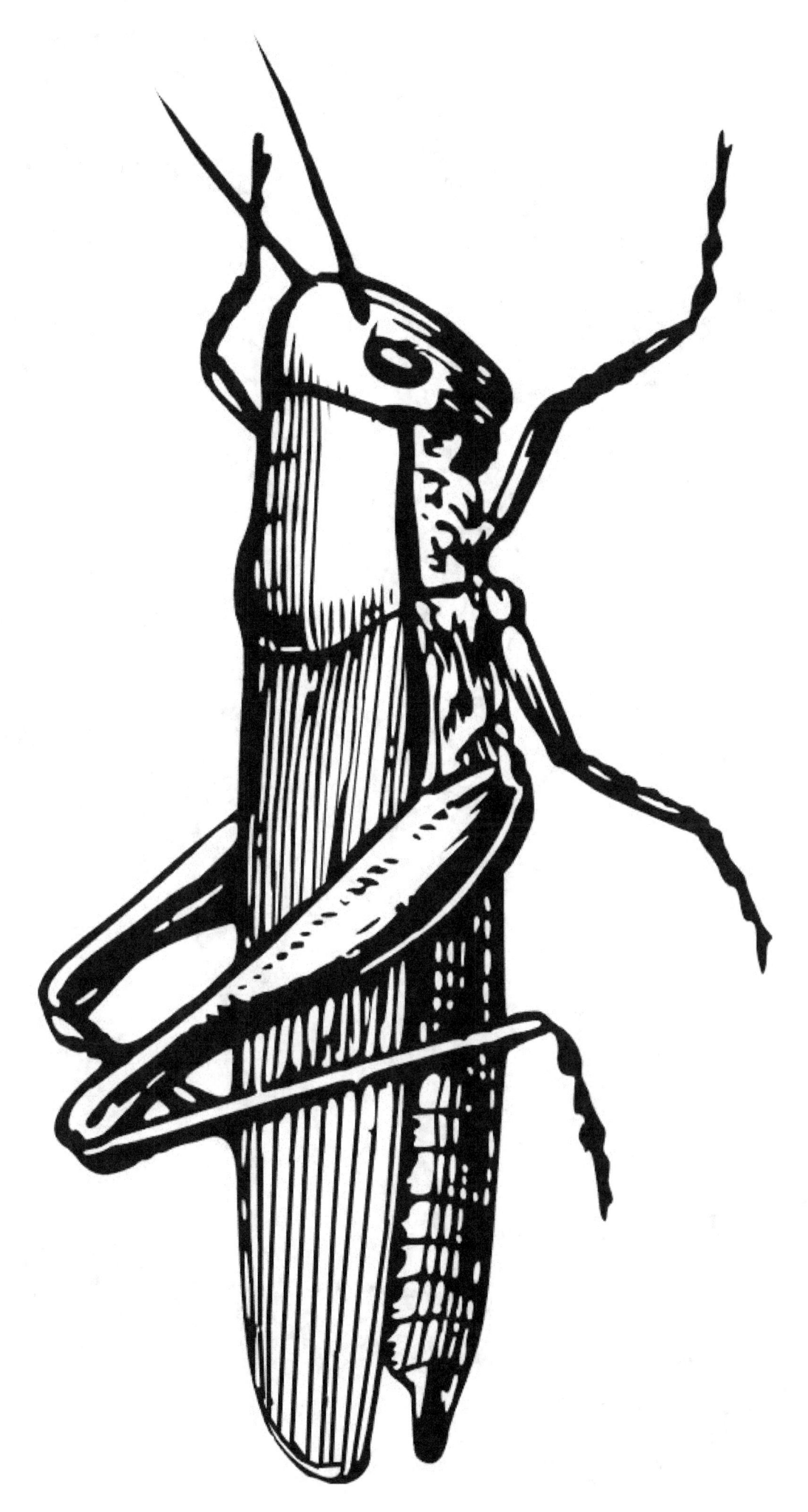

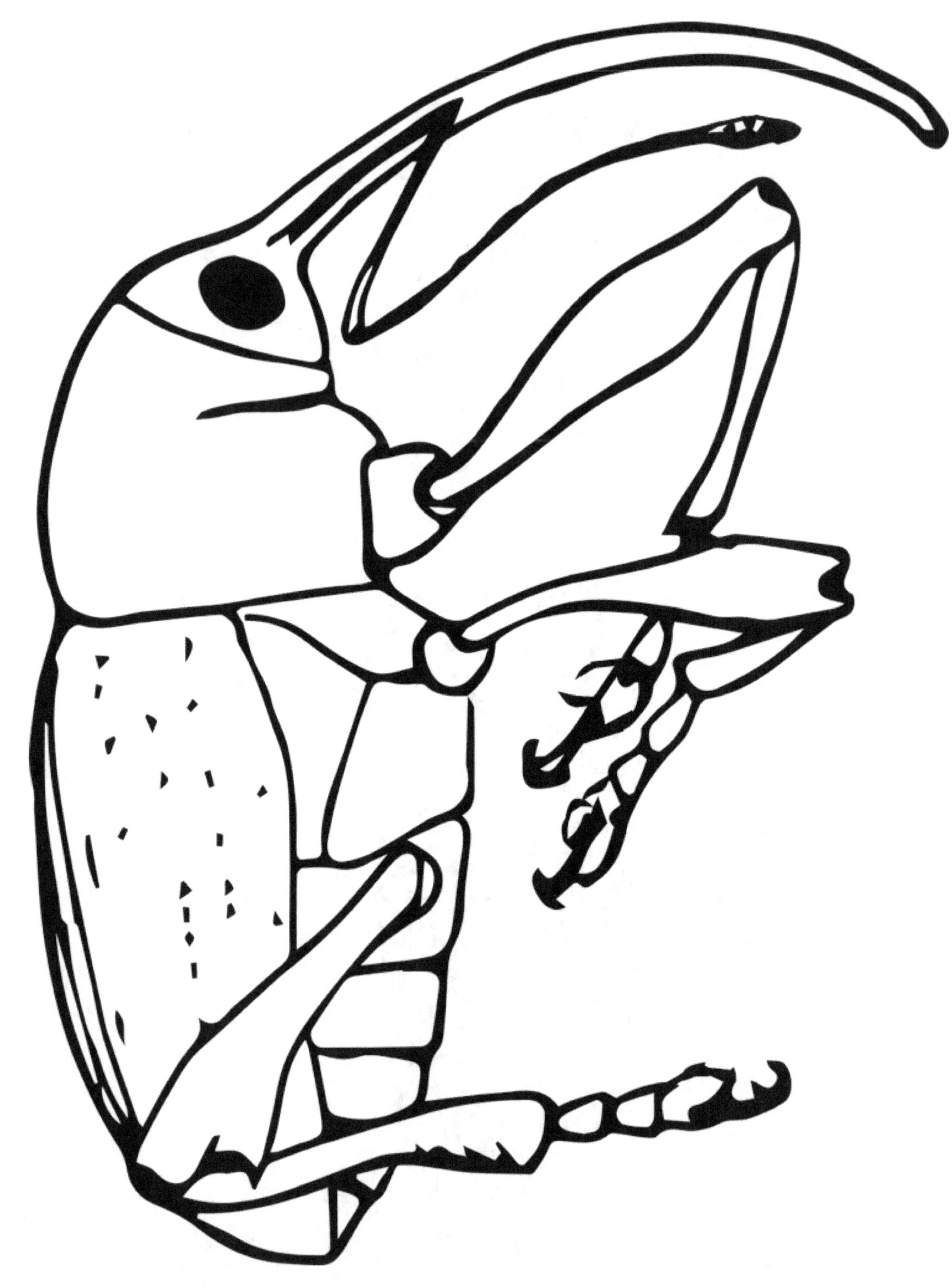

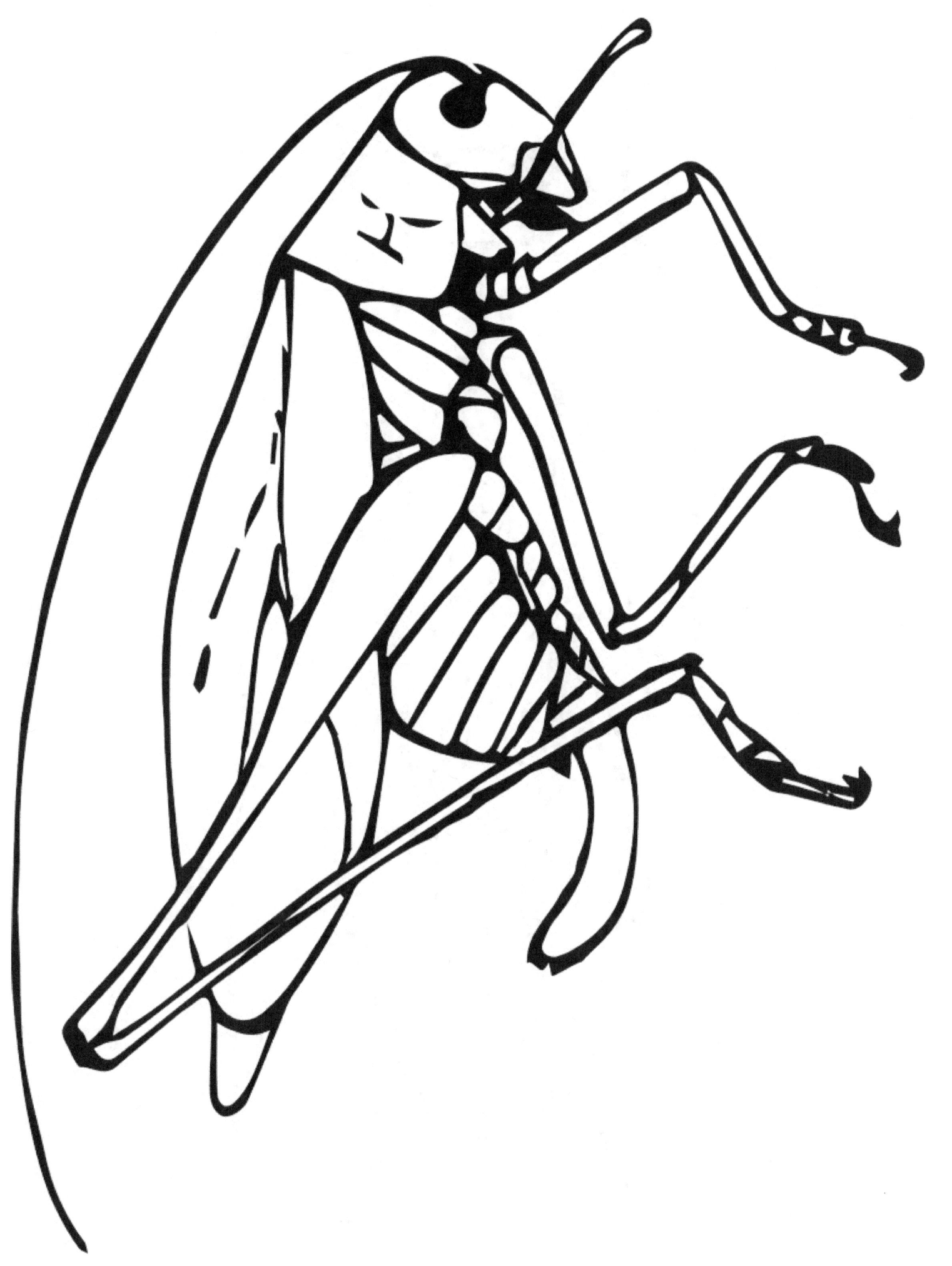

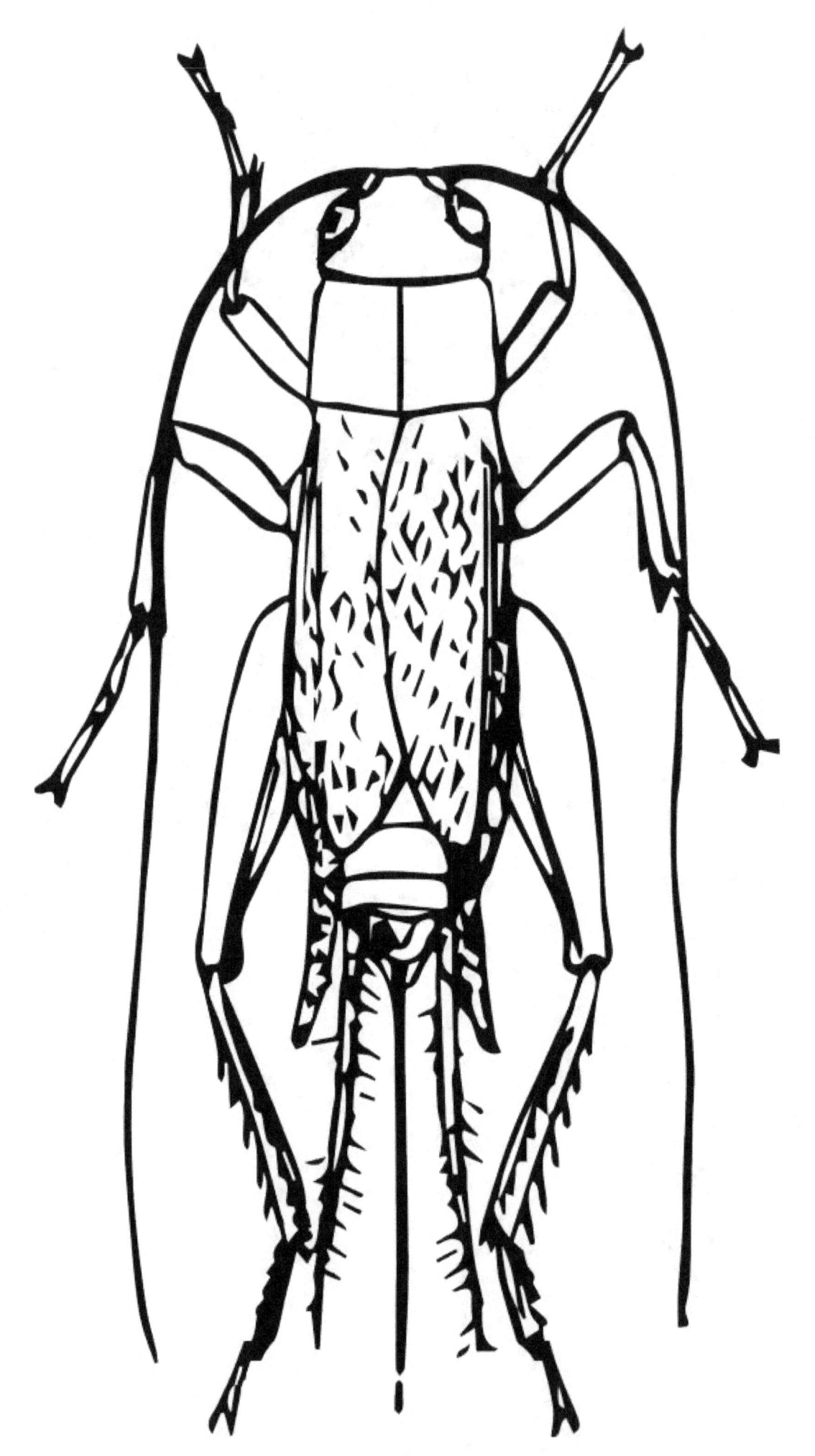

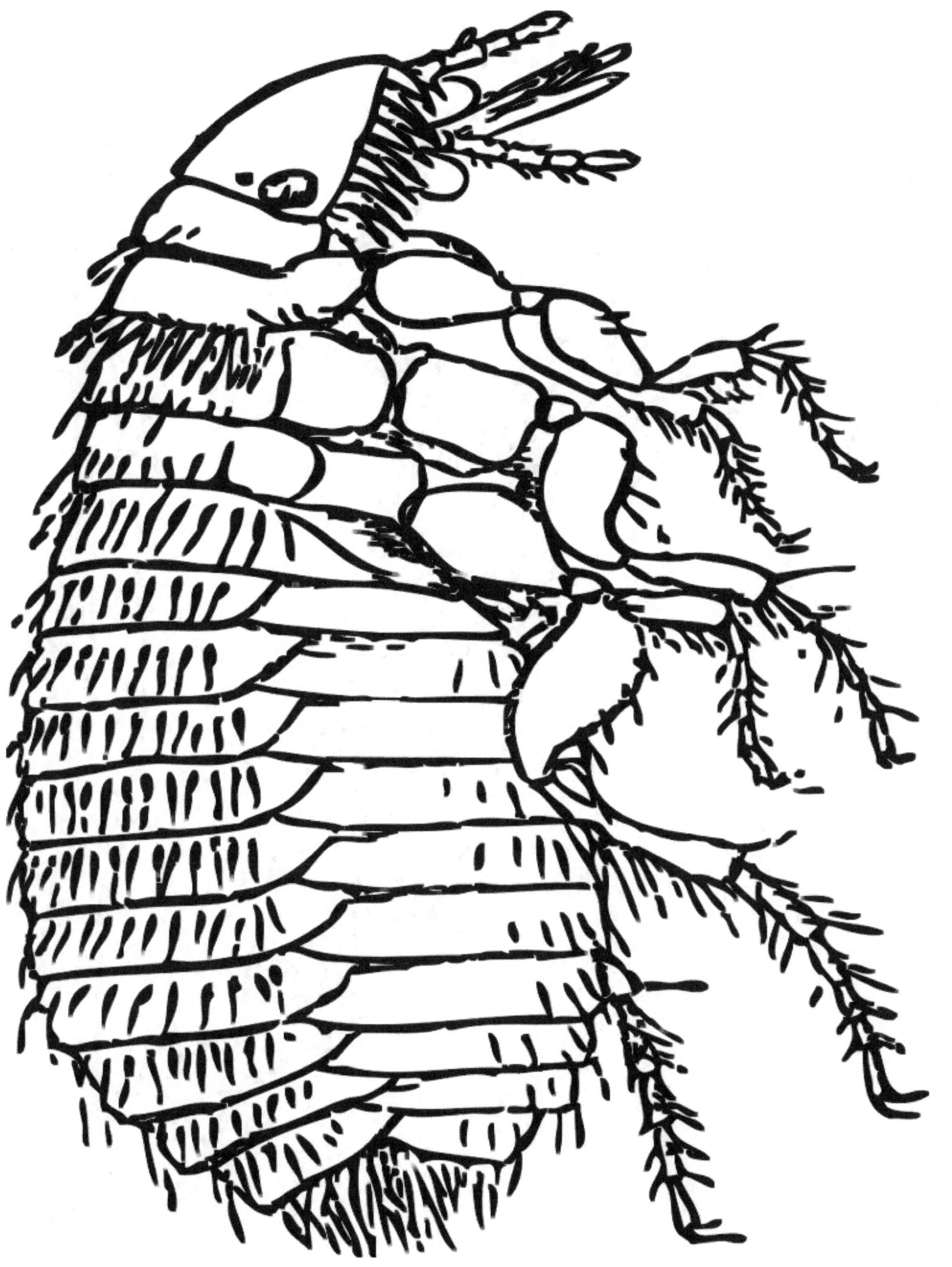

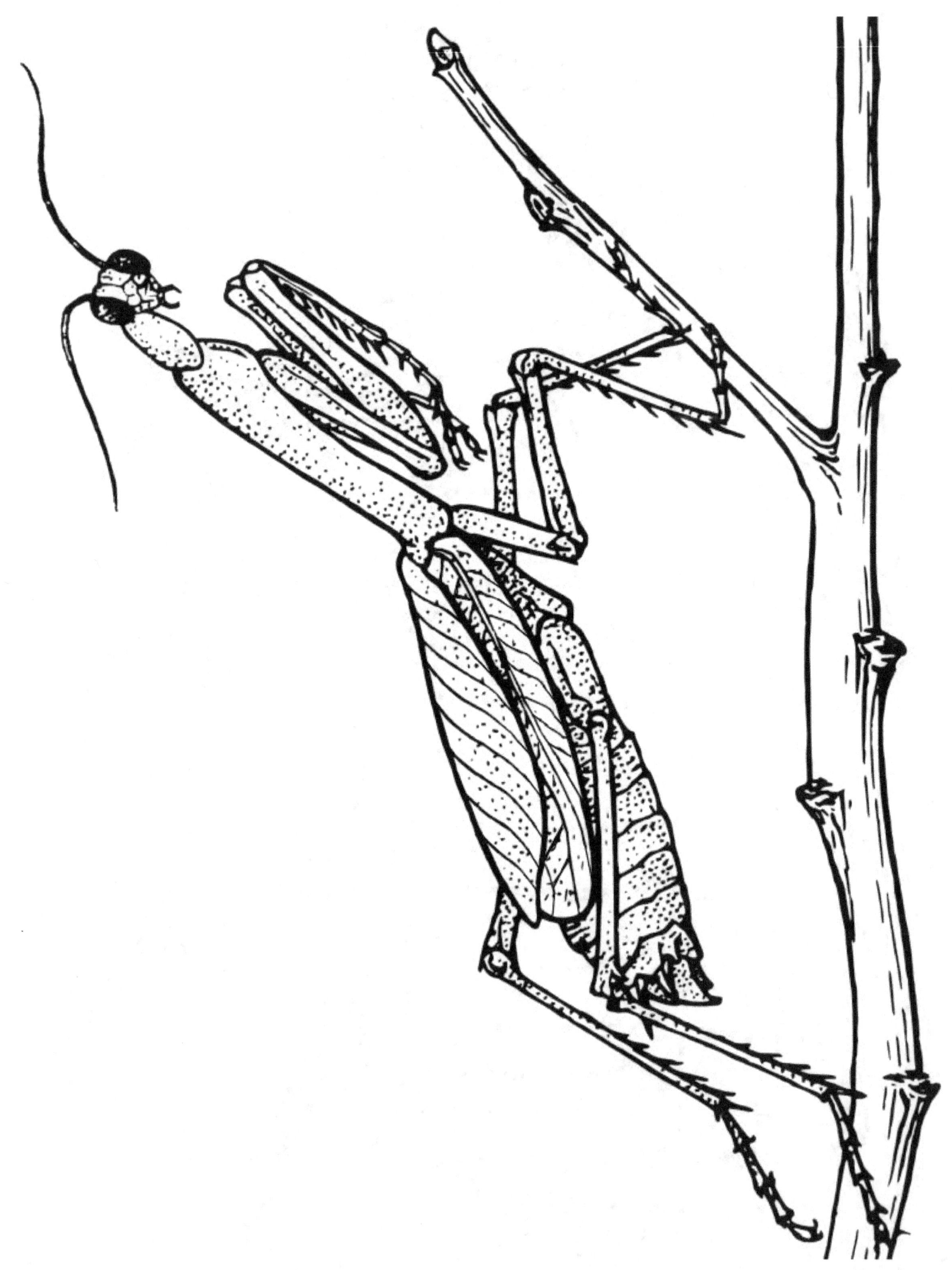

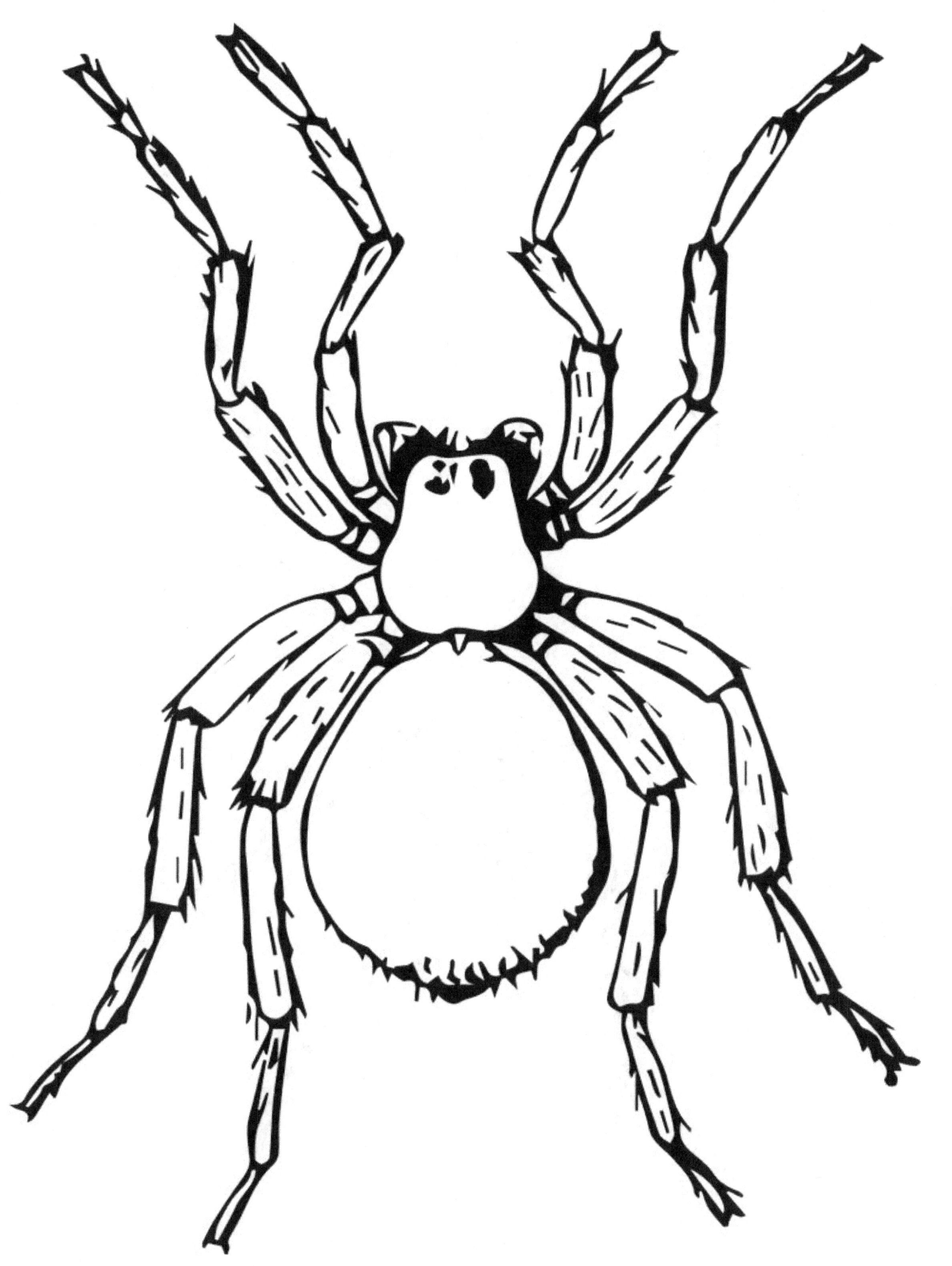

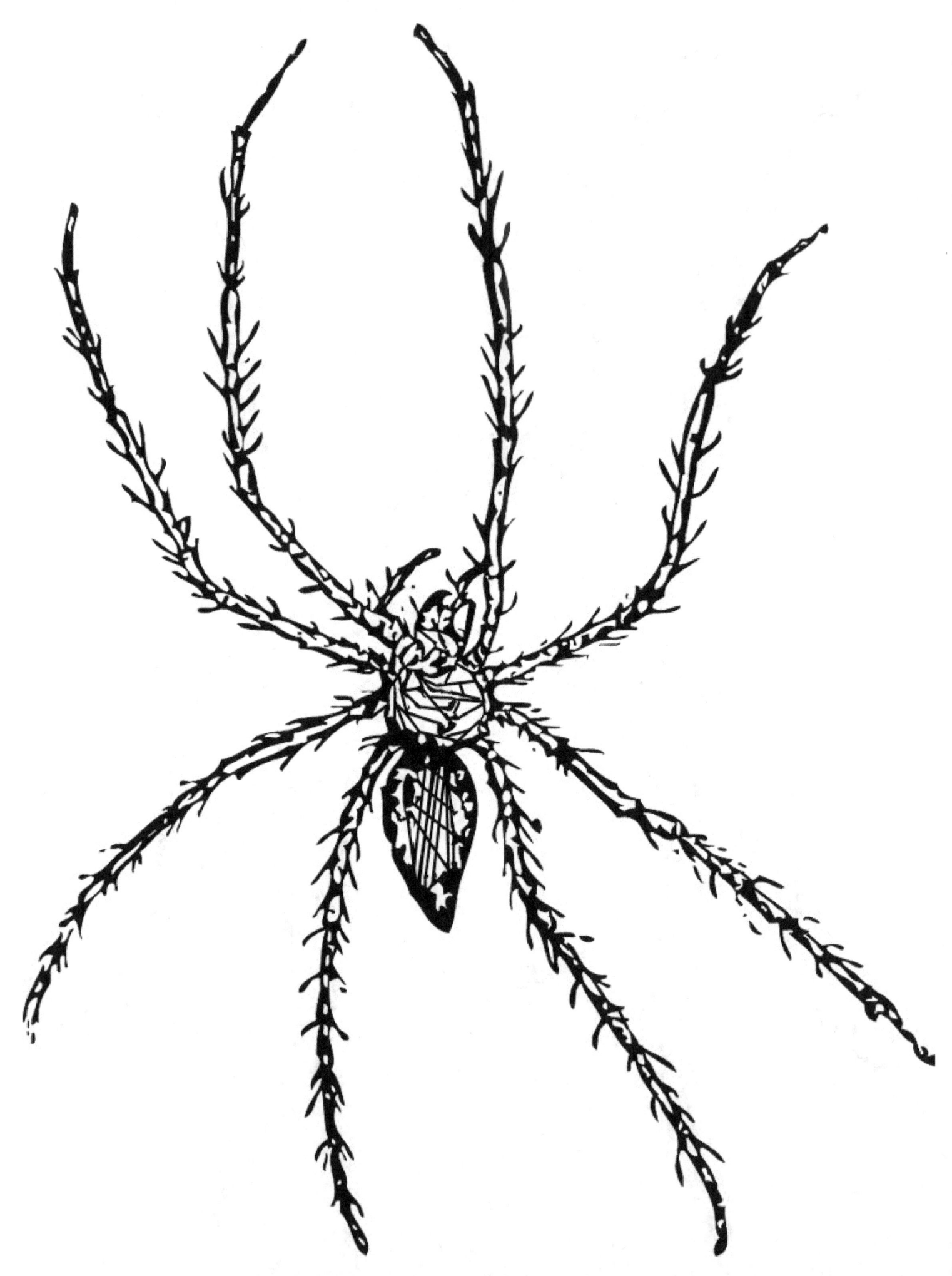

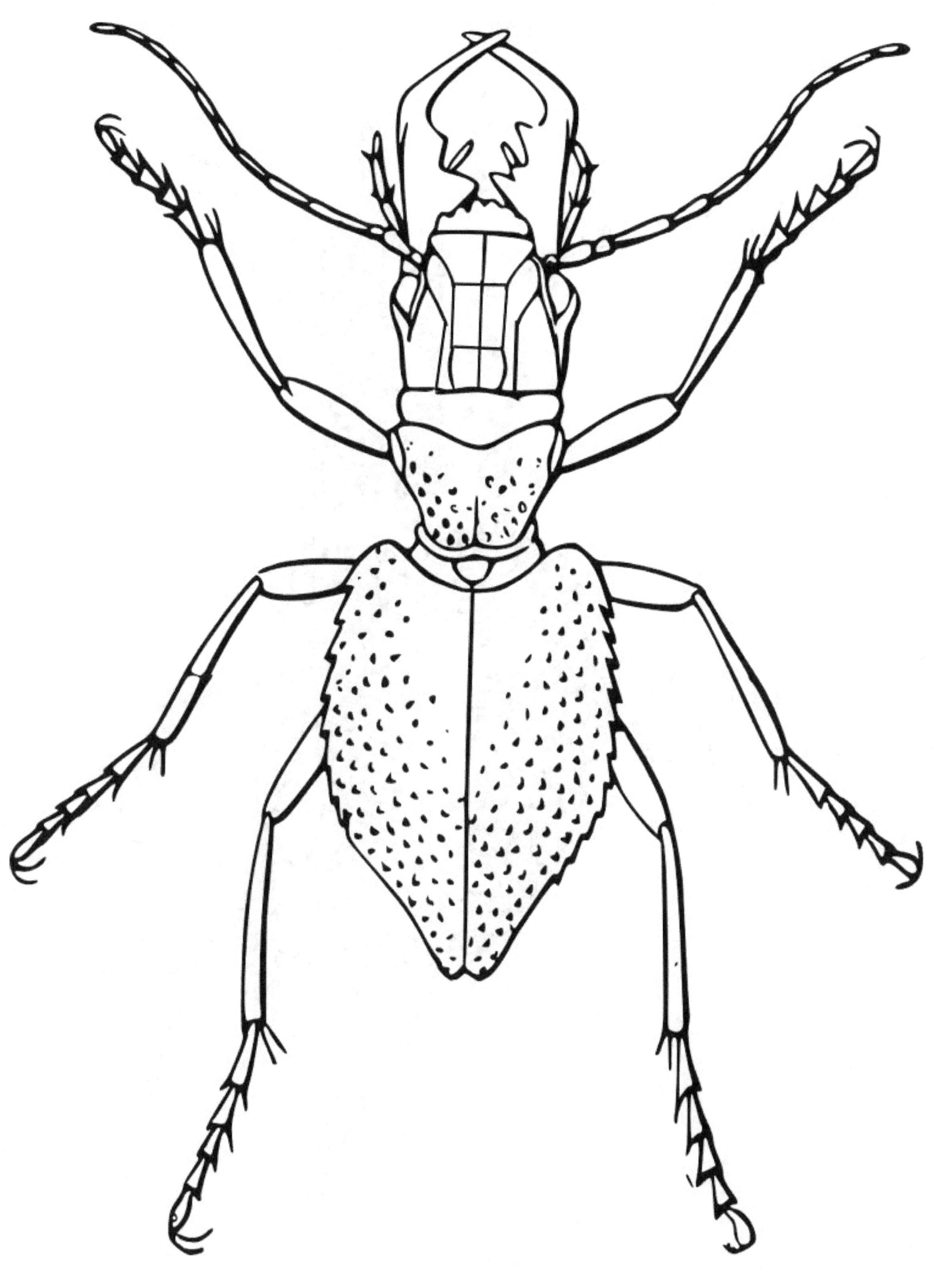

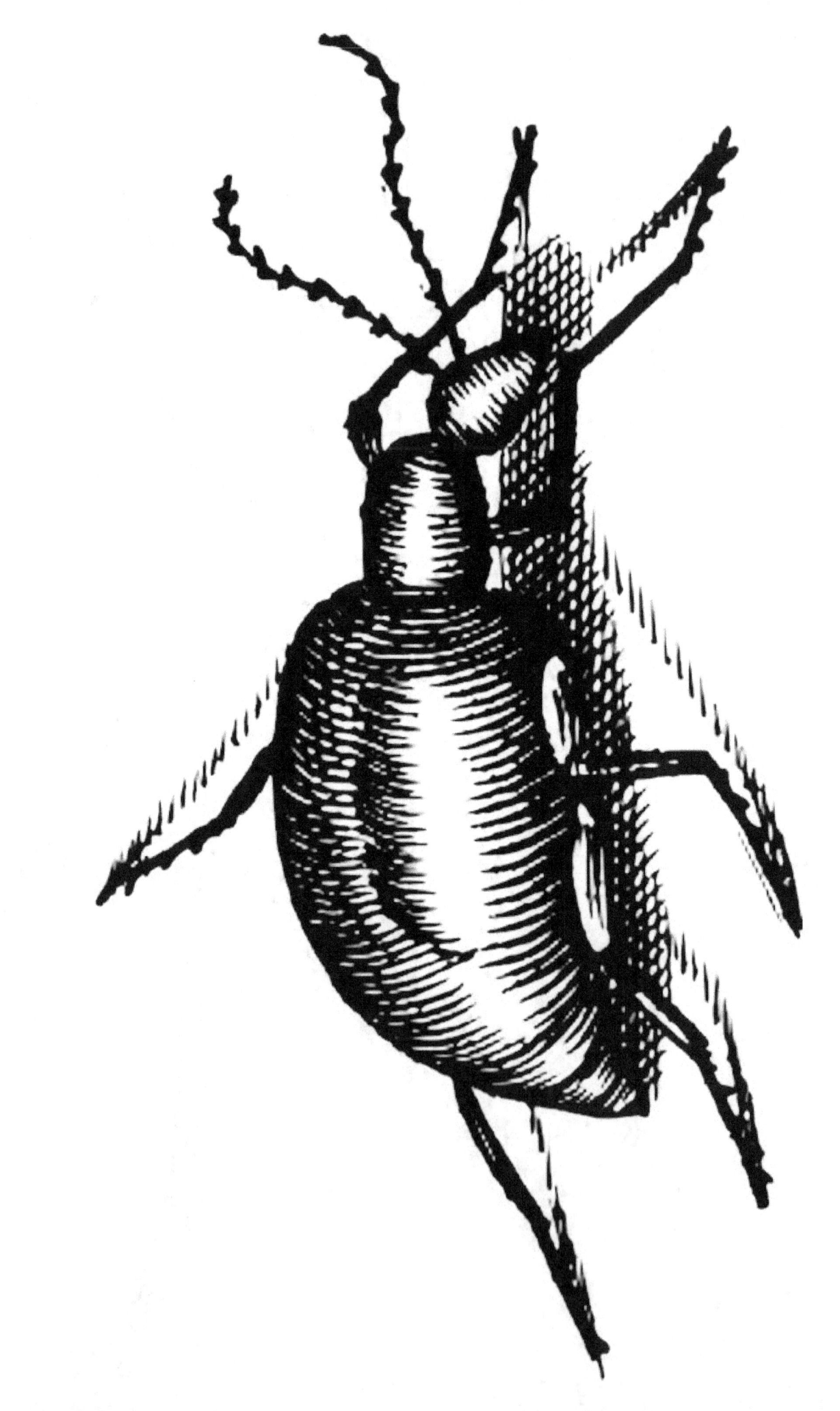

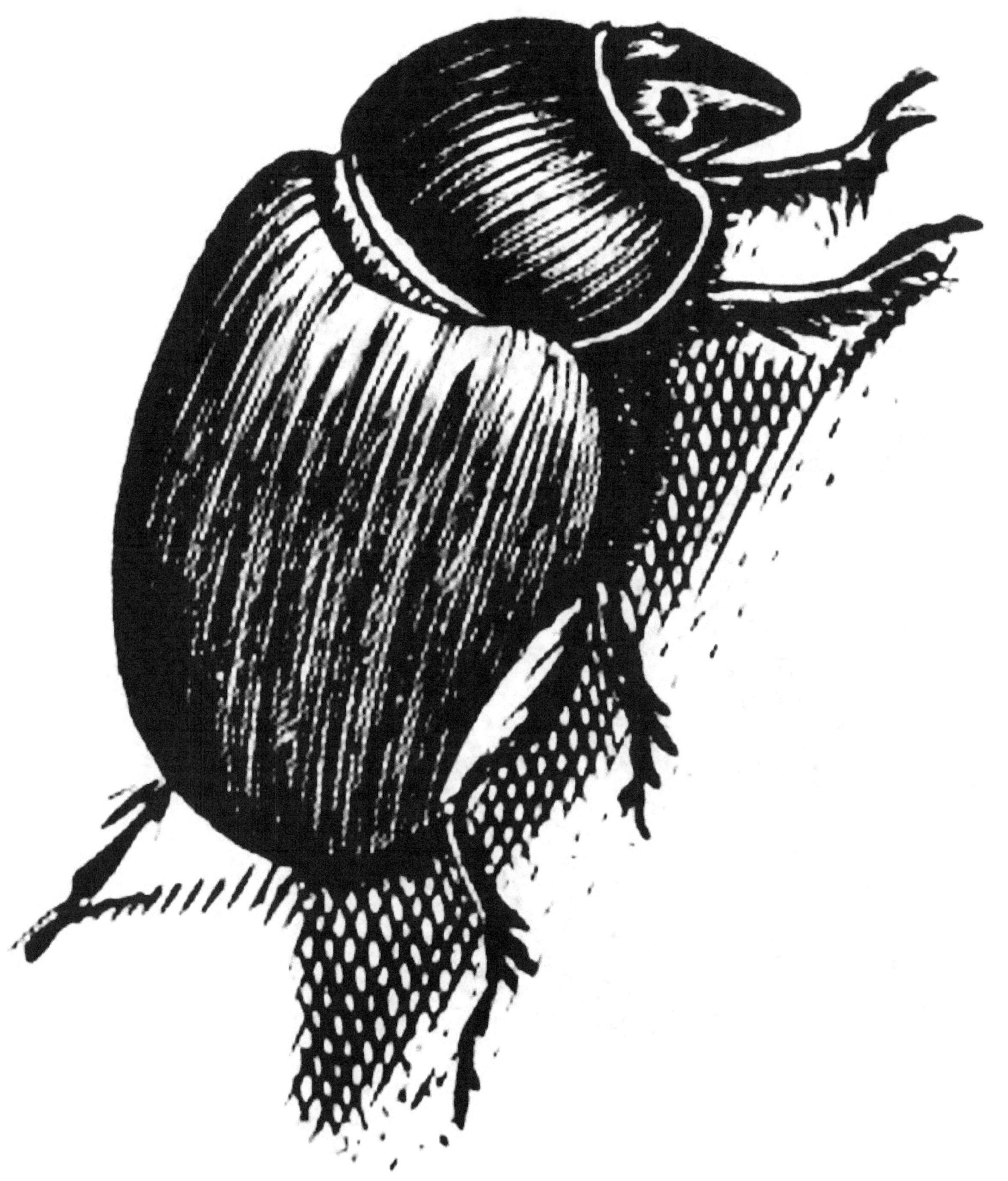

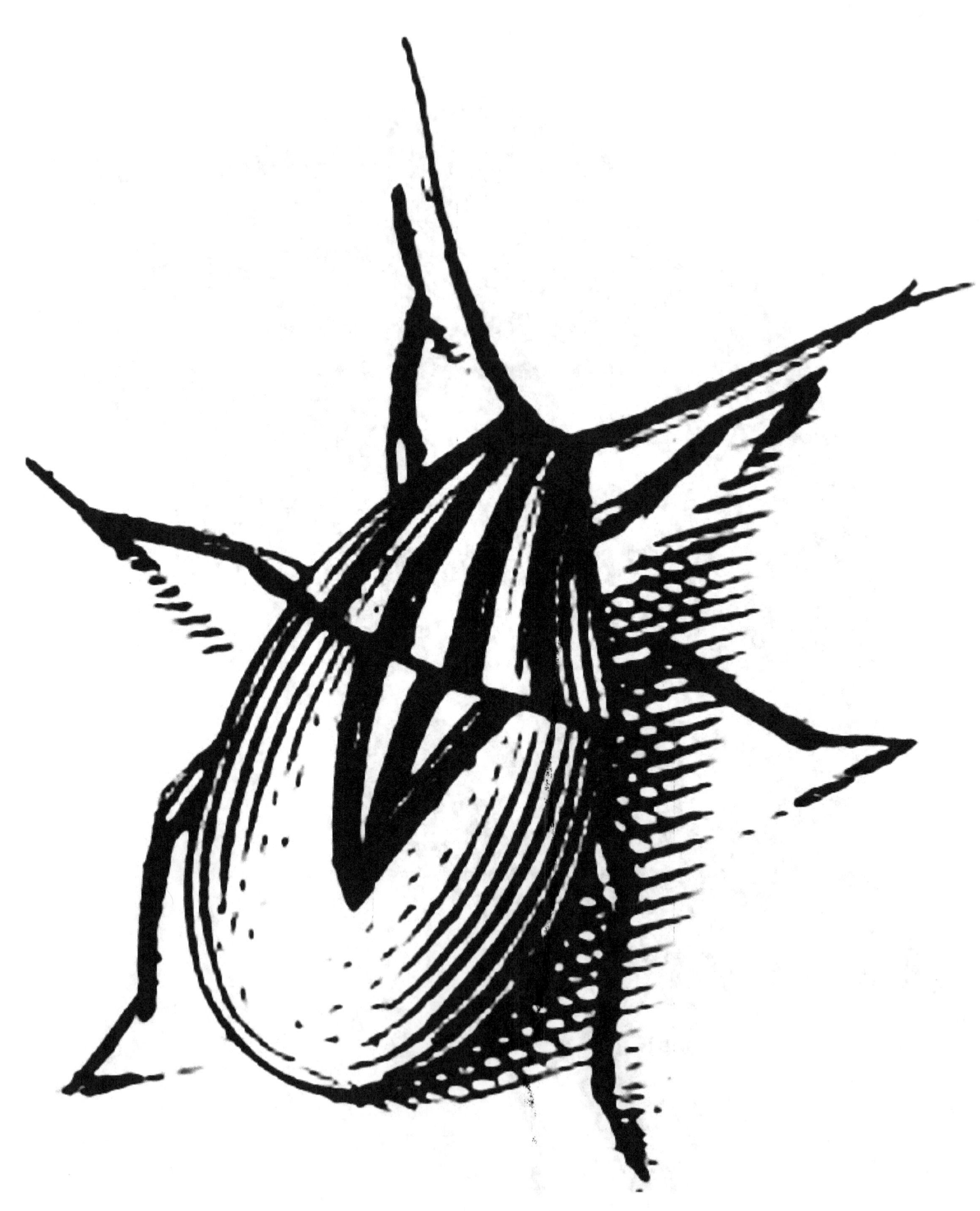

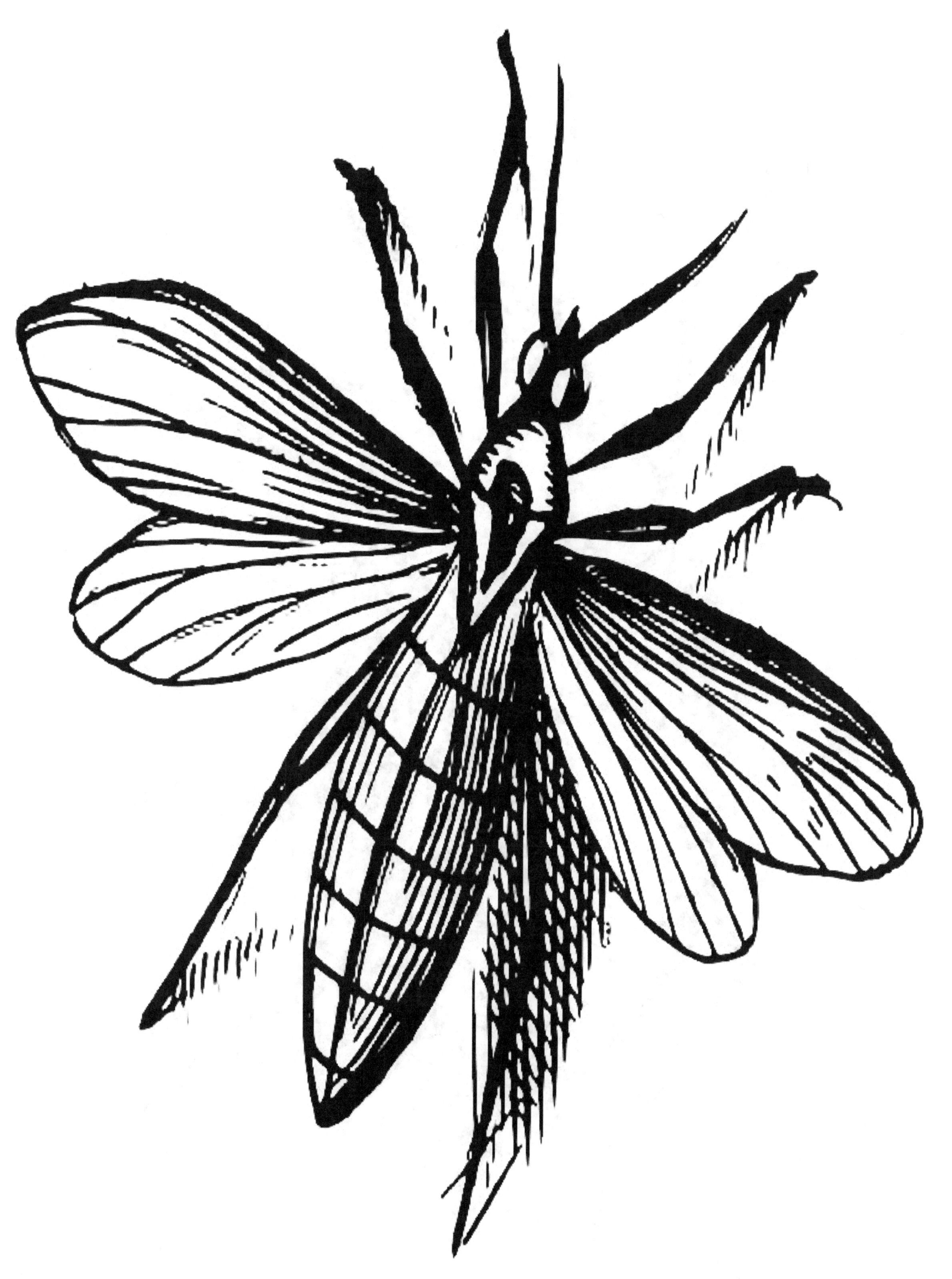

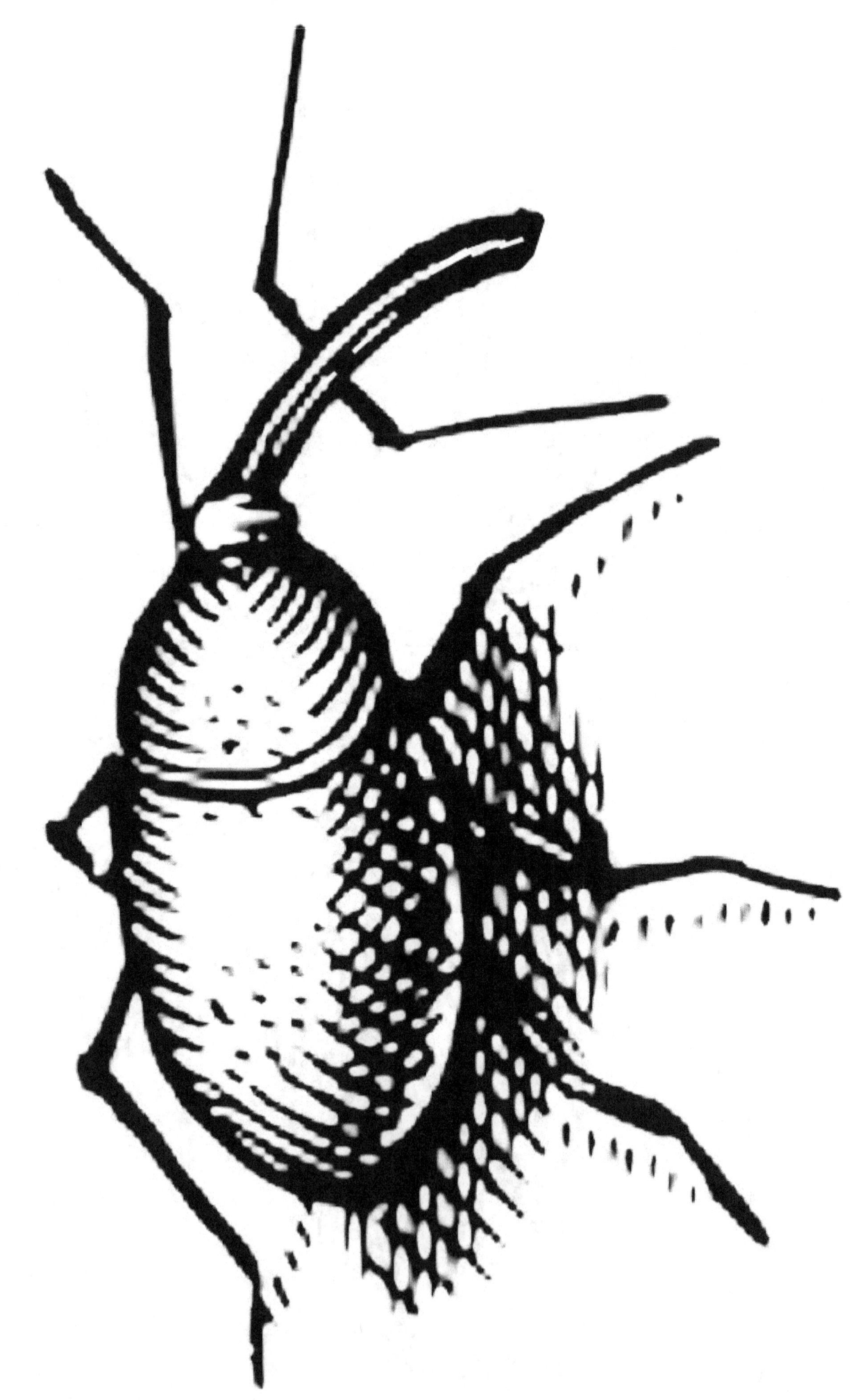

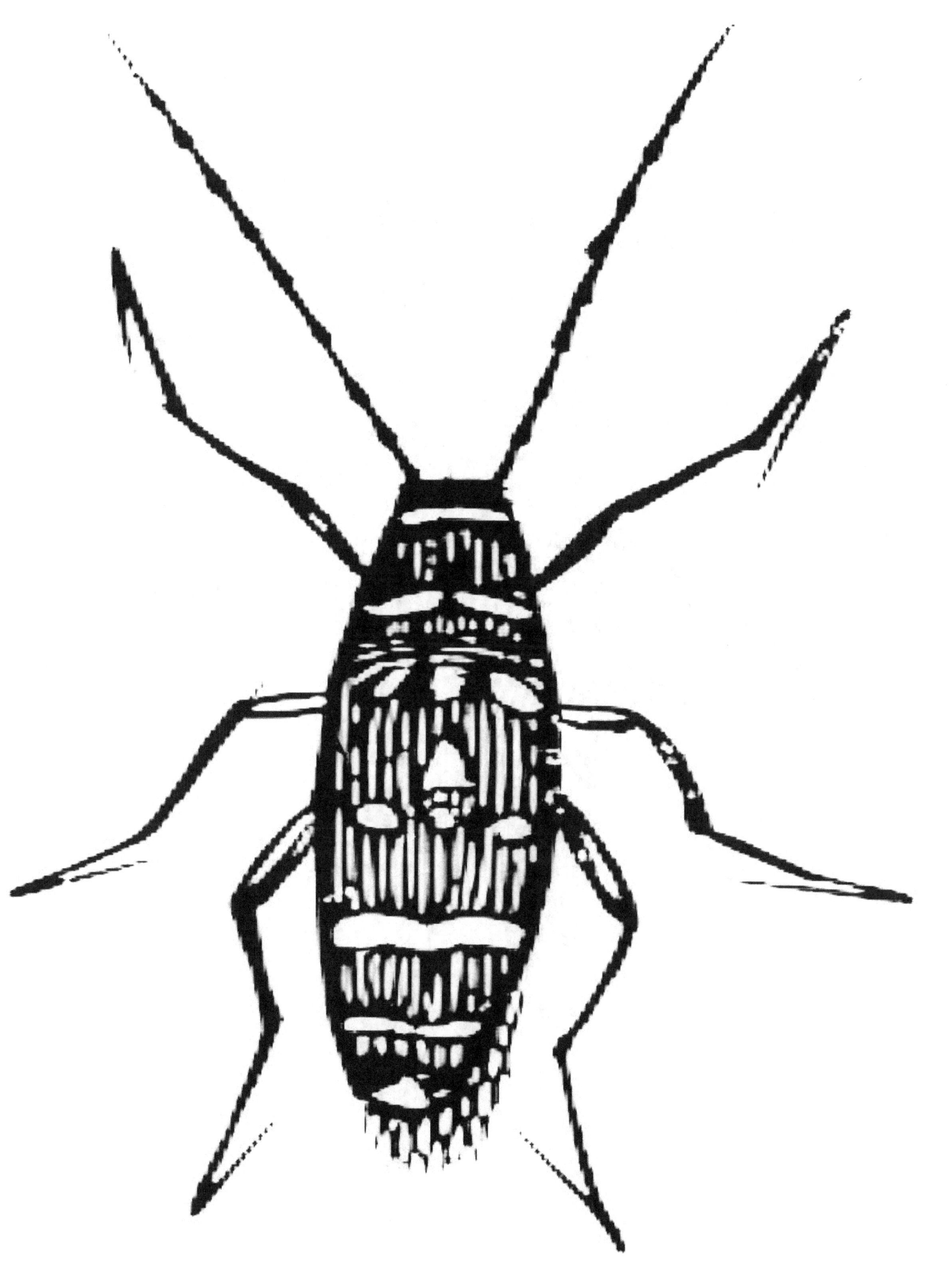

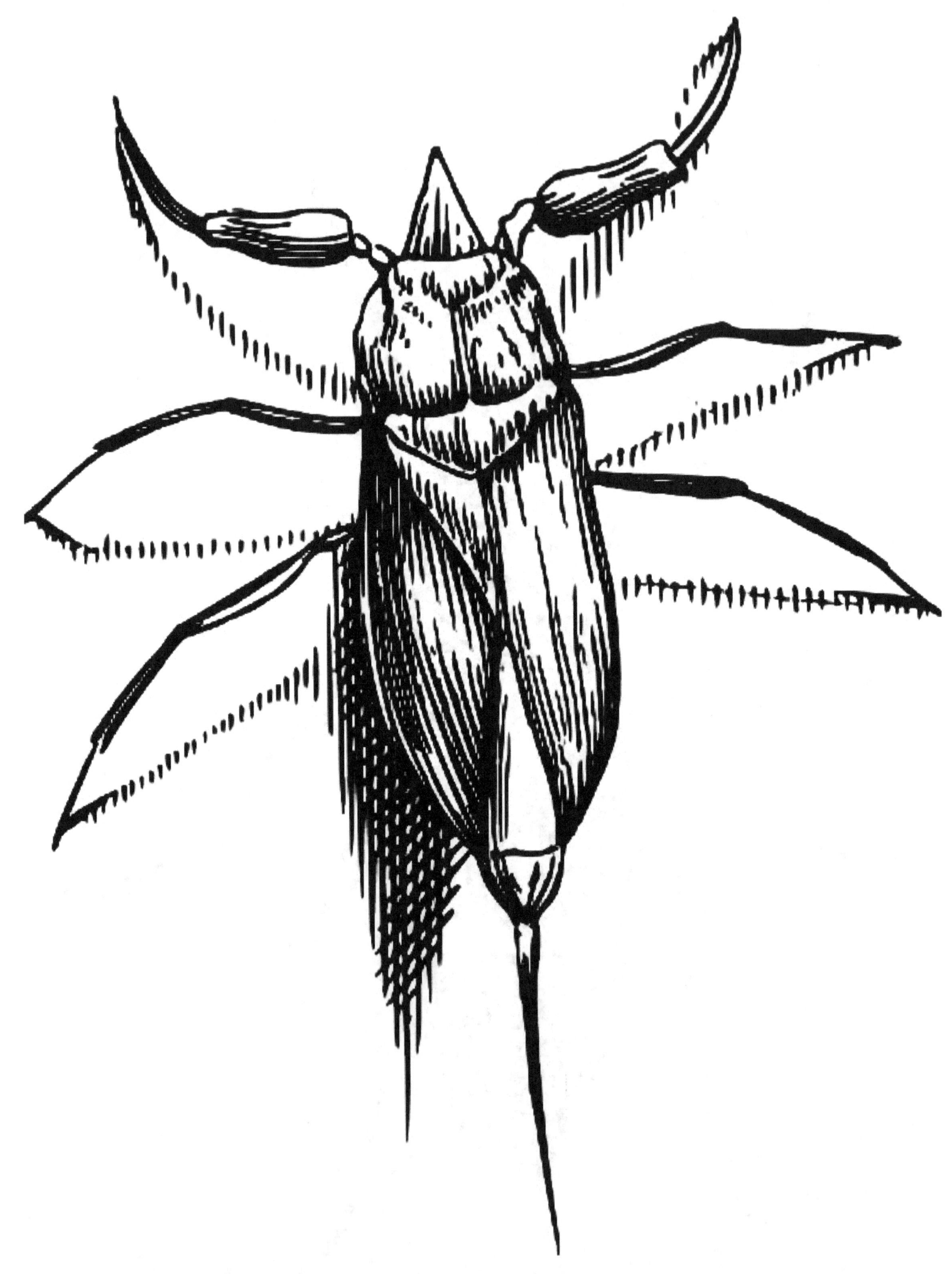

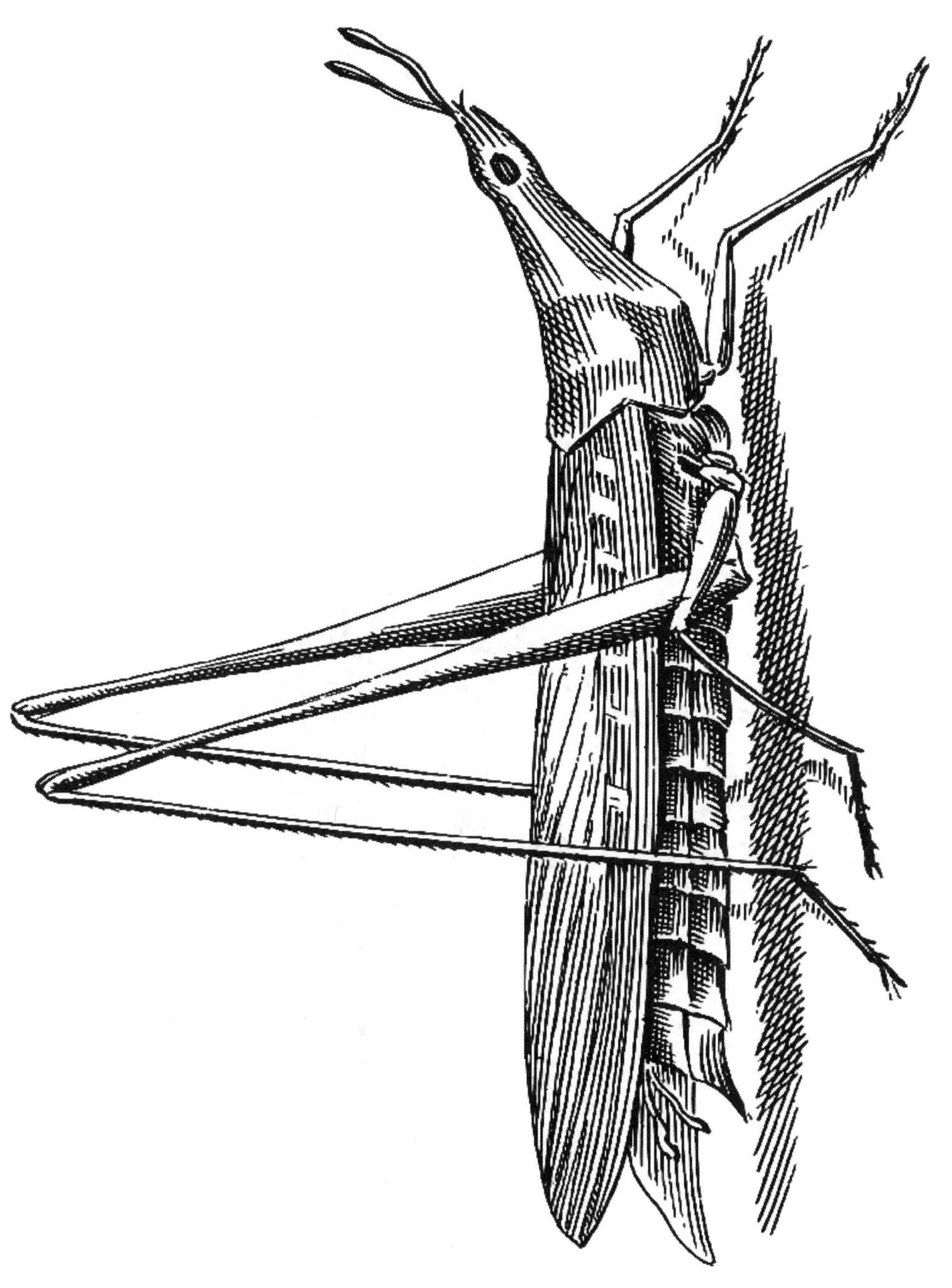

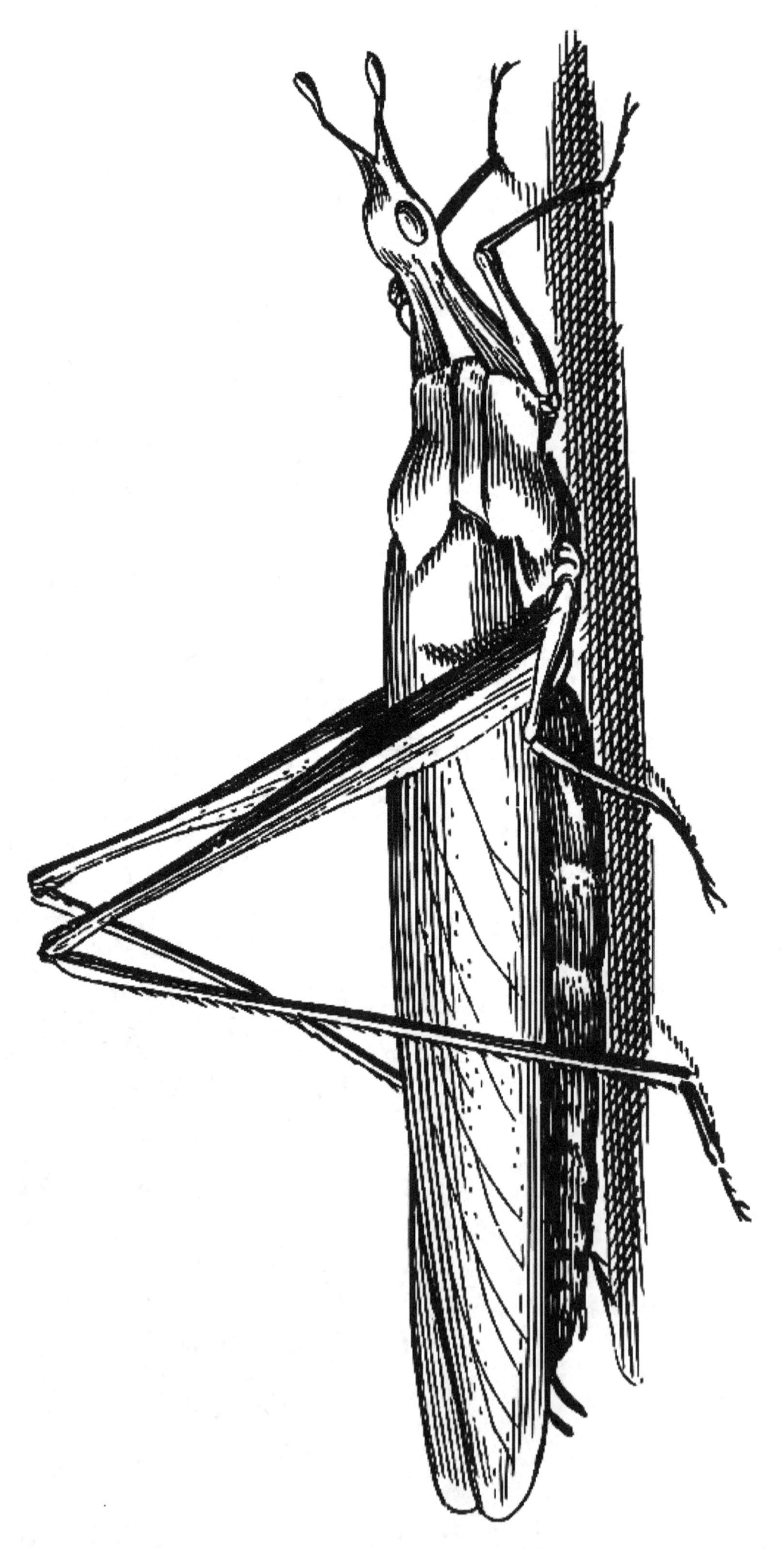

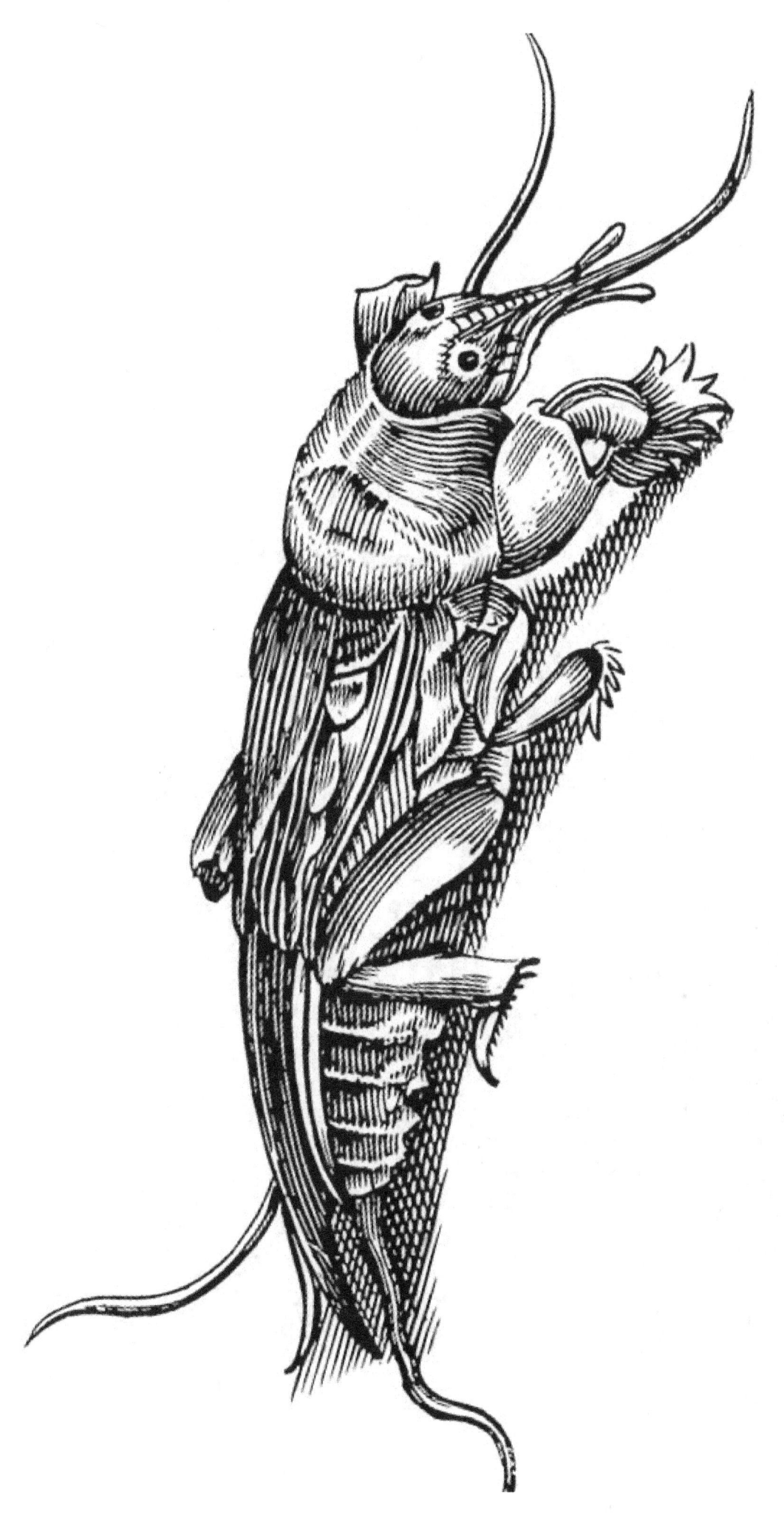

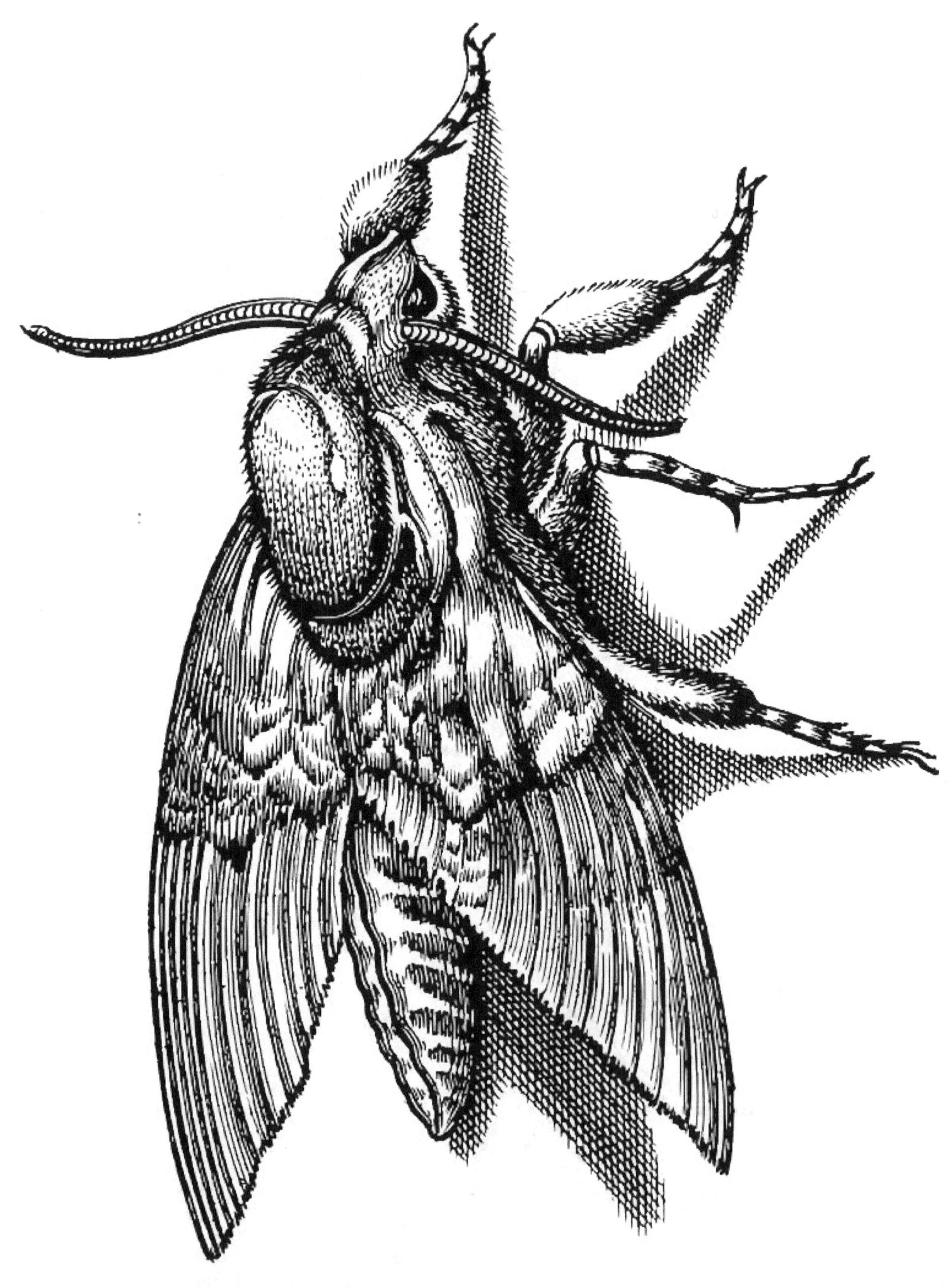

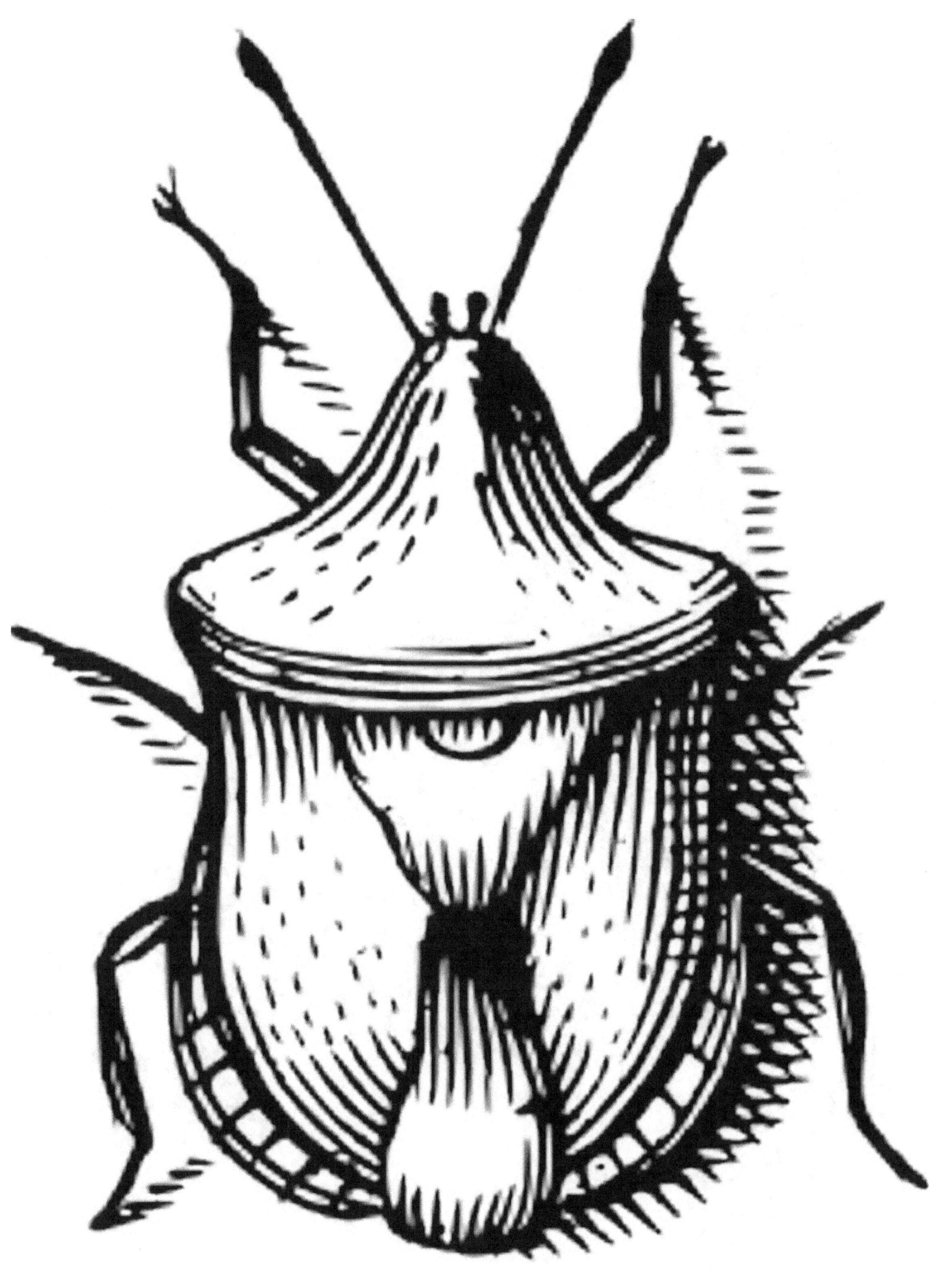

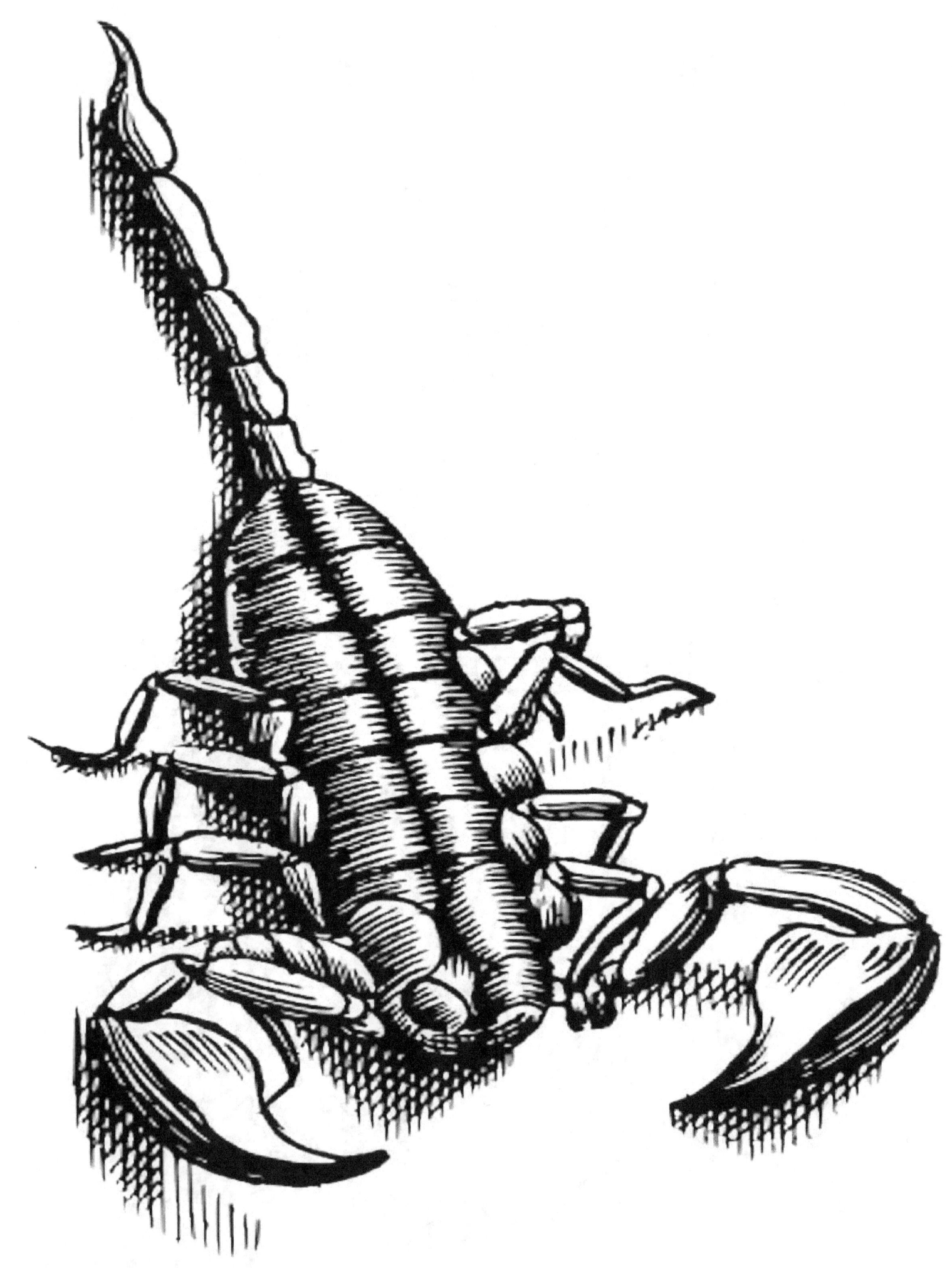

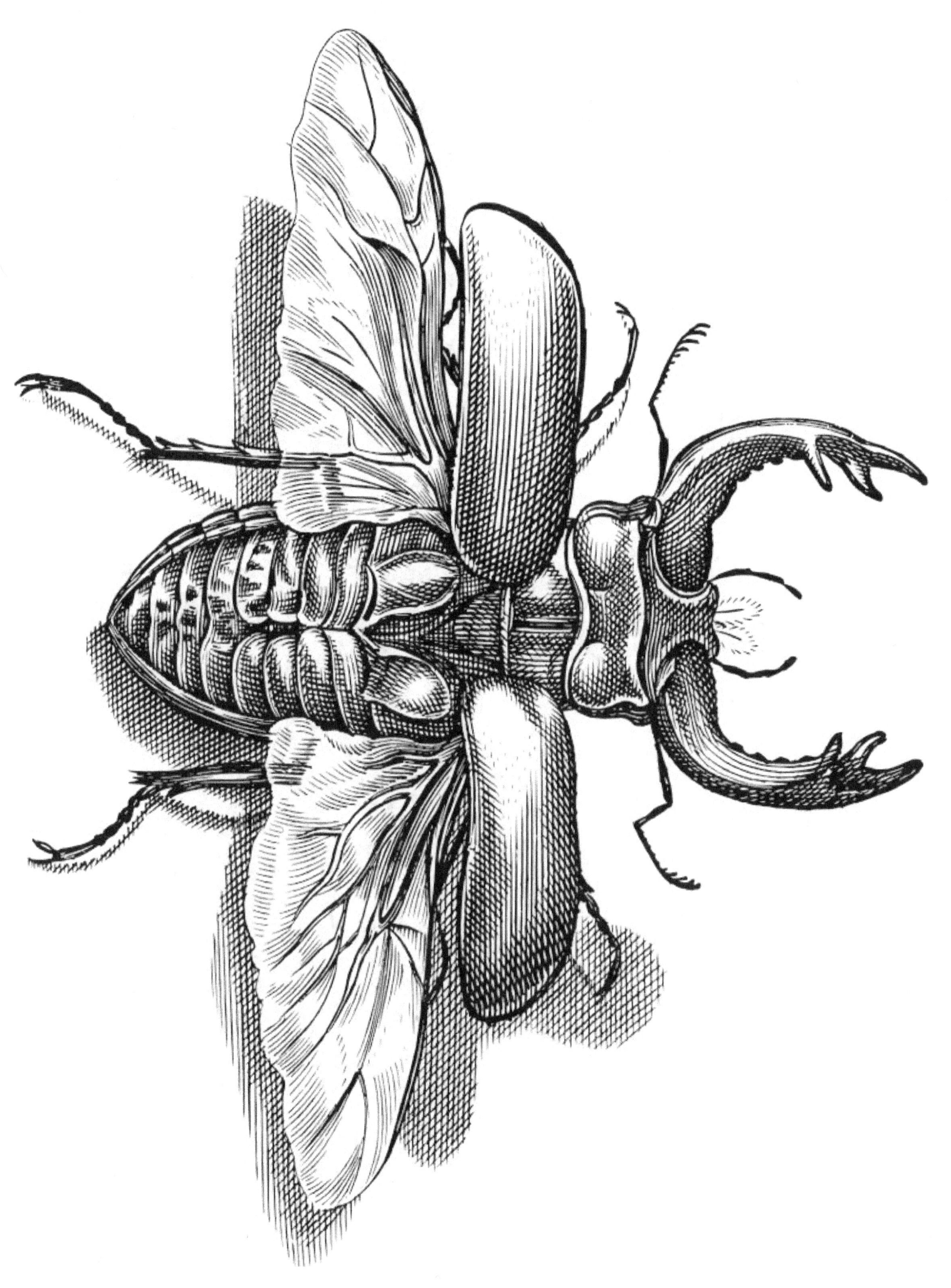

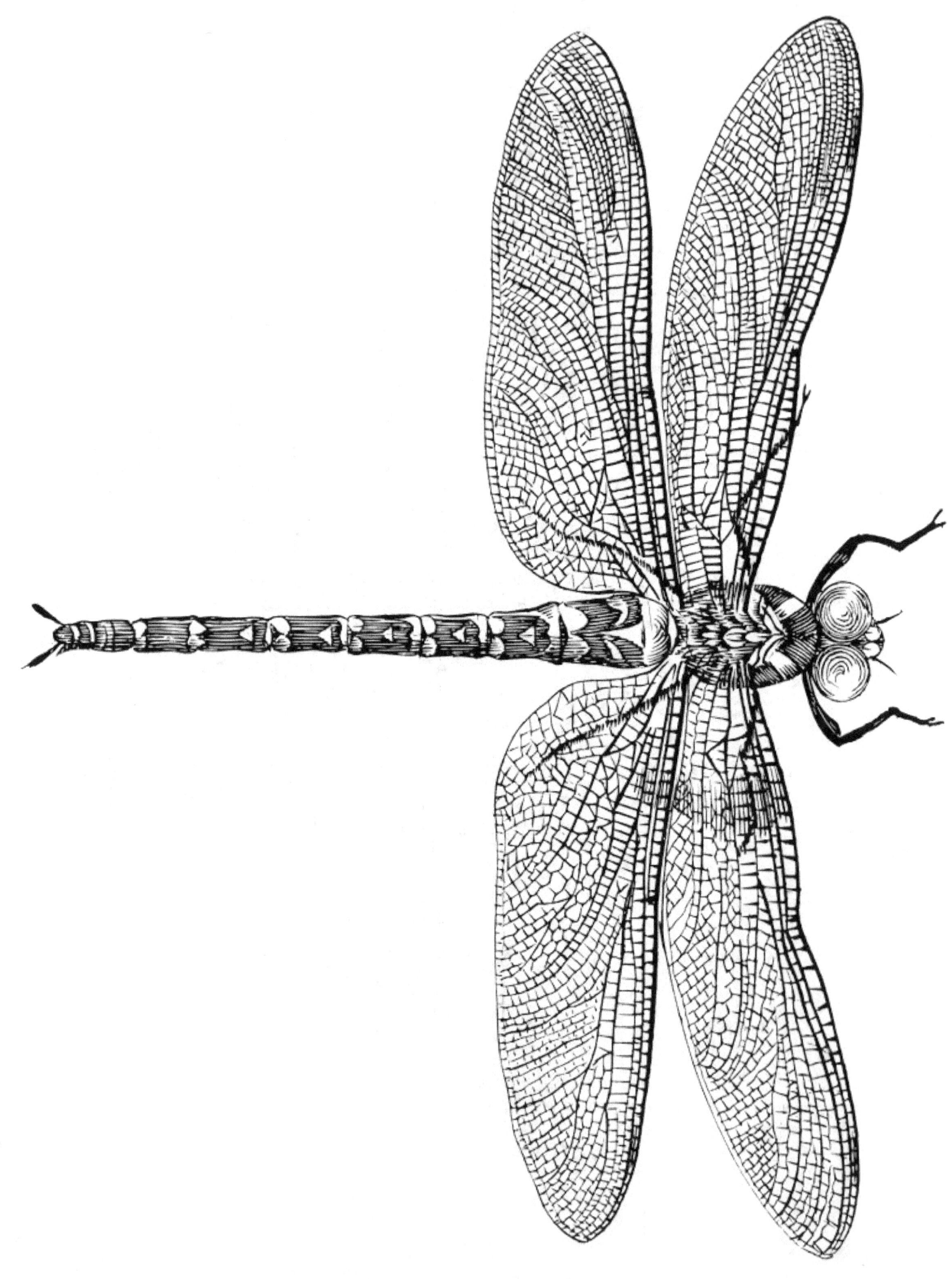

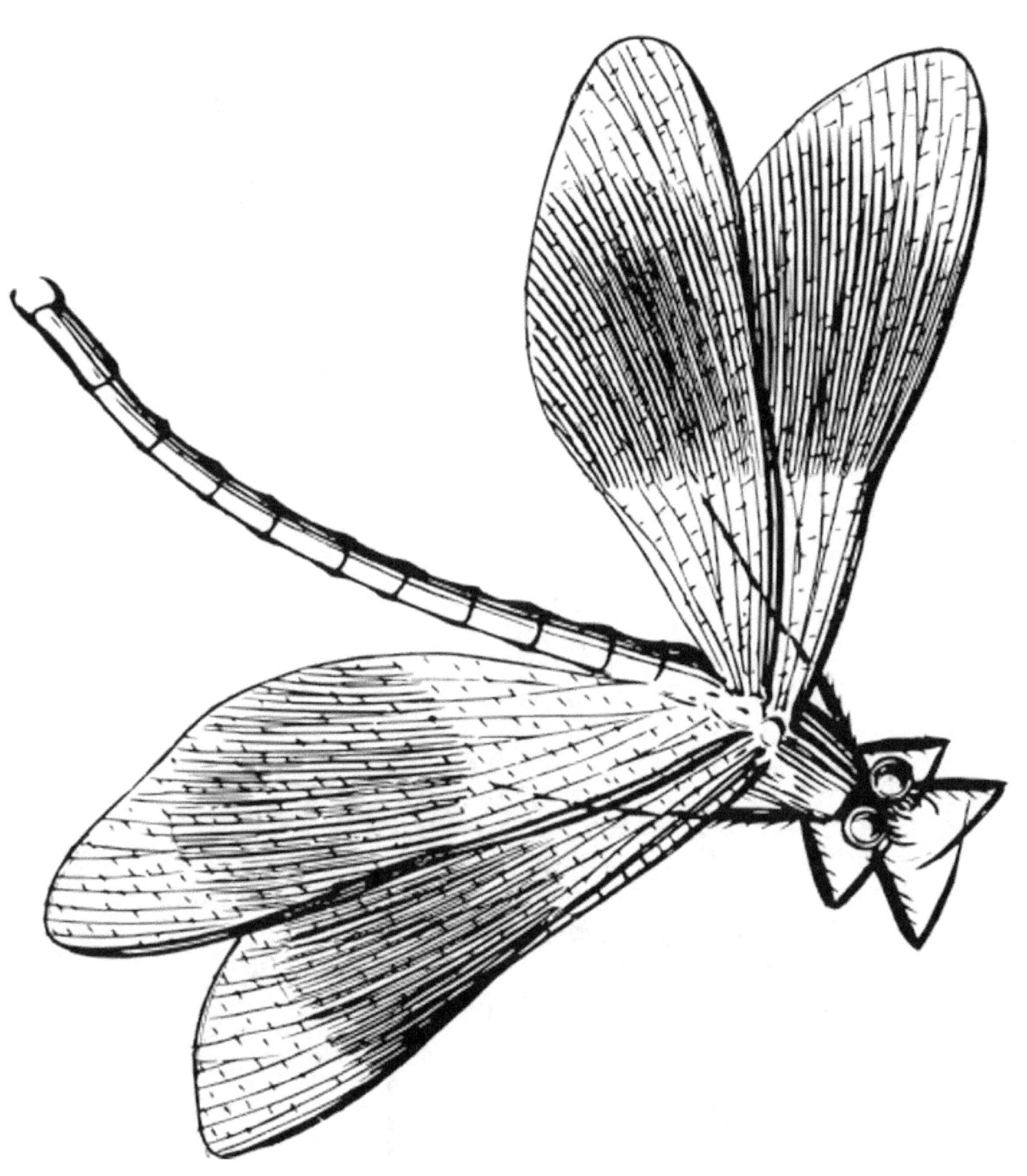

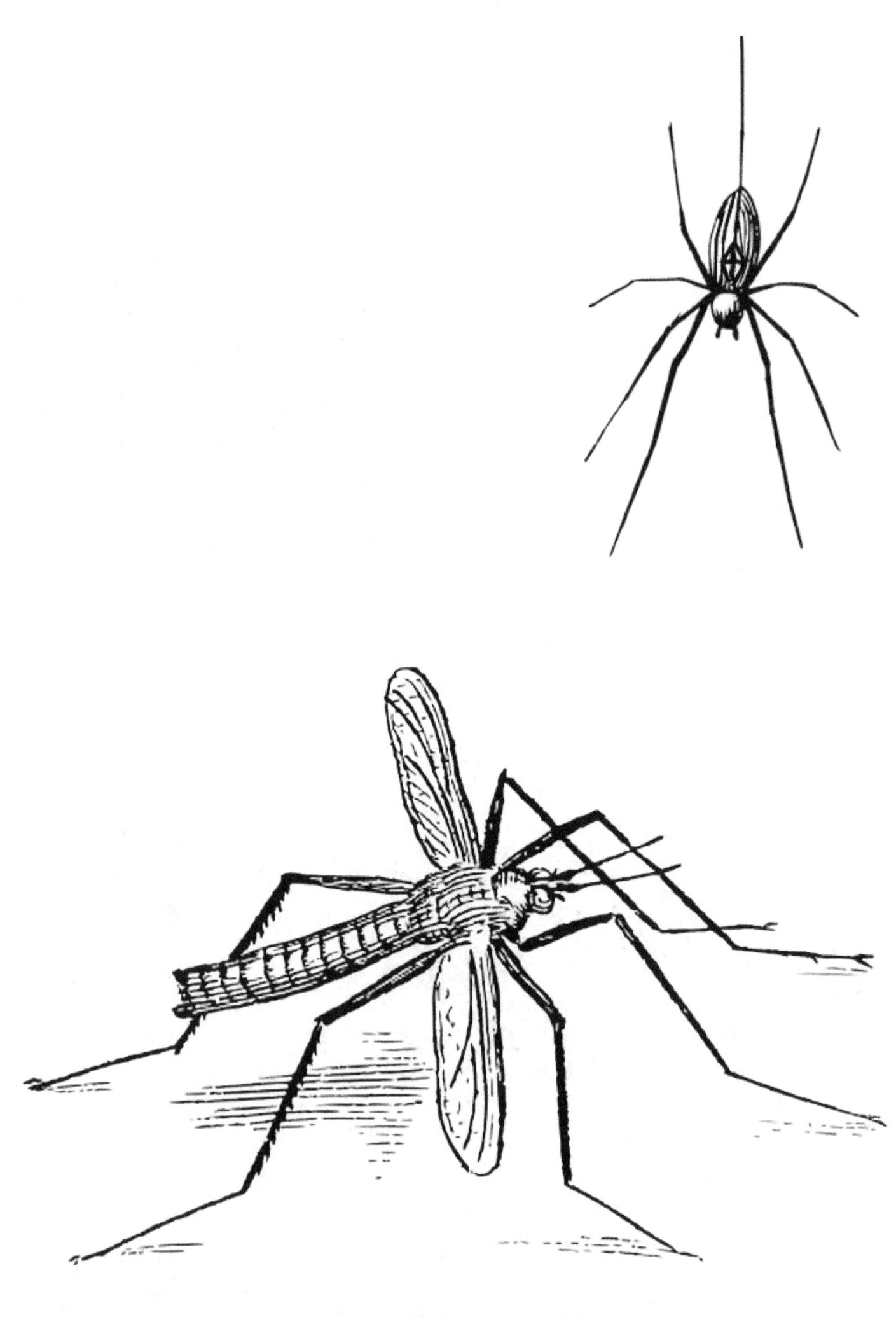

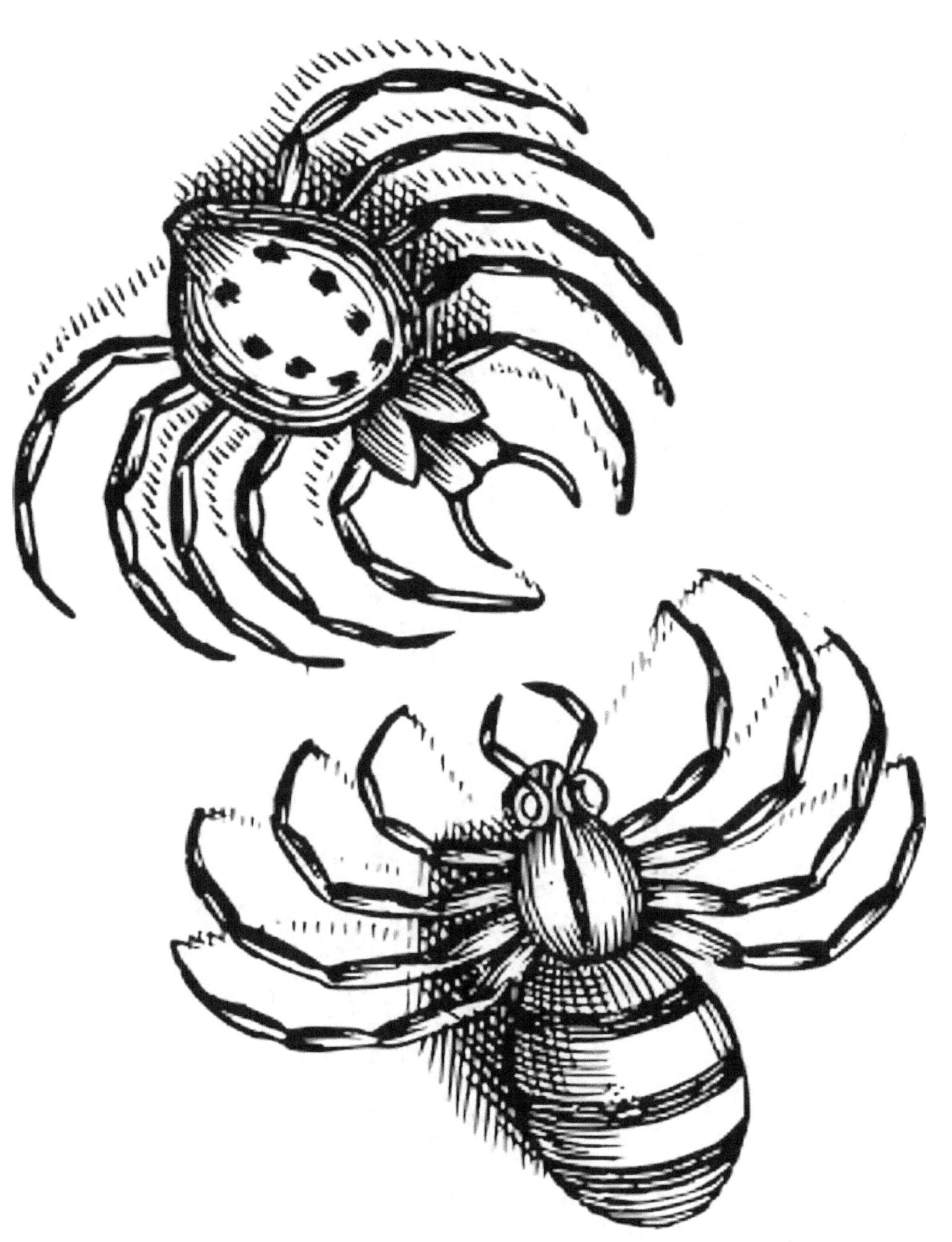

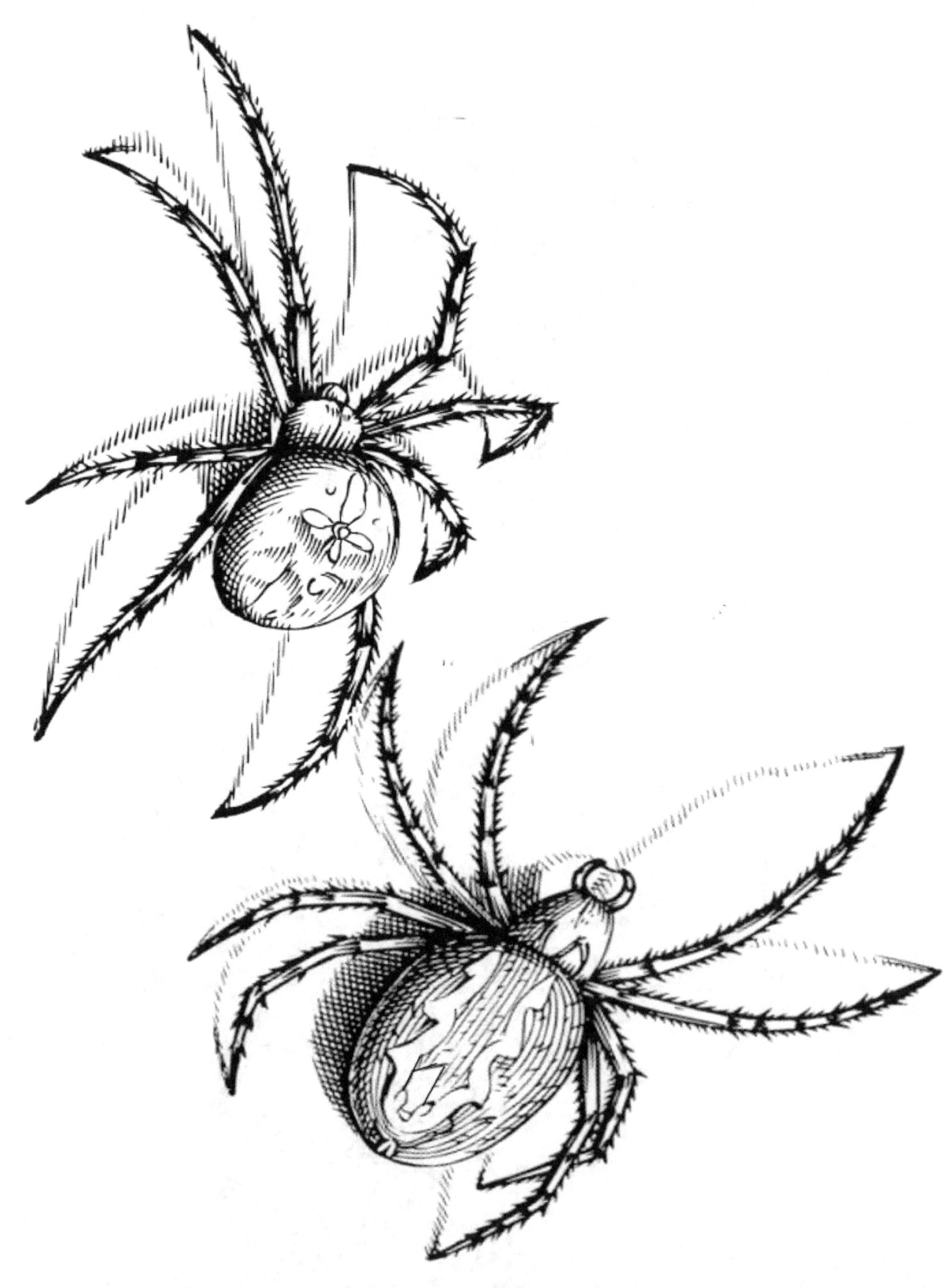

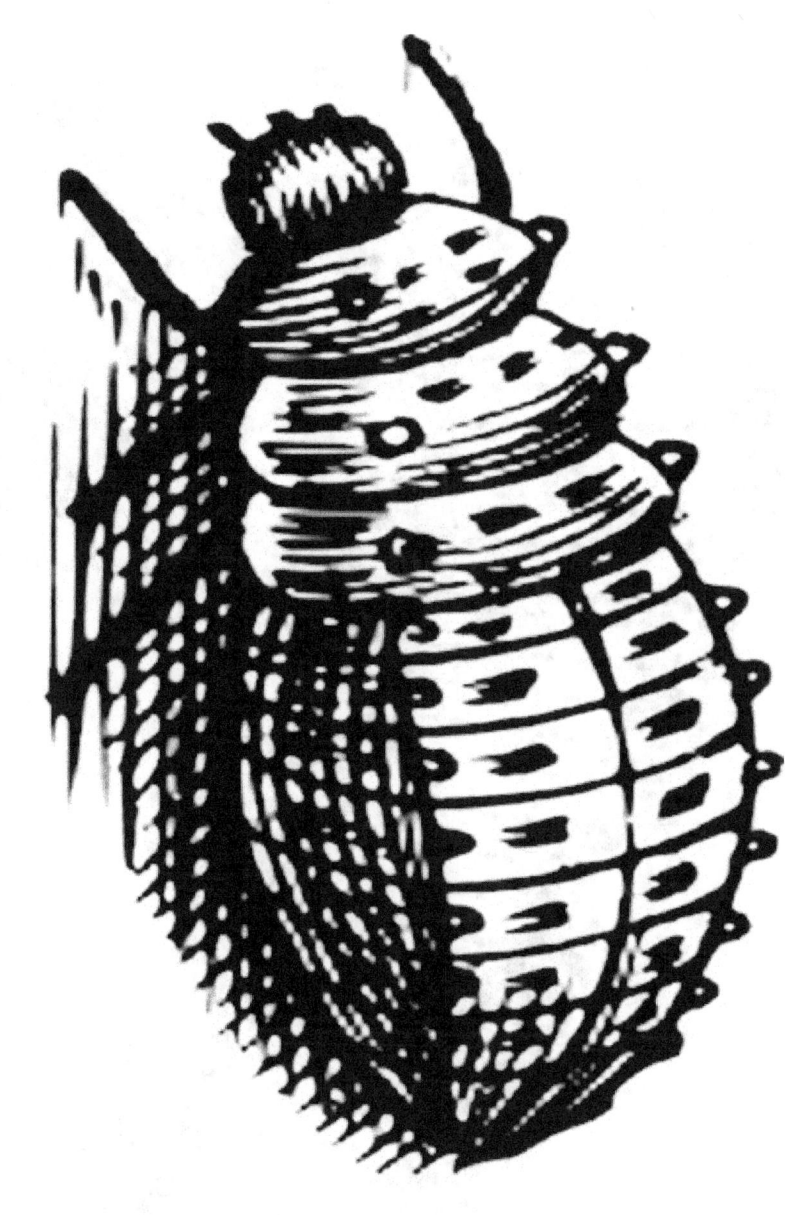
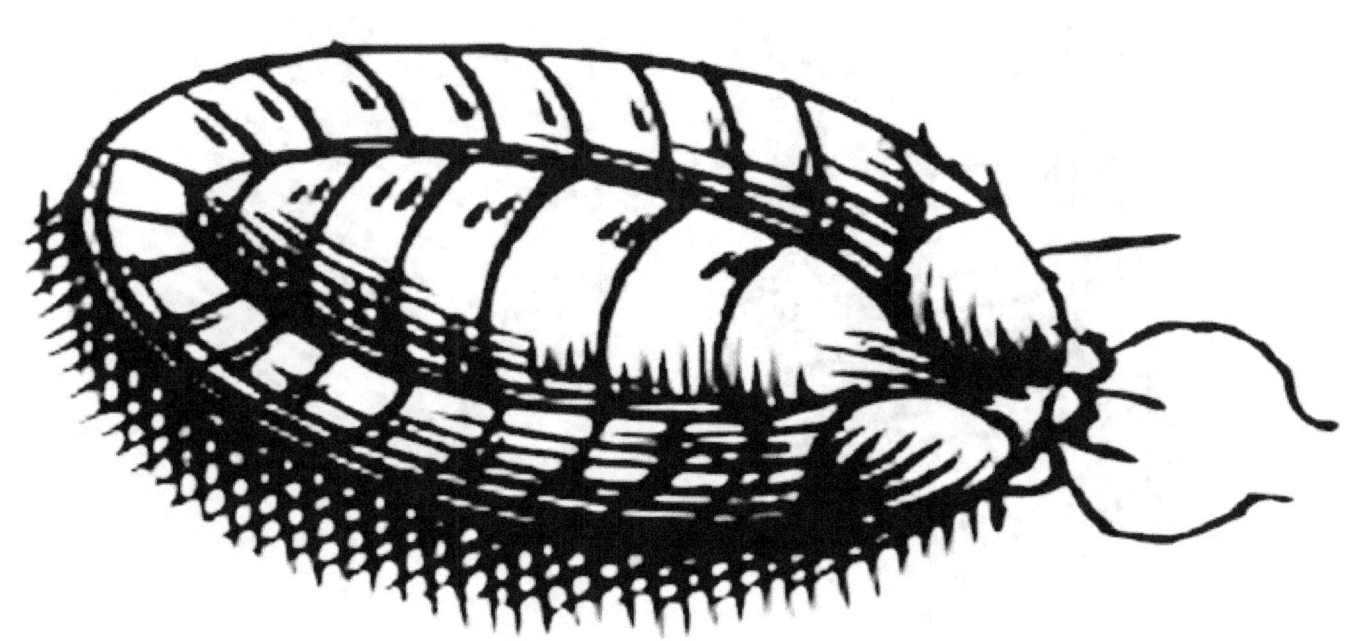

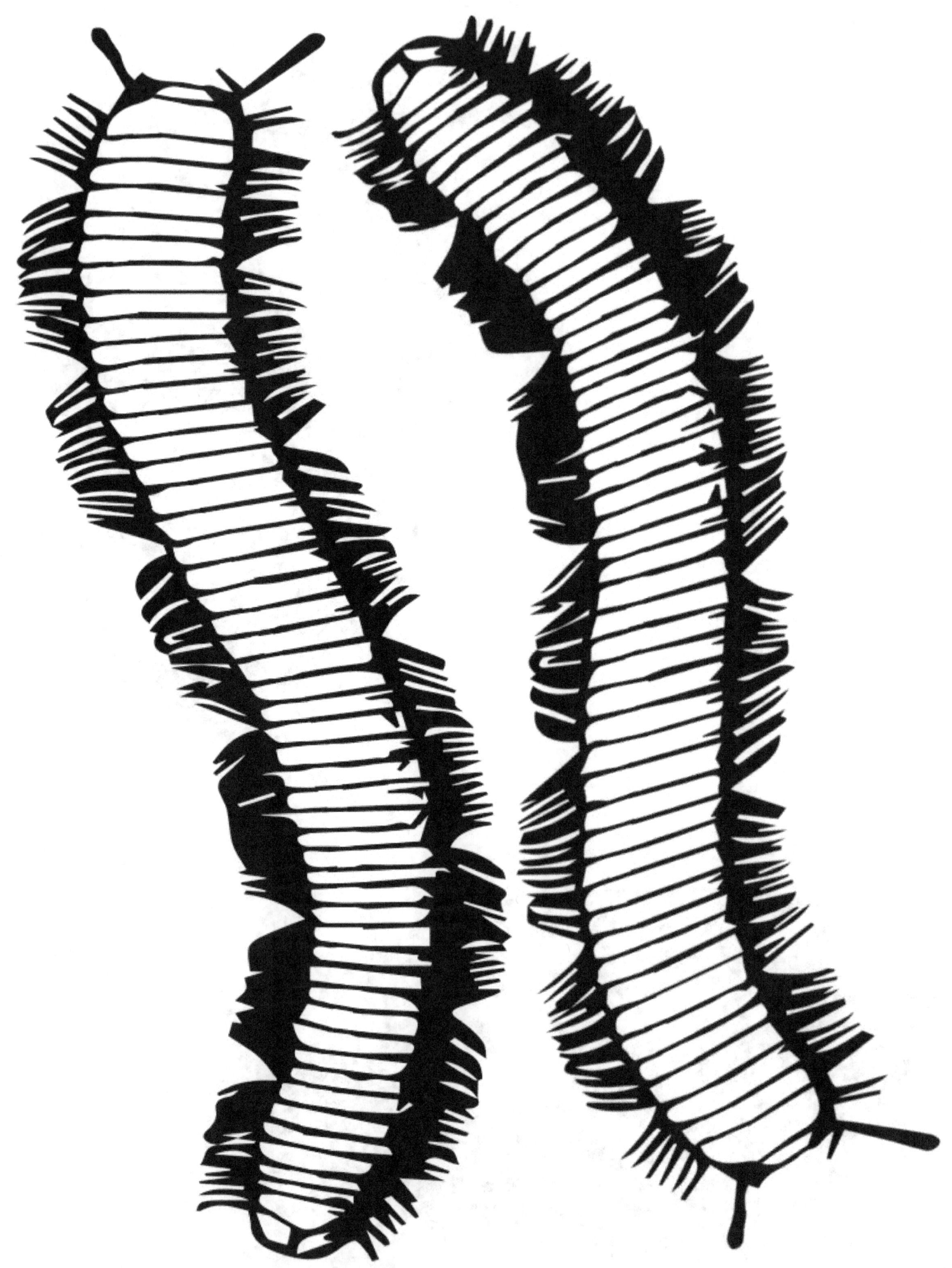

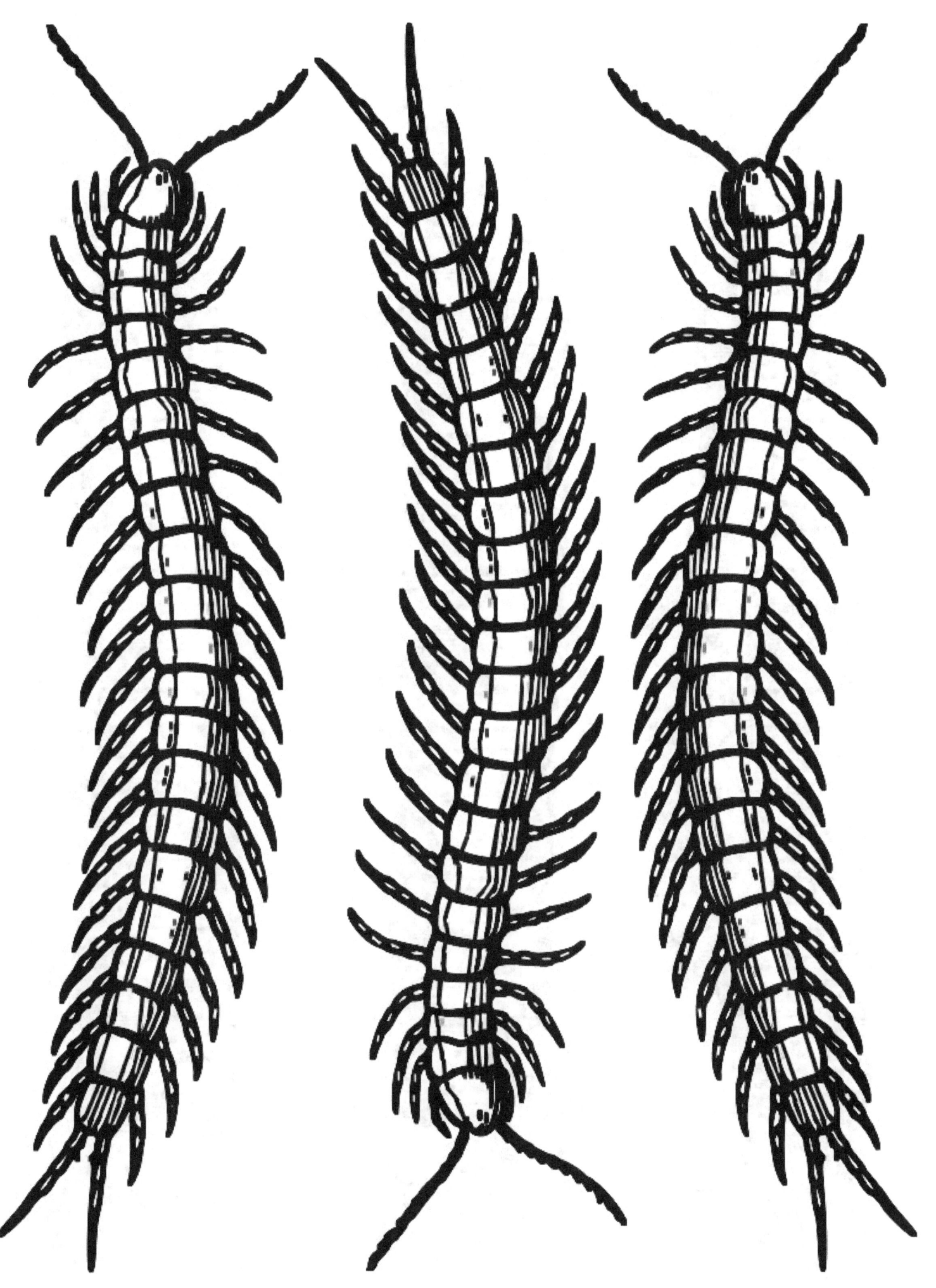

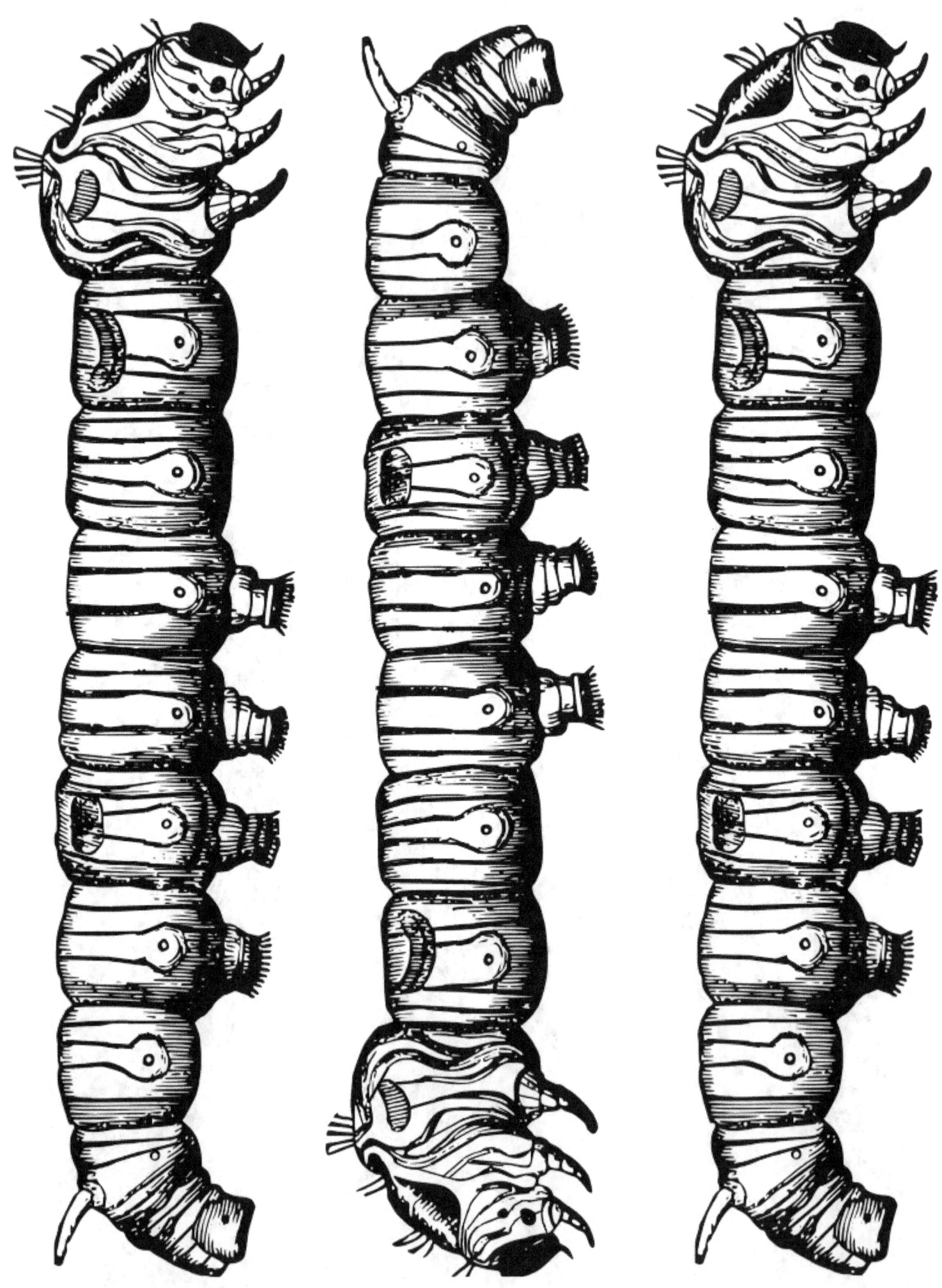

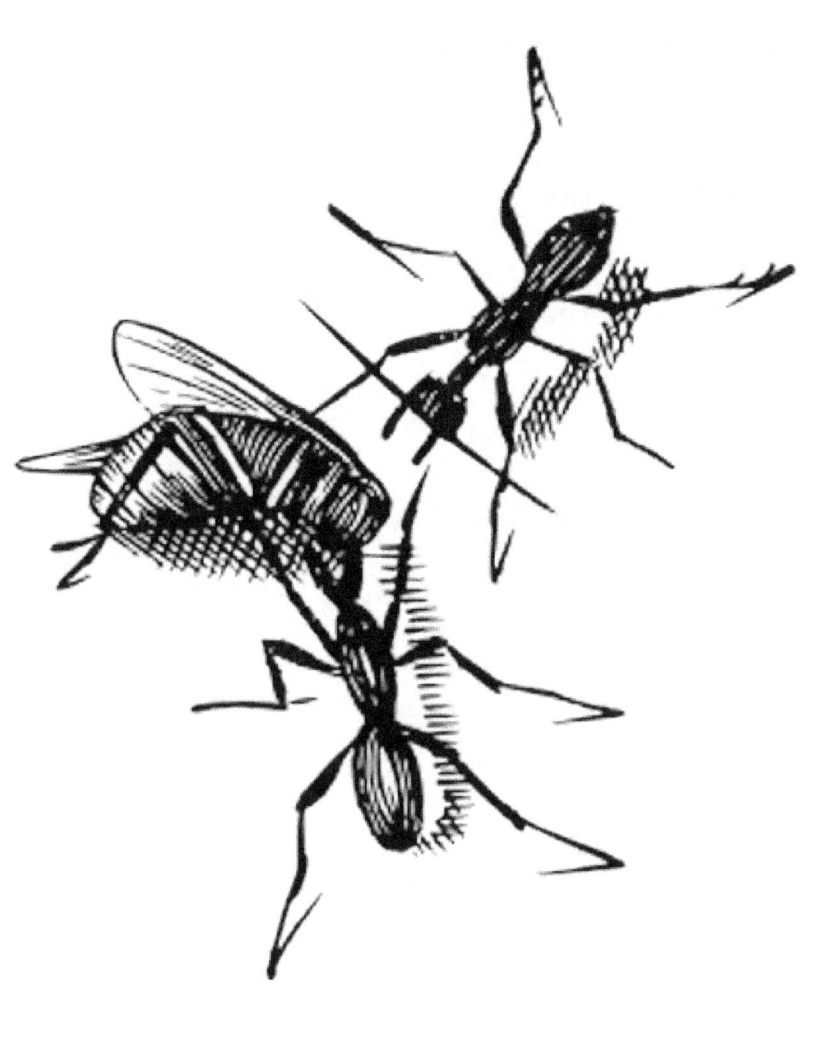
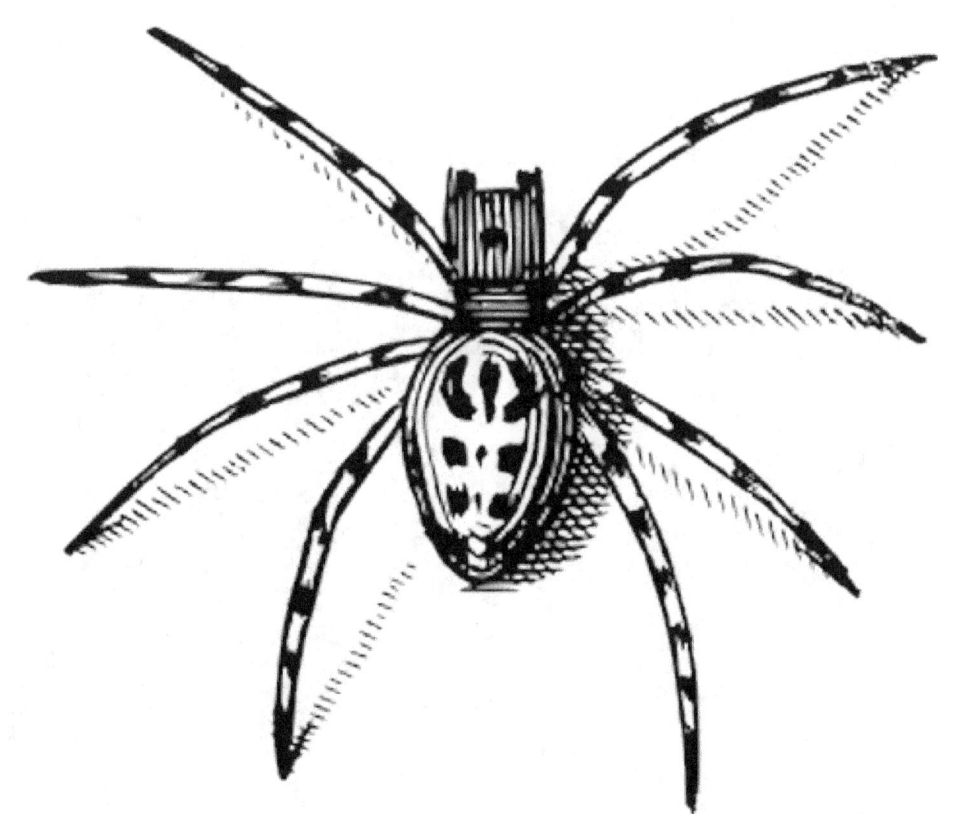

MORE BOOKS FROM DANO (Do a Google Search for Biker George Books by Dano)

DAILY DEVOTIONALS ~ THESE ARE ALSO AVAILABLE IN SPANISH & LARGE PRINT
01 - In The Wind With Biker George: Short Daily Rides Devotionals
02 - In The Breeze With Biker George: Short Daily Ride Devotionals

HUMOR & JOKES ~ THESE ARE ALSO AVAILABLE IN SPANISH & LARGE PRINT
Biker George Clean Humor + Biker Jokes: A Merry Heart Does Good Like A Medicine

CHILDREN'S BOOKS
Biker George Does The ABC's: For Toddlers & Future Bikers
The Sun, Moon, & Stars Book: A Biker George Nursery Rhyme
Once Upon Some Colorful Motorcycles: A Biker George Learn Your Colors Book (Adults like this too!)
Look Out For Colors! A Biker George Learn Your Colors Book

COLORING BOOKS
Biker George Bible Story Coloring Book 1
Biker George Bible Story Coloring Book 2
Coloring Fun With The ABCs & Scripture
Cool Designs & Patterns - Adult Chill Pill Coloring Book
Sugar Skulls - Adult Chill Pill Coloring Book
The Butterfly Coloring Pages - Adult Chill Pill Coloring Book

BIKER TESTIMONIES
Biker George Real Life Biker Testimonies
Biker George Real Life Biker Stories

BIBLES/REFERENCE
Biker George Biker Bible: & Real Life Biker Testimonies
Biker George Biker Bible: & Real Life Biker Stories
The Apocrypha - The Hidden Books: The 14 Secret Writings From King James Bible
4 Column Parallel & Chronological Harmony of the Gospels: Matthew, Mark, Luke & John

COMICS
Rabbit & Cat Comic Books - For Such A Time As This

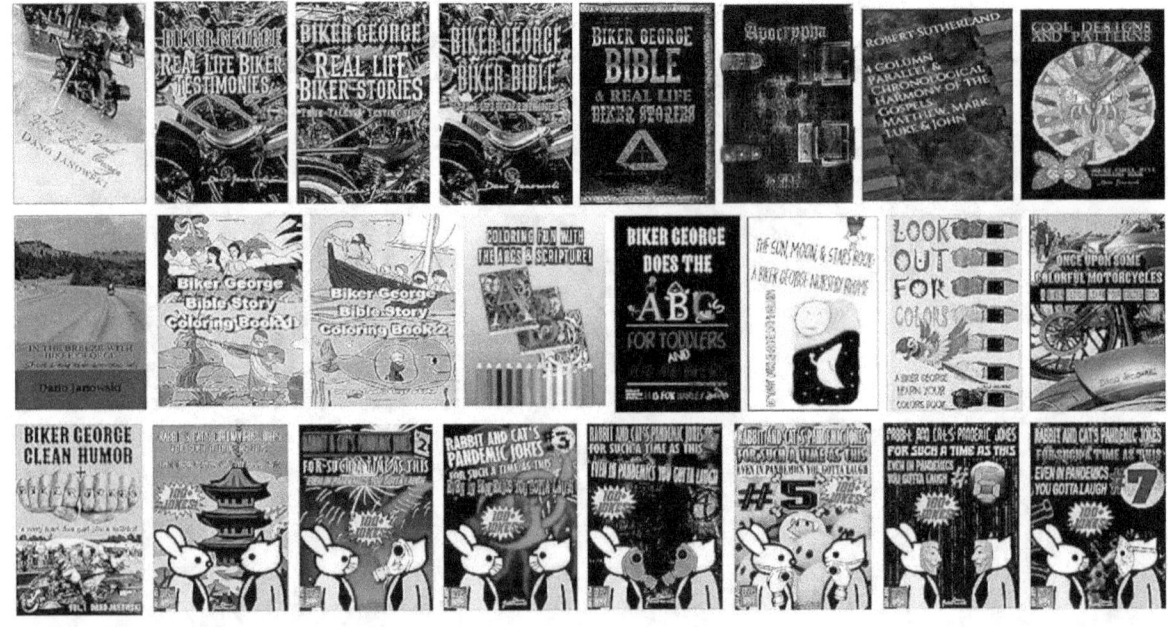